STRATEGIC FINANCIAL MANAGEMENT

Principles and Practices

DR. BEN EBO ATTOM
DR. YAW NDORI QUEKU
PROFESSOR EDWARD MARFO-YIADOM
PROFESSOR AFZALUR RAHMAN

BLUEROSE PUBLISHERS
India | U.K.

Copyright © Dr. Ben Ebo Attom 2024

All rights reserved by author. No part of this publication may be reproduced, stored in a retrieval system or transmitted in any form or by any means, electronic, mechanical, photocopying, recording or otherwise, without the prior permission of the author. Although every precaution has been taken to verify the accuracy of the information contained herein, the publisher assumes no responsibility for any errors or omissions. No liability is assumed for damages that may result from the use of information contained within.

BlueRose Publishers takes no responsibility for any damages, losses, or liabilities that may arise from the use or misuse of the information, products, or services provided in this publication.

For permissions requests or inquiries regarding this publication, please contact:

BLUEROSE PUBLISHERS
www.BlueRoseONE.com
info@bluerosepublishers.com
+91 8882 898 898
+4407342408967

ISBN: 978-93-6452-730-9

Cover design: Tahira
Typesetting: Tanya Raj Upadhyay

First Edition: August 2024

PREFACE

With a long and varied teaching experience in strategic financial management, financial management, financial analysis, business finance, strategic management, and applied corporate finance at the Higher National Diploma (HND), Bachelor of Technology (B-Tech), Masters in Business Administration (MBA) levels since 2009, we decided to come out with this succinct and comprehensive Strategic Financial Management (SFM) textbook. Strategic Financial Management: Principles and Practices, is being released, and it is particularly created for students at the Masters and Professional levels to satisfy their academic needs and expectations.

As a result, this textbook, which includes over 63 worked examples in the form of illustrations, has become essential to meet the current needs of students studying financial management-related courses. The goal of this book is to serve as study text for students enrolled in Masters of Business Administration programs, particularly at technical and traditional universities that offer accounting and finance Masters degrees (e.g., M-Tech and M.Com.), and also to provide them with additional illustrations.

This book provides a thorough study of strategic financial management for university students at all levels, with a focus on Masters students and those preparing for financial management professional examinations. The topics covered have been thoroughly chosen and systematically arranged to enable educators and students to pursue any specific aspects of the overall subjects with determination. The book is also useful for financial managers and professionals in their decision-making relating to the strategic financial management processes facing their businesses.

The book is divided into 13 chapters and includes over ninety (90) chapter review questions as well as over sixty-two (62) illustrations in the form of worked examples to help students prepare adequately for their examinations.

Each chapter begins with an introduction and an overview of the chapter's objectives as well as the key terms used in the chapter. Definitions and theoretical ideas are then presented, together with practical examples (where applicable), to offer users (students and teachers) a thorough knowledge of the issue at hand.

All errors and omissions, regardless of their form, are solely our fault, for which we sincerely apologize and accept responsibility. We would greatly appreciate and include your feedback and comments in subsequent versions.

Dr. Ben Ebo Attom
Dr. Yaw Ndori Queku
Professor Edward Marfo-Yiadom
Professor Afzalur Rahman

Department of Accounting and Finance
Cape Coast Technical University,
Cape Coast, Ghana.

AUGUST 2024

ACKNOWLEDGEMENTS

The development of this textbook, entitled "Strategic Financial Management," would not have been possible without the direct and indirect assistance of a substantial number of colleagues, faculty members, authors, researchers, and academic professionals.

We would like to convey our profoundest appreciation to every single author whose scholarly work (publications) was consulted during the development of this textbook.

We would like to express our appreciation for the encouragement we got from our academic colleagues at the department of accounting and finance and, in general, Cape Coast Technical University (CCTU), an institution of great renown.

Additionally, we extend our gratitude to our esteemed students and friends who have consistently encouraged us to achieve this academic feat, which features an abundance of worked examples that support students' financial education at the Masters and Professional levels and also across different proficiency levels.

In conclusion, we genuinely extend our appreciation to the Attom, Ndori, Marfo-Yiadom, and Afzalur families—particularly our spouses and children—for their unwavering encouragement, support, and selfless sacrifices during this scholarly endeavor.

We would like to extend our heartfelt apologies for any errors or oversights that may have occurred.

TABLE OF CONTENTS

PREFACE iii
ACKNOWLEDGEMENTS v
CHAPTER 1: OVERVIEW OF STRATEGIC FINANCIAL MANAGEMENT .. 1
    1.1 Overview 1
    1.2 Definition of Strategic Financial Management 2
    1.3 Strategic Financial Management Vs Financial Management 4
    1.4 Functions Performed by Strategic Financial Management 5
    1.5 Principles of Strategic Financial Management 7
    1.6 Importance of Strategic Financial Management 9
    1.7 Objectives of Strategic Financial Management 10
    1.8 Constraints to Strategic Financial Management 12
    1.9 Chapter Review Questions 14
    1.10 Chapter References and Bibliography 14
    1.11 Recommended Reading List 15
CHAPTER 2: FINANCIAL PLANNING 16
    2.1 Overview 16
    2.2 Definition of Financial Planning 17
    2.3 Objectives of Financial Planning 17
    2.4 Factors Affecting Financial Planning 18
    2.5 Importance of Financial Planning 21
    2.8 Types of Financial Planning 23
    2.7 Cumulative Capital Requirement (CCR) 24
    2.8 Key Financial Effect of Cumulative Capital Requirement 24
    2.9 Steps Involved in Financial Planning 26
    2.10 Chapter Review Questions 28
    2.11 Chapter References and Bibliography 28
    2.12 Recommended Reading List 29

CHAPTER 3: WORKING CAPITAL MANAGEMENT ... 30
3.1 Overview ... 30
3.2 Definition of Working Capital Management ... 31
3.3 Key Components of Working Capital ... 32
3.4 Scope of Working Capital ... 32
3.5 Types / Variations in Working Capital ... 35
3.5.1 Gross Working Capital and Net Working Capital ... 35
3.5.2 Permanent Working Capital & Temporary Working Capital ... 36
3.5.3 Working Capital Financing Strategies ... 37
3.5.4 Positive, Negative and Zero Working Capital ... 38
3.6 Types of Working Capital Policy (WCP) ... 39
3.6.1 Conservative Working Capital Policy ... 40
3.6.2 Aggressive Working Capital Policy ... 40
3.7 Factors that Affect the Size of Working Capital ... 41
3.8 Cash Conversion Cycle (CCC) ... 44
3.8.1 Interpretation of the Nature of CCC ... 47
3.8.2 Strategies to Improve Cash Conversion Cycle (CCC) ... 50
3.9 Working Capital Ratios ... 51
3.10 Computation of Working Capital Requirement ... 54
3.11 Chapter Review Questions ... 64
3.12 Chapter References and Bibliography ... 68
3.13 Recommended Reading List ... 69

CHAPTER 4: DIVIDEND POLICY ... 70
4.1 Overview ... 70
4.2 Definition of Dividend Policy ... 71
4.3 Factors Influencing Size of Dividend Payout ... 72
4.4 Types of Dividend Payments ... 75
4.5 Types of Dividend Policy ... 77

4.6 Firm's Life Cycle and Type of Dividend Payout..........................79
4.7 Advantages of Paying Regular Dividend................................81
4.8 Walter's Theory on Dividend Policy.....................................82
4.8.1 Ideas that led to the Creation of Walter's Model.....................82
4.8.2 Relationship between Dividend Decision and Value of Firm..83
4.8.3 Key Assumptions Under the Walter's Model..........................83
4.8.4 Walter's Model - Implications...90
4.8.5 Criticisms of Walter's Model...91
4.9 Chapter Review Questions..92
4.10 Chapter References and Bibliography..............................93
4.11 Recommended Reading List...94

CHAPTER 5: CAPITALIZATION...95
5.1 Overview..95
5.2 Definition of the term 'Capitalization'..................................96
5.3 Over- Capitalization..96
5.3.1 Causes of Over- Capitalization..97
5.3.2 Effects of Overcapitalization..98
5.4 Undercapitalization...100
5.4.1 Causes of Undercapitalization.......................................100
5.4.2 Effects of Undercapitalization..101
5.5 Fair Capitalization...102
5.6 Chapter Review Questions..102
5.7 Chapter References and Bibliography.............................102
5.8 Recommended Reading List...103

CHAPTER 6: CAPITAL STRUCTURE.......................................104
6.1 Overview..104
6.2 Definition of Capital Structure...105
6.3 Understanding Capital Structure.....................................105

6.4 Factors that Determine Capital Structure Composition 108

6.6 Components of Capital Structure 113

6.8 Benefits of Capital Structure 114

6.9 Principles Underlying the Theory of Capital Structure............. 115

6.10 Capital Structure and Point of Indifference 117

6.11 Calculation of Point of Indifference 117

6.12 Theories Underlying Capital Structure 123

6.12.1 Net Income (NI) Approach 124

6.12.1.1 Assumptions Underlying Net Income Approach............... 124

6.12.1.2 Criticisms of Net Income (NI) Approach........................... 129

6.12.2 Net Operating Income Approach- Irrelevance Approach ... 129

6.12.2.1 Assumptions Under Net Operating Income Approach 130

6.12.2.2 Criticisms/ Disadvantages of NOI 134

6.12.3 Traditional Approach to Capital Structure Theory 134

6.12.3.1 Key Assumptions Under the Traditionalist Approach 135

6.12.4 Trade-Off Theory 135

6.12.5 Pecking Order Theory.. 136

6.13 Chapter Review Questions 138

6.14 Chapter References and Bibliography 139

6.15 Recommended Reading List.. 140

CHAPTER 7: CAPITAL BUDGETING WITH RISK, PROBABILITY, INFLATION AND TAXATION 141

7.1 Overview.. 141

7.2 Capital Budgeting and Risk Consideration.............................. 142

7.3 Importance of Ascertaining Risk in Capital Budgeting 142

7.4 Factors Influencing Strategic Investment Decision 143

7.4.1 Company Factors... 144

7.4.2 Industry Factors 145

7.4.3 Fiscal Incentives and Non-Economic Factors 146

7.5 Definition of Risk 146
7.6 Types of Risk that Affect Capital Budgeting 147
7.7 Risk-Adjusted Discount Rate (RADR) 149
7.7.1 Reasons why Discount Rate takes into Account Risk 149
7.8 Determining Risk-adjusted Discount Rate with a Capital Assets Pricing Model (CAPM) 150
7.8.1 Advantages Using Risk-Adjusted Rates 153
7.8.2 Disadvantages of Using RADR 154
7.9 Certainty Equivalent Method (CEM) 154
7.9.1 Certainty Equivalent in Gambling 160
7.10 Sensitivity Analysis in Capital Budgeting 160
7.10.1 Understanding Sensitivity Analysis 161
7.11 Probability Technique in Capital Budgeting 166
7.12 Inflation and Capital Budgeting 169
7.12.1 Different Components Uniquely Affected by Inflation 170
7.12.2 Follow the Golden Rule 170
7.13 Impact of Income Tax on Capital Budgeting Decisions 179
7.13.1 Capital Budgeting with Income Tax 180
7.14 Capital Allowances in Capital Budgeting 185
7.14.1 Capital Allowances- Benefits 186
7.15 Decision Tree Analysis 189
7.15.1 Definition of Decision Tree 189
7.15.2 Steps in Decision Tree Analysis 189
7.15.3 Decision Tree Symbols 190
7.15.4 Steps in Decision Tree Analysis 191
7.15.5 Advantages of Decision Tree Analysis 193
7.15.6 Disadvantages of Decision Tree Analysis 194
7.17 Chapter Review Questions 208
7.18 Chapter References and Bibliography 211

7.19 Recommended Reading List...212

CHAPTER 8: VALUATION OF BUSINESSES 213

8.1 Overview..213

8.2 Definition of Valuation of Business...214

8.3 Standard of Value 215

8.4 Premise of Value..217

8.5 Reasons for Performing a Valuation 218

8.5.1 Factors that Influence Valuation of Businesses 219

8.5.2 Asset-Based Approach to Business Valuation 220

8.5.3 Going-Concern Approach 221

8.5.4 Liquidation Asset-based Approach 221

8.5.4.1 Limitations of Liquidation Assets-based approach 222

8.5.5 Income Approach to Business Valuation 222

8.6 Present Value of Future Receipts (PVFR) 223

8.6.1 Problems of PVFR Approach:..224

8.7 Valuation by Capitalizing Earnings...224

8.8 Super-Profit Approach 226

8.9 Discounted Cash Flow (DCF) method 229

8.10 Market Value Approach 231

8.11 Approaches to Market Comparison Methods 231

8.11.1 Key Comparison Indicators 232

8.12 Chapter Review Questions 233

8.13 Chapter References and Bibliography 235

8.14 Recommended Reading List..235

CHAPTER 9: BUSINESS ETHICS 236

9.1 Overview..236

9.2 Definition of Business Ethics..237

9.3 Principles of Business Ethics 239

9.4 Values of Business Ethics..240
9.5 Types of Business Ethics..242
9.6 Advantages of Ethics in Business 243
9.7 Drawbacks of Ethics in Business 244
9.8 Svensson and Wood's Model of Business Ethics 244
9.9 Chapter Review Questions 247
9.10 Chapter References and Bibliography 247
9.11 Recommended Reading List..248

CHAPTER 10: LEASE OR BUY DECISION 249
10.1 Overview..249
10.2 Meaning and Nature of Lease or Buy...........................250
10.3 Lease or Buy Decision Process 250
10.4 Financing Decision and Options in Asset Acquisition 250
10.5 Understanding Buying Decision 251
10.5.1 Implications of Acquisition Decision (Buying).............251
10.6 Understanding Leasing Decision 252
10.6.1 Type of Leasing Arrangement...................................252
10.6.2 Features of a Finance Lease 253
10.6.3 Advantages of Leasing..253
10.6.4 Disadvantages of Leasing...253
10.6.5 Implications of Lease Financing Decision 254
10.7 Fundamental Analyzes for Choosing Lease or Buy 254
10.7.1 Quantitative Analysis...254
10.7.1 Qualitative Analysis...254
10.7.2 Qualitative Factors to Consider in Lease vs. Buy Analysis 255
10.8 Relevant Cash Flow Analysis of Lease or Buy.....................258
10.8.1 Cash Flow Analysis for Buying Decision 258
10.8.2 Cash Flow Analysis of Lease Financing Decision..............259

10.9 Relevant Cash Flows for Lease or Buy Decision 259
10.10 Computation of Lease or Buy Decision 261
10.11 Chapter Review Questions 268
10.12 Chapter References and Bibliography 270

CHAPTER 11: FUNDAMENTALS OF MERGERS AND TAKEOVERS ... 272

11.1 Overview 272
11.2 The Concept of Mergers and Takeovers 273
11.3 Distinction Between Mergers and Takeovers 273
11.4 Types of Mergers 275
11.5 Types of Takeovers 276
11.6 Why Companies Merge and Takeover 277
11.6.1 Some Underlying Rationales 277
11.6.2 Merger and Takeover Drivers 278
11.7 Motives or Purpose of Mergers and Takeovers 280
11.8 Merger and Takeover Waves: Similarities and Differences .. 281
11.8.1 Key Determinants of Merger and Takeover Waves 281
11.8.2 Measuring the Success of Mergers and Acquisitions 282
11.8.3 Short-term Measures of Success 283
11.8.4 Long-term Measures of Success 283
11.9 Some Scenarios for Failure of Mergers and Acquisition 284
11.10 Reverse Takeovers 285
11.10.1 Uses of Reverse Takeovers 286
11.10.2 Benefits Reverse Takeovers 286
11.11 Due Diligence: Mergers and Takeovers 286
11.11.1 Types of Due Diligence 287
11.11.2 Objectives of Due Diligence 289
11.12 Mergers and Acquisition in Ghana- Motivation: 292
11.13 Laws that Support Mergers and Acquisitions in Ghana: 292

11.14 Examples of Mergers & Acquisitions in Ghana 293
11.15 Chapter Review Questions 293
11.16 Chapter References and Bibliography 293

CHPTER 12: VALUATION FOR MERGERS AND ACQUISITIONS 294

12.1 Overview 294
12.2 Overview and Nature of Valuation 295
12.3 Valuation as an Art or Science 295
12.4 Determinants of Pricing of a Merger or Takeover Bid 295
12.5 Valuation Methods 301
12.5.1 Stock Market Valuation 299
12.5.2 Asset Valuation 300
12.5.2.1 Book Value 300
12.5.2.2 Realizable or Break-up Value 300
12.5.2.3 Replacement Value 301
12.5.2.4 Factors to Consider in Selecting Assets Valuation Bases 301
12.5.3 Going-Concern Valuation 302
12.5.3.1 Capitalized Earnings Valuation 302
12.5.3.2 Price/Earnings Ratio Valuation 303
12.5.3.3 Significance of High P/E Ratio 304
12.5.3.4 Problems with Using P/E Ratios 304
12.5.4 Guidelines for a P/E Ratio-Based Valuation 305
12.5.4.1 Use of a Bidder's P/E Ratio 305
12.5.4.2 Use of Forecast Earnings 305
12.5.5 Dividend Valuation Model (Gordon Growth Model) 306
12.5.5.1 Assumptions in the Dividend Valuation Model 307
12.5.5.2 Discounted Cash Flow Valuation 307
12.6 Concept of Synergy and Determination 309
12.6.1 Categories of Synergy 309

12.6.2 Synergic Equation of Mergers and Takeovers 310
12.7 Chapter Review Questions 320
12.8 Chapter References and Bibliography 322

CHAPTER 13: FINANCING OPTIONS FOR ACQUISITIONS 324

13.1 Overview 324
13.2 Financing Methods 325
13.2.1 Cash Offers 325
13.2.2 Share-for-Share Offers 325
13.2.3 Vendor Placings and Vendor Rights 326
13.2.4 Security Packages 326
13.2.4.1 Problems of Associated with Security Packages 327
13.3 Strategic and Tactical Issues 327
13.3.1 Strategic Strategy Procedures 328
13.4 Shareholding and its Implication 328
13.5 Merger Regulation and Control 329
13.5.1 Legal Controls 329
13.5.2 Self-Regulatory Controls 329
13.6 The Bidding Processes 330
13.7 Takeover Bid Defenses 330
13.7.1 Pre-Bid Defenses 331
13.7.2 Post-bid Defenses 331
13.8 Estimating the Economic Gains and Cost of Mergers 331
13.9 All-Share Transaction 333
13.10 Chapter Review Questions 341
13.11 Chapter References and Bibliographies 344

GLOSSARY 345
SUBJECT INDEX 362

CHAPTER 1

OVERVIEW OF STRATEGIC FINANCIAL MANAGEMENT

1.1 Overview

This book discusses the principles, theories, analytical methods, and practical considerations that are helpful and relevant in addressing various issues in strategic financial management, a finance discipline that has greatly assumed enormous significance in the corporate world in recent times. This chapter provides an overview of the strategic financial management function that is crucial for the strategic positioning and long-term performance of the company.

> **Objectives of the Chapter**
>
> This chapter is organised into main objectives as follows:
> - To explain the term strategic financial management;
> - To distinguish between strategic financial management and financial management;
> - To explain the key functions performed by strategic financial management;
> - To ascertain the key principles of strategic financial management;
> - To explain the importance of strategic financial management;
> - To spell out the purpose of strategic financial management; and
> - To examine the constraints to strategic financial management.

> **Key Words Used in the Chapter**
> - Capital investment decisions
> - Financial management
> - Environmental assessment
> - Strategic financial management
> - Financial management
> - Strategy

1.2 Definition of Strategic Financial Management

The combination of the terms "strategy" and "finance" results in the term "strategic financial management." When planning strategically, one must always keep the big picture in mind. As has been demonstrated, strategic financial management (SFM) is the process by which the financial resources of any organization are managed to ensure that the organization's long-term goals can be achieved. It is presumed that the company has clear-cut plans for how it wants to spend its money. This is due to the fact that without such information, it is impossible to come to any kind of decision that will have a long-term or strategic impact on the firm.

Strategic financial management (SFM), as defined by Liu (2010), pertains to financial management theories that advocate for the most effective utilization and management of collected capital, prudent decision-making regarding profit distribution and reinvestment, and efficient financing practices within organizations.

Strategic financial management encompasses financial strategies that are intended to enhance and optimize financial management for the purpose of attaining corporate outcomes (Salazar et al., 2012). Financial strategy in particular "serves as a roadmap to attain and sustain business competitiveness while establishing a company as a global powerhouse."

Strategic management is defined as "a collection of managerial choices and activities that ascertain the enduring performance of an organization" (Wheelen & Hunger, 2010).

Karadag (2015) asserts that strategic financial management occupies a central position within the comprehensive management system of businesses. The performance and sustainability of profit-driven organizations are negatively impacted by the ineffectiveness and inefficiency of strategic financial management decisions.

Strategic financial management refers to the study of finance from a long-term perspective in line with the strategic goals of the business. In fact, financial management in its contemporary context is referred to as "strategic financial management," given that most of the issues considered are in line with the long-term perspectives of the firm.

Furthermore, the term strategic financial management, according to Delkhosh and Mousavi (2016), involves the collection of management decisions and actions that determine the long-term performance of a company. Strategic financial management includes environmental assessment, strategy formulation, strategy implementation, evaluation, and control. Therefore, strategic management focuses on and assesses the opportunities and external threats and emphasizes considering the strengths and weaknesses of a company. It relates to the identification of the internal weak and strong points of an organization, setting the long-term objectives, considering the various strategies, and selecting the specific strategies in order to continue the activity.

The term strategic financial management refers to a process for the identification, collection, selection, and analysis of financial data for the assistance of the management team in strategic decisions and organizational effectiveness assessment (Delkhosh & Mousavi 2016).

The function of strategic financial management starts with detecting the amount of funds required for the firm and then looking for the means or ways through which these funds are raised at cheaper rates so that the financial requirements of the business are fulfilled. In other words, it can also be termed applying the principles of management to the financial resources of a firm to achieve its business objectives.

1.3 Strategic Financial Management Versus Financial Management

Strategic financial management refers to the study of finance from a long-term perspective in line with the strategic goals of the business. There is a divergent viewpoint presented by strategic financial management. The practice of strategic financial management is to be aware of the fact that a positive net present value can be attained by a wide variety of projects. However, it is possible that the company does not have sufficient financial resources to carry out all of the initiatives that it has planned. As a consequence of this, it is possible that it will be necessary to prioritize certain projects more than others. If something like this happens, it may not be feasible to simply give precedence to the projects that have the highest net present value. The application of sound strategic financial management becomes extremely helpful at this point. It assists businesses in selecting projects that have the highest probability of being successful over the course of their operations.

The goal of conventional financial management is to maximize a company's value through the prudent accumulation and deployment of capital. As a direct result of this, it emphasizes how important it is to take on projects that have positive net present values. However, traditional methods of managing finances are useful for making decisions with a limited time horizon. For corporations, one of the primary functions of financial management is to act as a guide when it comes time to make three decisions: the decision regarding investments, the decision regarding financing, and the decision regarding dividends. On the other hand, these choices are made with a perspective that is either short- or medium-term.

In conclusion, strategic financial management is concerned with long-term financial decisions that generate profits for the company and the guarantee of a satisfactory return on investment (ROI) over an extended period of time. On the other hand, financial management refers to the process of planning the acquisition of funds, the investment of those funds, and the management of those funds in order to accomplish both short-term and long-term financial goals.

1.4 Functions Performed by Strategic Financial Management

Strategic financial management encompasses the entire spectrum of long-term financial activities performed by any organization. Some of the key decisions that are enabled by strategic financial management have been mentioned below.

- **Capital Investment Decisions**
  When viewed through the lens of strategic financial management, capital investment decisions made by an organization can be seen in a new light. For example, in the last 15 to 20 years, there has been a proliferation of asset-light businesses. Companies like Uber, Airbnb, and Facebook are currently at the top of their respective industries. They don't have many assets, however. Companies that specialize in strategic financial management would have been the first to notice this trend when making decisions about their long-term assets. As a result, they would have made a long-term commitment to illiquid assets, which could have resulted in a less-than-optimal return. Strategic financial management enables a company to anticipate the long-term consequences of its decisions. It is no coincidence that businesses that place a greater emphasis on strategic financial management have also invested more resources in digitising their operations.

- **Capital Structure Decisions**
  Once a firm has made a bold decision in respect of capital budgeting and working capital investment, it has to figure out the ways and means of adequately financing them in order to maximize return on such investments. The crucial issues in capital structure decisions include:
    - What is the best debt-to-equity ratio for the organization?
    - What is the necessary amount of finance for the investment?
    - What are the exact loan and equity instruments that the business should employ?
    - Where should the company raise funds (capital markets)?
    - What is the optimal time to raise the funds?
    - What is the cost of capital connected with the sources of financing?

- **Dividend Payout Decisions**
  This refers to the decision-making activities that relate to dividend payments to investors who have offered their financial resources by way of investment in share acquisition and ownership in the company. Dividend refers to the return that shareholders are paid for investing in the firm. Dividend payout decisions should be guided by the dividend policy that is being implemented by the firm at any given time. Strategic decisions should be made with respect to:
    - ✓ What form of dividend policy should the organization implement?
    - ✓ What is the optimal frequency of dividend payments to shareholders?
    - ✓ What is the appropriate dividend amount?
    - ✓ What method or kind of dividend should be used to distribute the dividend? etc.,

- **Location Decisions**
  When selecting a location for their operations, strategic investors and businesses frequently consider a wide range of factors. To cite merely one illustration, a great number of American corporations formerly maintained offices in China. If the decision were made today, fewer companies would select China as a location to locate their operations. This is a result of the ongoing hostilities and trade wars that are taking place between the two nations. As a result of this, establishing a business in China for the long term is fraught with greater peril than establishing a business in a country such as Ghana, which might be more expensive in the short-term but is less likely to experience trade wars in the long-term. When selecting a location for their operations, strategic investors and businesses frequently consider a wide range of factors.

- **Mergers and Acquisitions Decision**
  Businesses can benefit from conducting in-depth analyzes of their operational structures with the assistance of strategic financial management. During this in-depth analysis, businesses typically decide whether or not organic growth is their best option or whether or not they can also opt for inorganic expansion. This decision is typically made in order to

maximize profitability. The underlying idea has not been modified in any way. A company must be able to generate long-term benefits from an acquisition while also being able to bear the short-term expenses that are associated with the deal for the acquisition to be profitable for the company. On the other hand, strategic financial management ensures that businesses consider their long-term objectives prior to making any purchase decisions.

The bottom line is that strategic financial management is not a new technique for modeling financial data for making business decisions. In most cases, the tools and models used are the same. The change lies in the manner in which these results are interpreted. The long-term point of view changes how appealing each option looks and may influence the one that gets selected.

1.5 Principles of Strategic Financial Management

The outcomes of strategic financial management can be quite variable, and as a direct consequence of this need, a standardized set of guiding principles has been developed to ensure coherence among various institutions.

- **Matching resources with objectives**
  While implementing the principles of strategic financial management, an organization must be aware of the quantum of resources that it is likely to control in the long run. The company should also have a clear picture of how these assets will be distributed across their portfolio. The deployment of current resources must be based on the end goal. Strategic investments are costly to change. For example, it is difficult and costly to close a factory after it has been established. Financial experts assist in understanding the level of future economic activity and how resources can be best organised.

- **Maintaining productive capacity to meet current business objectives**
  The long-term is the primary consideration in terms of strategy in finance. In order for the company to be successful in the long run, it must first ensure that it will be profitable in the short-term. Therefore, preventing oneself from going bankrupt should be one of the aims of strategic financial management. Even if investments in R&D have the potential to make your company a market leader in the future, you should not continue making the

kind of massive investments that will drain your company's cash flow in the short-term. Instead, you should focus on making investments that will make your company more profitable in the long-term. If the company does not alter its pattern of spending, it may find itself susceptible to an unfriendly takeover in the not-too-distant future. As a result, the requirements of the current baseline must be satisfied. After the initial objectives have been met, the corporation will be able to put the surplus cash flow to use by investing in endeavors that have a more distant time horizon.

- **Keeping close eye on financing**
  With regards to strategic financial management, the investment decision may appear to be the most important. The choice of financing, however, is of equal significance (if not more important). Capital is a limited resource, and businesses implementing strategic financial management should recognize this. They ought to be familiar with the various financing options available to them. The cost of each potential funding option should also be considered. In the long run, most businesses aim to maintain a certain capital structure. This targeted financial structure is useful for linking tactical financing decisions with strategic ones over the long haul. The process of strategy and financial management become more cohesive with its aid. Companies should always keep a debt ceiling beyond which borrowing is strongly discouraged, as recommended by strategic financial management.

- **Evaluating strategic alternatives**
  Companies should constantly monitor their strategic options. In order to achieve their long-term goals, they may employ strategies such as partnerships and even outsourcing. In some cases, outsourcing may appear to be costly in the short-term. However, it allows the organization to scale its operations up and down at will. Many businesses value this option because they would rather invest their capital in core activities than build manufacturing hubs. Similarly, many businesses use franchising to expand over time. They can gain more market share even if it means losing control and dividing profits in the short run. The guiding principle here is that a company should try to maximize the long-term upside while minimizing the downside risks. Furthermore, when businesses see their relationships with

other organizations as long-term partnerships, they are less likely to be transactional. The philosophy of strategic financial management emphasises the use of tools such as a balanced scorecard. These tools can be modified to incorporate the financial aspect into the stated goals.

- **Integration of financial strategy with other strategies**
  The goal of strategic financial management is to ensure that the company's financial objectives are consistent with its other strategies. Only financial managers make financial decisions in a traditional financial management context. Strategic financial management, on the other hand, emphasises the importance of expanding the company's communication channels. Working in silos is discouraged. There is no such thing as a financial decision, according to this philosophy. The financial decision is simply the allocation of financial resources in the firm's strategic interests. Because the firm's strategic interests are shared, decisions must be shared as well.

1.6 Importance of Strategic Financial Management

1. **Aids in identifying the capital needs of the business**
   The earliest and most important job of financial management is to estimate the funds required for the business's smooth operation. This is a major responsibility of financial management. Due to differences in operation size, profit ambitions, and other aims and missions, the financial requirements of each organization will vary.

2. **Facilitates decision making pertaining to capital structure**
   After calculating the business's capital requirements, the finance manager's next task is to determine the appropriate capital structure. This entails deciding between short-term and long-term sources of financing and taking into account the costs associated with obtaining this financing.

3. **Aids in selecting the optimal source of financing**
   As several sources of obtaining capital are available on the market, the firm should be selecting the most relevant and correct option. Common ways of raising funds include the issuance of shares and debentures, taking out

loans from a financial institution, and the issuance of securities such as bonds.

4. **Allocation and investment of collected funds**
   Now, once the exact quantity of capital has been obtained, these funds are invested in a variety of revenue-generating and business-goal-aligned activities.

5. **Utilization of the excess money**
   It involves a choice about the firm's earnings and how they should be utilized. Depending on the company's future goals, there are two primary alternatives for profit utilization: excess profit should be distributed as a dividend or kept.

6. **Managing all cash expenditures**
   This basically refers to the management of funds so that no spending exceeds the budget. It includes numerous expenditures for which cash payments must be made, such as salary and wages, water and energy bills, and the amount necessary for the purchase of raw materials, etc.

7. **Controlling all finances**
   It is one of the essential functions since it contributes significantly to the achievement of the business's goals and objectives. It ensures that all operations are proceeding in line with the predetermined plans, and if not, it implements precise control measures.

1.7 Objectives of Strategic Financial Management

Strategic financial management aims to accomplish the following objectives within the context of the business world:

1. **To align the vision of the board and the management**
   The fact that it makes it easier to get everyone on the same page is the advantage of using strategic financial management, which stands out as being the most significant. When a company does not have strategic financial management in place, the board of directors and the management

team frequently disagree on the path that the company should take in the future. When dealing with issues that are related to strategic financial management, it is absolutely necessary for all parties involved to lay out their goals for the future in as much specific detail as possible. When every member of the group contributes to the planning process, it allows for more efficient management of the available funds. However, strategic financial management is advantageous due to the fact that businesses can be large and complicated, and their operations are frequently carried out in inefficient ways. This is why it is important to implement such management.

2. **To bring unity of purpose in setting common goals**
Strategic budgeting and planning help groups settle on shared goals. These unified goals are then communicated to the organization's lower ranks. The emphasis is on strategic goal attainment rather than impromptu creativity. In accordance with this unified strategy, the company's resources are allocated. This makes it easier to balance immediate needs with long-term objectives when allocating resources.

3. **To help to guide innovation and technology embracing**
Businesses today cannot afford to ignore the importance of technology. Due to the high price tag, information technology (IT) infrastructure must be constructed methodically. There is a need for strategic funding. Strategic financial planning requires thinking in terms of decades. In order to maintain its position as a market leader, the company must determine what technologies it requires. IT spending is not a linear process. A larger system will incorporate them within the next few years.

4. **To assists in new ideas acceptability**
Strategic financial management raises the level of consciousness in the upper echelons of an organization about the need for and impact of change. After this happens, executives and board members are more open to change. Introducing new projects is a great way to gain support. The Board of Directors is unlikely to make any changes if strategic financial management is lacking. Knowing that change is unavoidable but pleasant

if initiated voluntarily is one of the management skills learned from studying strategic financial management.

5. To help firms to focus on the competitive environment

A company with well-managed finances will keep an eye on its rivals. Strategic financial management is lacking, so the company's performance cannot be compared to its competitors. When businesses pay attention to competitive strategy and routinely monitor the business environment, they are better prepared to meet market challenges. Strategic financial management is the practice of using computer simulations to anticipate and plan for future changes in the business environment. Therefore, they can construct a more adaptable and robust organization that can weather the storm of intense competition.

1.8 Constraints to Strategic Financial Management

1. High cost of implementation

It is not easy to come up with a plan of action. Managers in charge of the day-to-day operations of a business cannot achieve this. Hiring managers with different backgrounds is necessary to create a long-term financial plan that fits in with the company's overall goals. These executives need a deep familiarity with recent and future developments in strategic thought. Extremely few people can boast this set of abilities. Therefore, it is costly to employ them.

2. Conflicting of varied goals

The biggest problem with strategic management is that it frequently causes a breakdown in interdepartmental communication and the consequent inability to meet either short-term or long-term goals. In theory, the answer is easy: the company should simply put long-term goals first. Unfortunately, this is easier said than done. Many companies feel serious pressure from shareholders to generate quarterly profits. That makes it so strategic that financial managers don't have much leeway to make their own decisions. Due to concerns from upper management and the Board of Directors about the company's stock price, strategic financial managers do not have unfettered freedom.

3. **Lack of flexibility**
The first step in formulating a plan of action is deciding on a set of goals. Choosing one set of goals automatically eliminates the possibility of achieving another. The flexibility of an organization will suffer if these goals are ignored. Strategic financial management is associated with less flexibility than other business models. This means they can't adjust as quickly to changes in their surroundings.

4. **Time constraints**
Every department should weigh in on the company's financial strategy as it is being developed. To be successful, a company's strategy requires that all of the organization's efforts and objectives align with one another. Many companies that have switched to a more strategic mode of management have discovered that it significantly slows down their operations. Since strategic financial management is a never-ending cycle, businesses must consistently invest in it if they hope to reap financial benefits.

5. **Lack of accuracy**
The practice of strategic financial management is predicated on the ability to accurately predict outcomes that will occur in the distant future. The decisions that are made by strategic financial management typically centre on the practitioners' projections of the external environment twenty years from now. The fact that the future very rarely plays out in the way that is anticipated is the primary factor contributing to the complexity of strategic management. Because of this, the strategy that is generated by this function frequently ends up being completely useless.

6. **Uncertainty in the external environment**
The conditions of the external environment are constantly shifting, and strategic financial management is unable to make adjustments to these conditions in a timely manner. As a result, strategic financial management presents a challenge for many businesses.

1.9 Chapter Review Questions

1. Explain the term strategic financial management (SFM).
2. Examine the main distinction between strategic financial management and financial management.
3. Explain the key functions involved in strategic financial management.
4. What are the main principles involved in strategic financial management?
5. Evaluate the importance of strategic financial management.
6. Explain the purpose of strategic financial management.
7. What are the main constraints confronting the smooth implementation of strategic financial management?

1.10 Chapter References and Bibliography

[1] Karadag, H. (2015). Financial management challenges in small and medium-sized enterprises: A strategic management approach. *EMAJ: Emerging Markets Journal*, 5(1), 26-40.

[2] Liu, Z. (2010). Strategic Financial Management in Small and MediumSized Enterprises, *International Journal of Business & Management*, 5(2): 887-894.

[3] McLean, R., (2003). *Financial management in healthcare organizations.* Clifton Park, NY: 331-349.

[4] Mishra, S. K., & Brahme, R. A. V. I. N. D. R. A. (2011). Study of strategic financial management and growth in micro and small-scale enterprises in Chhattisgarh. *The Indian Journal of Commerce*, 64(1), 70-84.

[5] Salazar, A. L.; Soto, R. C.; and Mosqueda, R. E. (2012). The impact of financial decisions and strategy on small business competitiveness, *Global Journal of Business Research (GJBR)*, 6(2): 332-349.

[6] Wheelen, L. T. & Hunger, D. (2010). *Strategic Management and Business Policy–Achieving Sustainability*. Pearson International Edition.

1.11 Recommended Reading List

[1] Bryce, H. J. (2017). *Financial and strategic management for nonprofit organizations*. Walter de Gruyter GmbH & Co KG.

[2] Chabotar, K. J. (2011). *Strategic finance*. Assoc. of Governing Boards.

[3] Sofat, R., & Hiro, P. (2015). *Strategic financial management*. PHI Learning Pvt. Ltd.

CHAPTER 2

FINANCIAL PLANNING

2.1 Overview

It is important to create a financial plan because it enables you to make the most of your assets, helps ensure that you meet your future goals, and gives you the confidence to weather any bumps along the way. Creating a financial plan is important because it enables you to make the most of your assets. It is critical to devise a strategy for one's financial future.

> **Objectives of the Chapter**
> This chapter is designed to achieve the following key objectives:
> - To explain what financial planning is;
> - To examine the objectives of financial planning;
> - To evaluate the factors that affect financial planning;
> - To explain the importance of financial planning;
> - To examine the types of financial planning;
> - To explain the key parts of cumulative capital requirement; and
> - to outline the key steps involved in the financial planning process.

> **Key Words Used in the Chapter**
> - ✓ Aggressive financing policy
> - ✓ Conservative financing policy
> - ✓ Cumulative capital requirement
> - ✓ Financial planning
> - ✓ Overcapitalization
> - ✓ Undercapitalization

2.2 Definition of Financial Planning

Financial planning is the process of forecasting the quantity of money that will be required in the future as well as analyzing the level of competition that exists in the market. The process of creating financial policies in connection with the acquisition, administration, and management of an organization's money is referred to as financial planning. In the framework of an organization's activities pertaining to the acquisition, administration, and management of finances, these policies are developed. Financial planning comprises an examination of the organization's internal and external environment, an assessment of the organization's mandate, mission, and values, and the identification of strategic issues (Bryson et al., 2028). In light of these evaluations, strategies, objectives, and plans are developed to tackle the identified issues.

Financial planning can be examined through the lens of both profit-oriented and public sector organizations, as stated by Bryson et al. (2018). The rationale for conducting strategic planning is evidently to optimize the performance of an entire organization or a subset of its units with regard to profit, market share, and other objectives associated with the business. Objective alignment, effort continuity, and performance-based effectiveness are critical justifications for engaging in strategic planning within the public sector.

Financial planning entails the examination and selection of opportunities that have the potential to generate financial success for the organization (McLean, 2003). Strategic and financial planning integration is the most effective method for ensuring that budget allocations are directed towards long-term solutions, according to Niles (2010). Strategic financial planning requires an examination of annual budgets from a long-term organizational standpoint to guarantee long-term financial success.

2.3 Objectives of Financial Planning

Through meticulous preparation of one's finances, the following objectives are intended to be attained:

- **To determining capital requirements**
  This will be decided based on a number of different factors, some of which include the cost of both current and fixed assets, the cost of promotional

activities, and long-range planning. When assessing the requirements for capital, it is important to look at the situation from the perspective of both the short-term and the long-term simultaneously.

- **To determining capital structure composition**
  The various forms of capital that are necessary for an organization to have in order for it to function properly are referred to as the "composition of capital," which is also known as the "capital structure." This includes decisions pertaining to the debt-equity ratio, both in the short-term and in the long-term, for the company.

- **To Frame financial policies**
  Planning your finances lays the groundwork for formulating effective financial policies in relation to cash control, lending, borrowing, and other aspects of finance by providing the foundation for doing so through the planning process.

- **To determine maximum utilization of scarce financial resources.**
  A financial manager's job is to make sure that the limited financial resources are utilized to the fullest extent of their potential, in the most effective manner possible, and at the lowest possible cost in order to generate the highest possible return on investment. This is the responsibility that falls on the shoulders of a financial manager.

- **To enhance the preparation of financial budgets**
  The process of financial planning allows for the gathering of the information that is necessary for the preparation of the financial estimates (budget) for the company.

2.4 Factors Affecting Financial Planning

It is important to keep in mind that the following factors, regardless of the size of the organization, are likely to have an influence on the tasks that are involved with financial planning:

1. Firm's spending habits

The spending patterns of a company have a direct bearing on the company's financial health. How the company chooses to spend its money today will determine whether or not it is successful in meeting its future financial goals. It is very important to stay within one's financial means if one wishes to have a successful future. When you spend more than you have, you risk losing the credibility that you have with your lenders. If one is unable to exercise proper financial restraint, they will be subjected to a number of additional severe and unanticipated consequences. In a nutshell, the firm has to keep a close eye on its spending if it really wants to be able to live comfortably within its means in the days ahead.

2. Financial potential

Your current savings, investments, and capacity to save for the future are the primary factors that will determine how far and how quickly you can advance financially. If you want to get places quickly and easily, you have no choice but to pay close attention to how well off your finances are right now.

3. Savings and investments

The manner in which you choose to invest in it is very important. In the event that you make even a small mistake, you run the risk of having a challenging time for the rest of your life. When it comes to savings, for instance, when one is planning for retirement, one should make sure to choose the best retirement plan. The same considerations should be made when selecting a vehicle for a retirement investment. Pick the very best option, and do not settle for anything less.

4. Provision for emergencies

If you do not include a section in your financial plan for unexpected expenses, then your planning is insufficient. It is irresponsible to keep one's attention solely on investments and to ignore the fact that unexpected events can occur at any time. Having adequate protection from your insurance provider is the most effective strategy for handling unexpected events. You will have peace of mind knowing that your savings will continue to be safe and sound, no matter what the future may bring.

5. Financial planner or advisor

When we are in need of assistance with our finances, there are people in the financial industry who can lend a helping hand. The act of having a conversation with or working with a certified financial expert has the potential to alter a person's viewpoint or perspective on financial planning. Consulting their friends, relatives, or other unqualified individuals on matters pertaining to their finances is a common but grave error that most people make when planning, and it is one that you must steer clear of. Although you might glean some useful information from them, only certified financial planners or advisors can point you in the right direction for your particular situation.

6. Financial decision responsibilities

How many people directly depend on you for their financial support? Be sure to include those who are dependent on you in your financial plan, such as your parents or your children, especially if they are financially dependent on you. In that case, no matter how hard you try to put money aside, it will not be possible for you to save up for either your short-term or your long-term goals.

7. Financial goals

How many different monetary objectives do you have? Is it possible to achieve them? It is important to set goals that can be accomplished. In the same vein, it is essential to rank them in order of importance. If you are serious about financial planning, you should try to avoid the practice of simply having goals without understanding which ones are more important. Just make sure that your financial plan is in line with your financial goals. After you have done that, it will be much simpler for you to transform something that is appealing on paper into something that is appealing in real life.

8. Age of the firm

The age of your company as of right now is a significant factor that will play a significant role in the state of your finances over the next few days. In most cases, a young company or one that has recently begun operations simply does not have the financial resources necessary to take many risks. Because of this, it is essential that it start working on your behalf as quickly as is humanly possible. The number of years that your company has been in business is another factor that should not be overlooked because it will influence the amount of time that it still has before it stops being profitable.

9. Changing culture
The culture of today is always evolving, and while some aspects of that culture can be disregarded, others must be embraced. Are you prepared monetarily to deal with what is inevitably going to happen? For instance, do you feel confident that you will be able to afford significant events such as your children's weddings and graduations? Adapting your financial strategy to meet the changing needs of your life without depleting your savings can be accomplished with the help of a good financial plan.

10. Economic condition of the country
The firm should always be concerned about the state of the economy because its performance can have a positive or negative impact on its life and financial fortunes. For instance, if the economy is growing, it may be in a position to increase the amount of money it saves and concentrate on achieving additional financial goals. On the other hand, when the economy is contracting, it may find it appealing to focus on the most important goals as a way to cushion itself against the challenging times that are likely to lay in waiting.

11. Solvency and liquidity
Only put your money into businesses or pursue goals related to your finances that have a good chance of generating a satisfactory return on investment. If the firm wants to defeat the purpose of financial planning, focusing on anything else will do it. This indicates that one needs to have a high degree of adaptability in order to shift toward goals or endeavors that are more appealing at any given point in time.

2.5 Importance of Financial Planning
The following is a concise explanation of the significance:

1. **Sufficiency in funding**
   The process of financial planning ensures that sufficient funds, both short-term and long-term, are made available to cater to working capital

requirements as well as capital budget decisions, respectively. This can be done by making sure that sufficient funds are made available in both the short-term and the long-term.

2. **Stability in operations**

   It is possible to keep operations and investments stable with the assistance of financial planning, which makes it easier to keep a reasonable balance between cash outflows and cash inflows. This, in turn, helps to maintain the stability of operations and investments by the firm.

3. **Propels growth and expansion**

   The development of growth and expansion plans, which are essential to the long-term viability of the business, can be facilitated by careful financial planning. This is because growth and expansion plans are essential to the long-term viability of the business.

4. **Better investment decisions**

   The preparations that are made using financial planning make it possible for businesses that engage in financial planning to more easily invest capital. This is made possible thanks to the fact that financial planning is practiced.

5. **Reduction of uncertainty**

   The process of financial planning helps reduce uncertainty in relation to shifting market trends, which can be easily dealt with if sufficient funds are available to cover unexpected expenses.

6. **Reduction in business risk**

   The expansion of the business may be hampered by a number of unknown factors; however, the risks associated with these factors may be reduced through careful financial planning. This helps to ensure that the concern will continue to be profitable in addition to maintaining its stability.

2.8 Types of Financial Planning

Basically, there are two main classes of financial plans, and these are:
- Short-term financial planning;
- Medium-term financial planning; and
- Log-term financial planning.

Short-term Financial Plan

The short-term financial plan outlines financial goals and the investment needs for up to a one-year period. Such a plan is less uncertain than a long-term plan and can be easily corrected if required. Plans that relate to working capital investments fall under short-term financial planning. The short-term financial plans include creating an emergency fund that is helpful in meeting unexpected expenditures such as increases in prices, medical emergencies, and temporary income losses. Emergency funds can be created by investing in short-term interest-yielding securities.

Medium-term Financial Plan

A financial plan for a period of three to five years comes under medium-term plans. This is the period wherein you have goals for investments in ventures that have a maturity range of 3-5 years. The firm can also look into creating a safe multipurpose corpus of the fund to retire a loan or cover your wedding expenses. The medium-term financial plans identify life goals that require an assured amount of money. It will also suggest that you make investments in bonds or time deposits in order to help you achieve your goals.

Long-term Financial Plan

The long-term financial plan is for periods over five (5) years and beyond. Planning for the long term is essential to enjoying financial security in your retirement years. Preparing for children's higher education and wedding also falls under long-term financial planning. This is because, over a longer horizon, the market volatility levels out and you have better chances of earning higher returns.

2.7 Cumulative Capital Requirement (CCR)

The cumulative capital requirement refers to the aggregate capital needed to finance the entire business activities (both short-term and long-term) of a firm for a given period of time. It refers to the total amount of capital that is required by a firm to achieve both short-term and long-term financial goals. The cumulative capital requirement (CCR) diagram below shows three (3) possible long-term financing paths a firm can pursue, as shown in Figure 2.1.

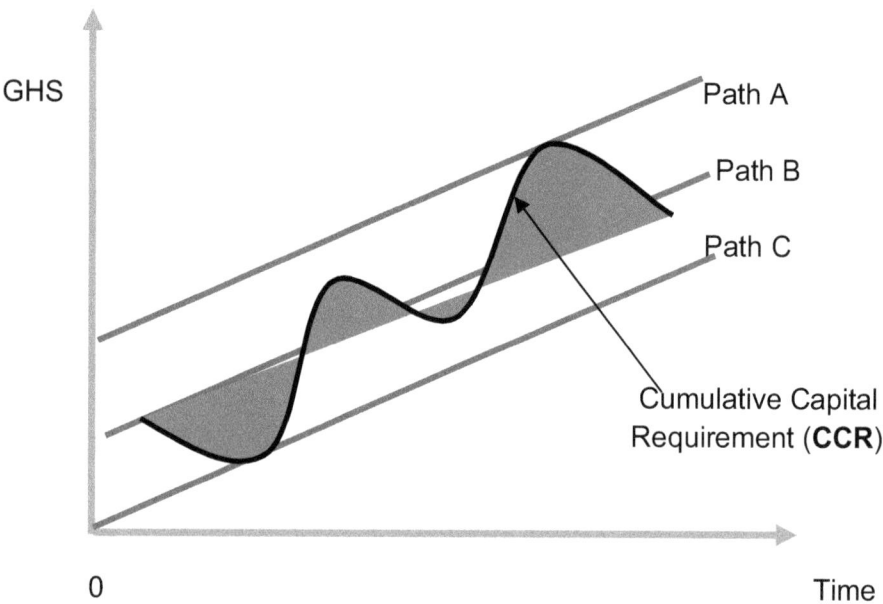

Figure 2.1: Cumulative Capital Requirement. Adopted from Brealey & Myers (1996)

2.8 Key Financial Effect of Cumulative Capital Requirement (CCR)

Path A

The company consistently maintains a level of financing that exceeds the CCR throughout this trajectory. Following this financial trajectory, the organization is inevitably going to encounter the following consequences:

- **Permanent cash surplus**
The consistent utilization of this financing route in excess of the CCR suggests that the company had surplus cash resources, rendering them unnecessary, without making a deliberate attempt to exercise cautious cash management.

- **Overcapitalization**

Because there is an abundance of cash, the company invests an excessive amount of money in the utilization of its working capital without giving adequate consideration to efficiency.

- **Conservative financing policy**

A less cautious financial strategy is implemented by the company. In light of the surplus monetary resources at hand, a lenient approach to financing (conservative) is consequently implemented.

Path B

The company pursues this course of action by maintaining a level of finances that varies intermittently above and below the CCR. In such a circumstance, the firm's financing strategy is unpredictable, contingent on the interplay between the available cash level and the CCR, and it experiences intermittent cash surpluses. The subsequent consequences are inevitable for the organization that proceeds down this financial trajectory.

- **Fluctuating cash balances**

The persistently higher value of this financing option relative to the CCR suggests the possibility of cash surpluses and deficits, which are contingent upon the magnitude of the CCR and the quantity of cash on hand.

- **Mixed of overcapitalization and undercapitalization**

When the firm's cash supply exceeds the critical cash balance (CCC), it engages in excessive investment in working capital (overcapitalization). Conversely, in the event of a cash balance shortfall, the firm employs an undercapitalization financing strategy.

- **Mixed financing policy**

In accordance with the interplay between available cash resources and the CCR, the business will employ both cautious and daring financing methods contingent on whether it is confronted with overcapitalization or undercapitalization.

Path C:
In this manner, the organization maintains a financial level that consistently falls below the CCR. Following this financial trajectory, the organization is inevitably going to encounter the subsequent consequences.

- **Permanent cash deficit**
The fact that this financing path is consistently below the CCR indicates that the organization has limited cash resources at its disposal, resulting in a scarcity of cash that necessitates a strong commitment to smart cash management and utilization.

- **Undercapitalization**
Due to the limited availability of cash, the company invests less on working capital use while being careful, in an effort to maximize efficiency.

- **Aggressive financing policy**
The company decides to pursue a more aggressive funding strategy. Consequently, as a result of the financial shortfall, a more stringent finance strategy is implemented.

2.9 Steps Involved in Financial Planning

The key steps involved in financial planning include the following:

- **Determine your present financial status or circumstances**
Determine your present financial condition in terms of income, savings, living expenditures, and debts as the initial stage in financial planning. This is your current wealth. One can compile a list of current assets, debt balances, and expenditures for numerous goods. This will establish a basis for financial planning efforts.

- **Determine the financial objectives**
Using the vision and mission statement you have produced for your organization as a guide, one must have a vision for the company as a whole. Creating a comprehensive financial plan requires the identification of certain financial goals. You must choose your financial objectives. Your financial

objectives might range from spending all of your present income to building substantial savings and investment strategies for future stability and independence. Developing financial objectives involves examining and defining how and why you feel about money, your profit expectations, maximization of return on investment, shareholder wealth maximization etc. The purpose of this analysis is to distinguish between your financial necessities and your desires.

- **Identify and evaluate alternatives and collect data**
  It is essential to be creative while planning since it assists in the process of arriving at options that are beneficial. If you think about everything that could be done differently, you will be able to come to decisions that are both more useful and more enjoyable to you. Hence, you must keep on obtaining relevant information related to your financial plans and possible alternatives.

- **Measure the level of risks**
  Every decision-making process includes a risk component. For example, it may be impossible to amass multibillion-dollar retirement savings. Other options, such as placing money into a savings account or purchasing popular items, incur minimal or no risk. In such situations, the possibility of losing something of significant value is small or nonexistent. In many situations involving financial decision-making, recognising and assessing risk is difficult.

- **Implement a financial action plan**
  Create a strategy for achieving your financial goals as the next phase in the financial planning process. Specifically, this means picking a methodical path toward success. Once the immediate objectives are met, the next most pressing ones will take centre stage, and so on, until your immediate (short-term), intermediate (medium), and long-term monetary needs are met. To prevent spending too much money, it is important to put a budget (financial estimates) into action and make sure it is followed to the letter.

- **Examine and adjust your budget through evaluation**
  The process of financial planning is dynamic and does not end when a decision is made and your budget is drawn and implemented. As such, it is important to regularly evaluate the choices you make about your money. Given the dynamic nature of individual, societal, and economic issues, periodic evaluations become obligatory. The current financial planning method will become a useful tool for reacting to unanticipated events, such as medical problems or accidents. Identify whether there is a dissimilarity (variance) between actual performance and the target stated in the budget, and then address any discrepancies that were uncovered.

2.10 Chapter Review Questions

1. Define the term 'Financial Planning'
2. Evaluate the main objectives of financial planning.
3. Examine the key factors that affect financial planning activities.
4. What are the main types of financial planning?
5. Evaluate the key financial planning strategies that are adopted in the concept of cumulative capital requirement (CCR).
6. What are the main steps involved in the financial planning activities?

2.11 Chapter References and Bibliography

[1] Brealey, R. A & Myers, S. C. (1996). Principles of corporate finance, (5th. Ed)., New York: McGraw-Hill.

[2] Bryson, J. M., Edwards, L. H., & Van Slyke, D. M. (2018). Getting strategic about strategic planning research. *Public management review*, 20(3), 317-339.

[3] George, B., Walker, R. M., & Monster, J. (2019). Does strategic planning improve organizational performance? A meta-analysis. *Public Administration Review*, 79(6), 810-819.

[4] Hunger, J. D. (2020). *Essentials of strategic management*.

[5] Niles, N. J. (2010). A case study in strategic financial planning in health service organizations. *Journal of Business Case Studies (JBCS)*, 6(5).

2.12 Recommended Reading List

[1] Bryson, J. M. (2018). *Strategic planning for public and nonprofit organizations: A guide to strengthening and sustaining organizational achievement*. John Wiley & Sons.

[2] Kapoor, J. R., Dlabay, L. R., Hughes, R. J., & Stevenson, L. (2018). *Personal finance*. Pearson.

[3] Smith, R. D. (2020). *Strategic planning for public relations*. Routledge.

CHAPTER 3

WORKING CAPITAL MANAGEMENT

3.1 Overview

Firms require efficient management of their working capital to ensure continuous business operations. The main aim of working capital management is to ensure that a firm is able to continue its operations and that it has the ability to sufficiently satisfy both maturing short-term debt and all operational expenses in order not to fall into the trap of over-trading.

Objectives of the Chapter

The chapter seeks to address the following objectives:

- To explain the meaning of working capital management;
- To examine the key components of working capital;
- To identify the scope of working capital;
- To examine the variation in working capital;
- To identify the types of working capital policies;
- To identify the objectives of working capital management;
- To examine the effect of working capital management on profitability;
- To identify the importance of working capital management;
- To examine the cash conversion cycle;
- To examine cash management, accounts receivables management, and inventory management; and
- to compute and analyze the key working capital ratios.

> **Key Words Used in the Chapter**
>
> - ✓ Aggressive working capital financing
> - ✓ Cash conversion cycle
> - ✓ Cash management
> - ✓ Conservative working capital
> - ✓ Gross working capital
> - ✓ Inventory management
> - ✓ Net working capital
> - ✓ Permanent working capital
> - ✓ Receivables management
> - ✓ Regular working capital
> - ✓ Reserve working capital
> - ✓ Seasonal working capital
> - ✓ Temporary working capital
> - ✓ Working capital management

3.2 Definition of Working Capital Management

Working capital is defined as the total short-term resources available to the firm (both current assets and current liabilities). The reason for this definition is that it is believed that working capital comprises the totality or summation of current assets and current liabilities, which are constantly recycled in the course of the day-to-day operations of the business. In addition, working capital has a short-term investment focus that is easily reversible to meet the changing circumstances of the business. Working capital is often regarded as the livelihood of every successful business. If a firm's current assets are greater than its current liabilities, then it has positive working capital. The ideal working capital ratio is 2:1. This means that the total current liabilities should be financed by half (50%) of the total current assets (short-term assets). Positive working capital is required to ensure that a firm is able to continue its operations and that it has sufficient funds to settle both maturing short-term debt and upcoming operational expenses.

Working capital management involves decisions relating to short-term assets and short-term financing; hence, it is a short-term financial planning tool. Working capital management involves managing the relationship between a firm's short-term assets and its current liabilities.

Attom & Afzalur (2022) posit that working capital management (WCM) is a set of rules and procedures for keeping an eye on short-term loans and current assets, like inventory, receivables, cash, and cash equivalents. This is done to make sure that cash flows and returns stay within generally acceptable limits, which helps the business grow and expand.

3.3 Key Components of Working Capital
Working capital management practices strictly involve the management of a firm's current assets and current liabilities, as categorized below:

Current assets
Current assets include cash and cash equivalents; inventory of raw materials; work-in-progress; and finished goods; marketable securities such as Treasury bills; and amounts receivable from account receivables, etc.

Current liabilities
Current liabilities include account payables falling due within one year and may involve amounts owed to trade account payables, taxation payable, dividend payments due, short-term loans, long-term debts maturing within one year, etc.

3.4 Scope of Working Capital
Working capital management involves the following key areas:

- **Cash Management**

This involves determining the amount of cash that will allow the firm to meet its day-to-day obligations while simultaneously reducing the expenditures that are involved with maintaining a cash reserve. Cash management is to determine the optimal cash balances that will be required by the company to finance ongoing and short-term business activities in order to guarantee that operations run smoothly without any difficulties caused by a lack of liquidity. Cash flow management pertains to the effective utilization of an organization's short-term investments and cash. Cash flow management decision-making is predicated on maintaining a balance between the organization's cash holdings and short-term investments, including treasury bills and deposit accounts (Salas-Molina et al. 2018).

As a result, Ross et al. (2002) state that retaining an excessive amount of cash is inefficient, and holding an insufficient amount of cash may result in significant shortfall costs. In contrast, transaction costs are involved with the movement of cash from or from a cash account into or from any other short-term asset that is accessible. These assets include Treasury bills and other marketable securities, among others.

Salas-Molina et al. (2018) define the cash management problem as typically involving two categories of assets: the cash balance and short-term assets, including marketable securities and interest-bearing accounts. Managing cash balances typically requires the implementation of control limits or a set of boundaries.

The purpose of this is to determine the optimal cash balances that will be required by the company to finance ongoing and short-term business activities.

- **Inventory Management**.

Find the optimal level of inventory that not only enables continuous production but also reduces the amount of money invested in raw materials, reduces the amount of money spent on reordering, and, as a result, boosts cash flow. This level of inventory should be determined so that it not only enables continuous production but also reduces the amount of money invested in reordering. This strategy makes use of a number of different approaches, some of which include just-in-time (JIT), economic order quantity (EOQ), and economic production quantity (EPQ), among others.

- **Account Receivables Management.**

Determine the appropriate credit policy, that is, the credit terms that will attract customers, in such a way that any impact on cash flows and the cash conversion cycle will be offset by increased revenue and, consequently, return on capital, such as trade discounts and other allowances. This should be done in order to ensure that any impact on cash flows and the cash conversion cycle will be offset by increased revenue and return on capital. By doing so, any impact on cash flows will be neutralized as a result of this action. Because it prevents the tying up of cash in the form of a huge sum due by borrowers, which has a negative influence on the cash operating cycle, the management of receivables is of the utmost significance.

The firm must have a credit policy guiding its credit management system. Credit scoring and credit risk assessment must be the cardinal principles in approving credits. Credit scoring is an approach used to assess the creditworthiness of an individual by examining their information in order to ascertain the probability that they will fail to repay a loan (Abdou & Pointon, 2011).

The current economic significance of credit risk assessment has been demonstrated by Zhang et al. (2018). This is not only due to the yearly increase in the volume of individual unsecured loans but also to the rapidly rising probability of default risk.

Credit risk assessment frequently relies on credit scoring models that are established within the credit industry. These models are extensively employed to assess the likelihood of an applicant defaulting (Sousa et al., 2016).

- **Account Payables Management (i.e., Short-term financing)**

Determine the most appropriate kind of financing, taking into account the cash conversion cycle, and consider the following: The credit that is granted by the supplier is the preferred method of financing the inventory; nevertheless, it is conceivable that financial help from a bank may be necessary in some circumstances (or an overdraft). As stated by Samuels (1994), effective working capital management necessitates the provision of solutions to the subsequent issues:

- What amount of currency must be available for calls at different times throughout the upcoming planning period?
- At what extent of inventory should the company operate?
- What is the firm's ability and speed of repayment for its short-term loans and overdraft?
- Which credit period ought the company to extend to its clientele?
- Should the company expedite supplier payments in order to capitalize on the cash discount that is being extended?
- What percentage of current assets ought to be funded through short-term investments?
- In what ways does the firm's working capital level change?

3.5 Variations in Working Capital

Working capital may be categorized using the following key based on its intrinsic characteristics:

3.5.1 Gross Working Capital (GWC) and Net Working Capital (NWC)

The term "GWC" refers to the aggregate value of short-term assets that are frequently issued by businesses. In contrast, NWC is calculated by deducting all short-term obligations of the company from its total current assets. This metric is based on the classification of working capital components that make up GWC. These components belong to current assets and are needed to make cash flow from ongoing activities. It is common to refer to the level of demand a company has for financing its current assets as its "overall current asset financing requirements." It encompasses all investments in present assets as a component of working capital. Thus, it computes the comprehensive expense associated with the effective operation of a company. Samuels et al. (1990) suggest that at least twice the magnitude of short-term debts owed should constitute gross working capital so as to maintain a working capital ratio of 2:1. Working capital, as established by subtracting current liabilities from current assets, is denoted as NWC.

3.5.2 Permanent Working Capital (PWC) and Temporary Working Capital (TWC)

Working capital can be broadly categorized into two types, namely, long-term and short-term. Fletcher et al. (2018) argue that a critical element of the theory of working capital management that requires sufficient consideration is the explicit and unambiguous differentiation between short-term and long-term characteristics.

- **Permanent Working Capital (PWC)**

Permanent working capital is the proportion of working capital that remains constant during any particular period, irrespective of sales or business activity. Therefore, PWC represents the portion of a business's working capital that it is necessary to retain in order to sustain its operations, irrespective of the operational cycle. Therefore, it denotes the bare minimum working capital requirement upon which the operation of the business is predicated. Permanent working capital, on the other hand, fluctuates throughout the business's existence in response to evolving business opportunities and expansion or contraction. Permanent working capital guarantees that investments made in working capital requirements are utilized effectively in order to ensure the continued existence of the business. It is subdivided further into:

- **Regular Working Capital**

The minimal quantity of a firm's liquid capital is required in order for the company to be able to transfer money between its bank accounts, inventory, and accounts receivable and vice versa.

- **Reserve Working Capital**

When a firm is confronted with an unanticipated or unanticipated occurrence, such as an increase in the prices of inputs and outputs, economic lockdowns, failures, depressions, lock-outs, or strikes, it may be required for the company to have additional standby working capital.

- **Temporary Working Capital (TWC)**

This category pertains to working capital needs that are generally considerably greater than permanent working capital due to various factors, including advantageous business conditions, seasonal peaks, and favorable trade cycles (Brigham & Houston, 1999). On the contrary, temporary working capital is defined as working capital that exceeds permanent working capital. Temporary working capital is primarily required to address economic emergencies and seasonal demand increases. Frequently, temporary working capital exhibits attributes such as being unique and seasonal in nature. The following are several primary methods by which temporary working capital can be allocated to groups:

- ✓ **Special Working Capital**

This pertains to the provisional funds necessary to support distinctive business operations, such as expanding production methods, conducting more research and development, and implementing effective marketing and promotion strategies for a one-of-a-kind product.

- ✓ **Seasonal Working Capital**

A variety of current asset components are incorporated into seasonal working capital. Enhanced working capital needs for current assets are a consequence of business expansions driven by seasonal and special event factors during periods of strong economic activity.

3.5.3 Working Capital Financing Strategies: (Conservative, Aggressive, and Moderate)

Depending on how an organization chooses to manage its short-term funds, working capital can be further subdivided into numerous categories. The management of working capital is commonly categorized into three distinct approaches, as identified by Ukaegbu (2014) as; conservative, moderate, or aggressive. Corporate working capital financing can be approached with either prudence or aggression.

✓ **Conservative Working Capital (CWC) Financing**
When a company has current asset components in excess of what its current liabilities can finance, this is referred to as the conservative working capital financing strategy (Sohail et al. 2016). Consequentially, both short-term and long-term financing sources are utilized to jointly finance the components of current assets. Further, in terms of short-term financial management outcomes, a conservative approach to working capital financing typically results in mediocrity.

✓ **Aggressive Working Capital (AWC) Financing**
When the current assets and working capital components of a company are inadequate to fulfill the firm's trading requirements, an AWC is declared. A significant working capital challenge confronts the organization. While an organization may use its short-term debts to fund its short-term investments, its current asset investment can only be financed through short-term debts due to the aggressive working capital strategy of the company. In contrast to aggressive working capital, which carries a higher level of risk, conservative working capital does not yield a high rate of return and does the opposite. Cash flow generated by a business is directly proportional to its capacity to enhance its operations, according to this theory. Nevertheless, in the event that a business inquires for additional credit from its suppliers, it risks impairing its operations by potentially forgoing cost reductions.

✓ **Moderate Working Capital (MWC) Financing**
The "moderate working capital strategy" is a framework proposed by Mansoori et al. (2019) that aims to strike a balance between conservative and aggressive approaches to working capital financing. Investments in working capital components that are well-balanced in light of the risk profile should be the focal point of a modest strategy for financing working capital.

3.5.4 Positive, Negative and Zero Working Capital
Another way to classify the components of working capital is according to the proportional magnitudes of current assets and short-term liabilities. "Net working capital" thus emerges as the central concern. As determined by

deducting current liabilities from current assets, the surplus or deficit in "net working capital" is defined (Mandal & Goswami, 2010).

✓ **Positive Working Capital (PWC)**
A company has positive working capital if the value of its current assets surpasses the value of its current liabilities. This signifies that the company's current assets exceed its total current liabilities, thereby establishing a favorable position for the company that guarantees adequate capital infusion for ongoing business activities due to the adequacy of current asset components.

✓ **Negative Working Capital (NWC)**
On the contrary, a company incurs a "negative working capital" position when its current assets are significantly lower than its current liabilities. This suggests that the company's current liabilities exceed the capacity of its current assets to settle them, thereby creating precarious circumstances that may swiftly escalate into business insolvency due to the burdensome nature of short-term obligations to account payables. A company in this predicament is perpetually inundated with increasing levels of recurring financial obligations. This is highly detrimental to the survival of the firm.

✓ **Zero Working Capital (ZWC)**
In this case, the current asset and current liability components are of equal magnitude to signify parity between the two primary components of working capital. Therefore, the current asset components correspond to an equivalent amount of the requirement for short-term financing. (current liabilities minus current assets) According to Brigham & Houston (1999), there is a current global perception among business managers that achieving zero working capital is equivalent to increasing the efficacy of their working capital through the implementation of a moderate financing strategy.

3.6 Types of Working Capital Policy (WCP)
Working capital policy is an established set of regulations and processes intended to oversee current asset components, including cash equivalents and short-term financing, in order to maintain the company's liquidity at a level

sufficient to support its growth and development. Brigham & Houston (1999) define "WCP" as the process by which an organization determines its short-term financing in accordance with the values of its current and desired assets. The following are the two most prevalent strategies utilized by businesses to regulate their working capital:

3.6.1 Conservative Working Capital Policy

When current asset components are funded through a combination of current liabilities and alternative long-term capital sources, an organization is considered to have adopted a conservative working capital policy. To clarify, the organization possesses readily convertible current assets. A prudent working capital plan is a risk-free working capital financing technique distinguished by diminished risk and lower returns. The research conducted by Sohail et al. (2016) indicates that the predominant origins of a firm's working capital are classified as long-term sources, which encompass equity, debt, and other forms of long-term credits, among others. Financial managers are virtually never able to make prudent financing decisions due to the availability of current asset components within the framework of the conservative financing approach. This is due to the method's incorporation of a conventional funding approach, which distinguishes it from alternative methods.

3.6.2 Aggressive Working Capital Policy

Conversely, within the framework of this policy, the operational capital elements of an organization that are categorized as current assets are not eligible for long-term financing, as their sustenance is limited to immediate obligations (Gitman & Zutter, 2012). Typically, organizations that embrace an aggressive working capital policy are cognizant of the substantial risk associated with this approach. As a result, they exert considerable efforts to maintain optimal levels of current asset components, or even a minimal quantity in certain situations, which are consistently covered by current liabilities. The organization encounters an aggressive working capital phenomenon if its trading capacity is not met.

3.7 Factors that Affect the Size of Working Capital

An overabundance of working capital results in unwarranted inventory accumulation and capital waste, whereas a shortfall of working capital disrupts operational continuity and hinders the organization from fulfilling its commitments. Consequently, the organization must possess a highly precise estimation of its working capital. Consequently, the financial manager bears the obligation of approximating the appropriate amount of working capital. Prior to determining the working capital amount, the financial management must consider the following elements:

1. Duration of Cash Conversion Cycle

There is a direct correlation between the total amount of working capital required and the duration of the cash conversion cycle. The duration encompassing the industrial process is denoted by the term "conversion cycle." It continues until payment is received subsequent to the transaction's conclusion, commencing with the procurement of basic materials. For the seamless operation of the business cycle, working capital is of the utmost importance. The working capital requirement is greater or heftier for organizations with a lengthy conversion cycle; nevertheless, businesses with a short conversion cycle generally have a reduced working capital requirement.

2. Nature of the Business

The subsequent consideration in calculating the required working capital for a given organization is the characteristics of the enterprise in which the organization operates. The short conversion cycle requirements of a retail establishment or trading firm substantially diminish the necessity for working capital. In contrast to retail establishments, wholesalers necessitate a more substantial working capital investment due to the expansion of their inventory holdings and the prevailing practice of selling products on credit, both of which contribute to an extended conversion cycle for the enterprise. Operating on credit, maintaining an inventory of raw materials and finished goods, and transforming raw materials into finished goods all require the manufacturing company to maintain a significant working capital position.

3. Size of Business Operations

Keeping a larger number of products in inventory, clients, and other things is necessary for the corporation because of the size at which the business is done. As a consequence of this, they normally own a substantial quantity of working capital, in contrast to businesses that operate on a smaller scale, which typically have a reduced requirement for working capital.

4. Variations in the Business Cycle:

Due to the positive market conditions that characterize the prosperity era—including heightened demand, increased production, expanded inventory, and an accumulation of account receivables—a greater amount of working capital is necessary. More financial resources are necessary to address each of these factors. Conversely, during a period of economic distress, when demand is low, there is a reduction in the need for working capital as there are fewer accounts receivable and inventory to maintain.

5. Seasonal Factors:

Working capital requirements for a company that sells goods throughout the year are constant. However, for a company that sells seasonal goods, working capital requirements increase substantially due to increased demand, the need to maintain a larger inventory, and the requirement for a fast supply. On the contrary, the quantity of working capital needed decreases during the off-season or idle season due to the substantial reduction in demand.

6. Technology and the Production Cycle.

When an organization employs a labour-intensive production method, it necessitates a greater amount of working capital to ensure sufficient cash flow for labour payments. Conversely, in the event that an organization employs a machine-intensive production method, it will necessitate a smaller amount of working capital due to the fixed capital investment in machinery and the resulting reduction in operational expenses. A prolonged production cycle necessitates a greater amount of working capital due to the extended duration required for the transformation of basic materials into finished products. Conversely, a shorter production cycle leads to reduced financial investment in inventory and basic materials, thereby reducing the need for working capital.

7. Extent of Credit is Granted and its Availability
The duration typically allocated for the collection of funds from credit transactions is referred to as the "credit policy." It depends on a variety of factors, including the creditworthiness of customers and clients, business regulations, and so forth. A company that maintains a lax credit policy will require additional working capital investments (requirements). Conversely, a business that adheres to a stringent or short-term credit policy could potentially operate with reduced working capital. The credit policy also encompasses the availability of credit, which pertains to the quantity and duration of credit received by the organization from its suppliers. A reduction in the company's working capital requirement is feasible if the suppliers of raw materials are amenable to extending credit for a prolonged duration. Conversely, should the suppliers solely offer credit on a temporary basis, the organization will require a more substantial quantity of working capital to settle its account payables.

9. Operating Efficiency
A firm characterized by a high degree of operating efficiency requires a reduced amount of working capital, as opposed to one with a low degree of operating efficiency that requires an increased amount of working capital. Furthermore, firms experience reduced expenditures throughout the operational cycle, allowing them to function with a diminished working capital.

10. Availability of Raw Materials
Businesses can operate efficiently while requiring a reduced quantity of working capital if two conditions are met: primary materials and inputs are readily available and easily accessible. This is due to the fact that they are either able to operate efficiently with a negligible inventory of basic materials or neither are required to maintain an inventory. Conversely, in the event of a disruption in the raw material supply chain, enterprises will be compelled to maintain substantial inventories to ensure uninterrupted operational cycles. They require a greater quantity of capital for operations as a result.

11. Intensity of the Competition
In the event that market competition is intense, the company will be required to maintain a flexible credit policy and ensure timely delivery of the products. An

increase in inventory levels necessitates the provision of supplementary working capital. A business with monopoly power or minimal competition will require less working capital to meet its conditions of demand, as it will be able to dictate those conditions according to its own preferences.

12. Inflationary Level
An increase in price will inevitably lead to a corresponding rise in the expenses associated with labour and basic materials, thereby effectuating an expansion in the need for working capital. Conversely, should the organization succeed in increasing the prices of its own products, the concern regarding inadequate working capital will be alleviated. The degree to which an increase in price affects the working capital of a business will differ among entrepreneurs.

13. Potential for Business Growth or Prospects
Companies that want to expand their operations will need a larger amount of working capital. The expansion of operations requires firms to increase the scale of their production, which in turn requires more raw materials, more inputs, etc., and therefore also requires more working capital. Businesses that want to expand their operations will need to have more working capital available. Those companies that have existing activities and want to grow those operations will need to raise the quantity of accessible working capital.

3.8 Cash Conversion Cycle (CCC)
The cash conversion cycle (CCC) refers to the period of time during which an organization can transform its resources into cash. The CCC quantifies the interval of time between the cash inflow generated from the sale of products and the company's expenditures on raw materials, wages, and other related items. The measurement of a company's ability to convert its current operational assets into currency on hand is referred to as the working capital cycle. As of the end of the cash conversion cycle (CCC), cash is generated from current liabilities and net current assets. A protracted cycle refers to the perpetual commitment of funds with no anticipated return. A company can generate cash more rapidly and function with greater agility when cycles are shorter.

The CCC is the straightforward process by which cash is transferred to inventory, then to account receivables, and finally back to cash (Higgins, 2001). A multitude of activity and working capital ratios may be computed in order to evaluate the financial health of a company. The current ratio, the acid test ratio, the inventory turnover ratio, the collection period for accounts receivable, and the payment period for account payables are examples of such ratios.

In essence, the calculation of these ratios as an element of a working capital management instrument will assist in ascertaining whether the organization is functioning within the "ideal" current ratio of 2:1 (Samuels 1990). This is critical because it will allow the company to assess its liquidity position and prevent overtrading, even when profitability is increasing.

The CCC encompasses three primary tiers of operations within the institution. These include resource acquisition (purchasing of basic materials), production process transformation, and sales (primarily credit sales).

It is important to acknowledge that purchases of raw materials and sales are typically able to be conducted on credit, eliminating the need for immediate cash payments. Consequently, the discrepancy between the cash collected from sales and the cash paid to suppliers should be duly considered.

An essential concept for the management of cash and/or working capital is the cash conversion cycle. This is because an organization requires additional financial resources to function efficiently for the duration of its operational cycle. Certain activity ratios are computed to evaluate the working capital cycle in order to determine whether or not it is deteriorating and, if so, what remedial actions are necessary. As illustrated in Figure 3.2, the cash conversion cycle consists of such recurrent occurrences.

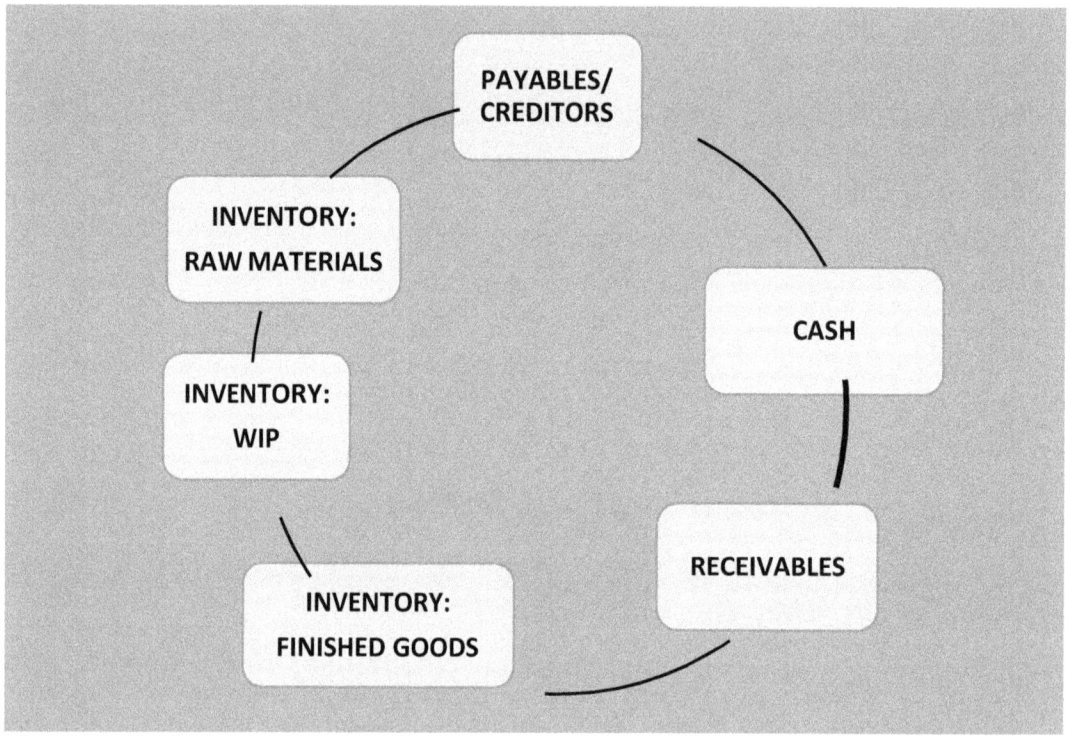

Figure 3.1   *Cash Conversion Cycle (CCC)*

Note:
The diagram above illustrates the cash conversion cycle, which denotes the duration required for the firm to receive cash from credit sales subsequent to settling payments for resources obtained through credit purchases. The typical depiction of the working capital cycle for manufacturing firms is as follows:

CCC = Cash Conversion Cycle
[Process holding period for inventory of basic materials plus process working period plus conversion/holding period for inventory of produced goods plus receivables' period minus accounts payable' period].

3.8.1 Interpretation of the Nature of CCC

The CCC reflects the efficiency with which an organization handles its working capital and cash flow.

✓ **Negative CCC**

When the company's CCC is negative, it indicates that it has sufficient cash on hand to cover its supplier payments. A currency surplus is the consequence that arises when a firm's revenues surpass its expenditures during a designated period. The firm ought to take pleasure in a negative CCC. When the CCC is negative, it indicates that an entity has obtained funds before the designated payment due date to its suppliers. Consequently, the organization will sustain a cash surplus for a specified period of time, denoting that its cash inflows surpass its cash outflows. In actuality, a negative CCC is advantageous for a business. This exemplifies the organization's capability to remunerate its suppliers prior to incurring any obligations to collect payments from its clients.

✓ **Positive or Favorable CCC**

A positive cash conversion cycle (CCC) indicates that the organization experienced a deficit in funds during a designated time frame, indicating that its cash outflow, measured in days, surpassed its cash inflow. This indicates that the firm can sustain a cash deficit for a specified period of time, denoting that its cash inflows are limited as compared to its cash outflows, leading to liquidity challenges. In actuality, the firm will be facing an overtrading situation, as a huge positive CCC is disadvantageous for a business in terms of cash availability.

✓ **Reduced CCC**

A reduction in a company's CCC serves as a positive indicator of its ability to expedite cash generation and reduce reliance on external funding. Nonetheless, a WCC that is too low could indicate that the company is underinvesting in inventory or extending credit to consumers insufficiently, both of which could have a negative impact on sales and profits. A company that maintains a lower CCC than its competitors or the average may be indicative of effective inventory management, prompt recovery of receivables, or adherence to stringent payment terms with suppliers. The working capital and cash flow of the organization might be enhanced by implementing these variables.

✓ Extended CCC

A prevalent indication of subpar performance is extended cash denials anticipating receipt of funds from trade activities; this, in turn, extends the cash conversion cycle (CCC). The organization's increased dependence on external financing will stem from its diminished capacity to generate cash at a quicker rate. A working capital ratio that is above average or in comparison to its competitors may indicate that a company has inadequate inventory management, sluggish collection of receivables, or lenient payment terms with suppliers. The aforementioned concerns may impair both cash flow and CCC.

Illustration 3.1

Raw materials are purchased by Kwakye Company Ltd. on a three-month credit basis, and the inventory is held in storage for two months prior to distribution to the production department. Prior to sale, finished products are held for one month. Credit is extended for account receivables for 0.5 months. Determine the revenue cycle.

Solution:

	Months
Raw material inventory holding period	2.0
Less: Credit taken from suppliers	(3.0)
Finished goods holding period	1.0
Account receivables' Payment period	0.5
	0.5 (in months)

This indicates that a period of 0.5 months (i.e., two weeks) would elapse between the cash payment for production raw materials and the cash receipt from accounts receivable, profit margin included.

Illustration 3.2

Kwaawam Company Ltd. has the following data appearing in its end of year of 2022.

Financial statement:

	GHS
Credit Sales	3,350,000.00
Cost of Sales	2,250,000.00
Credit Purchases	5,180,500.00
Inventory	250,000.00
Trade Account receivables	380,000.00
Trade Account payables	460,000.00

Required: Calculate the length of cash operating cycle in days.

Solution:

Inventory holding period:

$$\frac{\text{Inventory}}{\text{Cost of Sales}} \times 365 = \frac{250,000}{2,250,000} \times 365 = \textbf{40.56 days}$$

Accounts receivables' period:

$$\frac{\text{Closing receivables}}{\text{Credit Sales}} \times 365 = \frac{380,000}{3,350,000} \times 365 = \textbf{41.40 days}$$

Accounts payables' payment:

$$\frac{\text{Closing payables}}{\text{Credit Purchases}} \times 365 = \frac{460,000}{5,180,500} \times 365 = \textbf{32.41 days}$$

Kwaawam Company Ltd.
Computation of Cash Conversion Cycle

	Days
Inventory conversion period	40.56
Less: Credit taken from suppliers	(32.41)
Receivables' payment period	41.40
Cash conversion cycle (in days)	**54.95days**

3.8.2 Strategies to Improve Cash Conversion Cycle (CCC)

Enhancing the firm's working capital cycle (through cycle reduction) will result in decreased liquidity risk and increased profitability. This may be accomplished by implementing any of the subsequent approaches:

i. Increasing the debt collection rate. In other words, the accounts receivable period of the company ought to be reduced.

ii. Promotions extended to customers who make prompt payments, such as cash discounts and free deliveries of inventory purchased;

iii. Reduce the level of the outstanding receivables balance by taking steps to collect the delinquent debt through the services of factors.

iv. Prioritize the use of the cheque system for payments. In order to delay payments to suppliers, the firm ought to use the cheque system as its principal mode of payment.

v. Negotiate for a longer payables period. The firm should engage in negotiations with suppliers for an extension of the account payables period by way of extended credits.

vi. Reduction in the manufacturing cycle (if feasible) and this will result in an equivalent decrease in production time, subsequently leading to a reduction in the duration of inventory holding.

vii. Invest in more state-of-the-art automation to reduce the length of the work-in-progress inventory holding period in order to accelerate the transformation of raw materials into finished products.

3.9 Working Capital Ratios

As stated previously, the responsibility of ensuring that working capital is consistently adequate to support uninterrupted business operations lies with the financial manager. In the process of conducting a financial analysis of working capital, ratios prove to be valuable instruments. Operating capital ratios serve as a valuable instrument in demonstrating the efficiency with which a business utilizes its accessible working capital. Presented below is a compilation of the most frequently employed ratios utilized in the assessment of a business's working capital levels.

i. Current ratios:

The term "working capital ratio" is another name for this concept. It is used to demonstrate whether or not a company's current assets are capable of covering its short-term liabilities in a manner that is sufficient and adequate. This is how it is measured:

$$\text{Current Ratio (CR)} = \frac{\text{Current Assets}}{\text{Current Liabilities}} = \frac{CA}{CL} \qquad \text{Equation-------3.1}$$

Where:

CA = Inventory + Account receivables + Cash in hand + Cash at bank + Bills Receivables + Prepaid expense + Accrued income

CL = Account payables + Bills payable + Bank overdraft + Outstanding expenses + Income received in advance

ii. Quick Ratio (QR) or Acid-test Ratio

This is a measurement of the ratio between the company's quick assets and current liabilities. This ratio is also known as the acid-test ratio or the liquid ratio. It is measured as, and indicates, the immediate liquid position of the company, and its values are as follows:

$$\frac{\text{Current assets – Inventories - Prepaid expenses}}{\text{Current Liabilities}} \quad \text{Equation ---------3.2}$$

iii. Cash Ratio (CR)

The cash ratio, often known as the absolute liquidity ratio, is one of the most common methods utilized for determining a company's liquidity. The following is how it is measured:

$$= \frac{\text{Cash in hand + Cash at bank+ Marketable securities}}{\text{Current Liabilities}} \quad \text{Equation----3.3}$$

iv. Account Receivables Period (ARP)

When it comes to credit sales, this ratio determines how many days in a year the company's receivable, also known as account receivables, are handed over or rotated. It communicates the connection between the account receivables period and the total net sales on credit for a given year. Additionally, it evaluates the effectiveness of the company's credit policy by determining the number of days necessary for the company to recover cash from sales made on credit. This is how it is measured:

$$= \frac{\text{Closing Account Receivables (measured in days)}}{\text{Credit Sales}} \quad \text{Equation----3.4}$$

v. Account Receivables Turnover Ratio (ARTR)

In terms of credit sales, it is a measurement of the number of times that receivables, also known as account receivables, are handed over or rotated in a given year. It conveys the relationship between the total amount of credit sales made and the annual average amount of accounts receivable for a particular year. This ratio determines how effective the company's overall credit management strategy is. This is how it is measured:

$$= \frac{\text{Credit Sales}}{\text{Closing Account Receivables (measured in times)}} \quad \text{Equation --------3.5}$$

vi. Inventory Conversion Period (ICP)

This ratio determines the relationship between the cost of goods sold and the average inventory at cost by calculating the number of days it takes the company to turn its inventories into cash through sales. This is how it is measured:

$$= \frac{\text{Closing Inventory}}{\text{Cost of Goods sold}} \quad \text{(measured in days)} \qquad \text{Equation --------- 3.6}$$

vii. Inventories Turnover Ratio (ITR)

This ratio determines the degree to which the average inventory cost and the cost of goods sold are related to one another. This metric is utilized to determine how rapidly (in terms of the number of times) sales are generated from available inventory. This is how it is measured:

$$= \frac{\text{Cost of Goods sold}}{\text{Closing Inventory}} \quad \text{(measured in times)} \qquad \text{Equation -----------3.7}$$

Where:

Cost of Goods Sold = Sales – Gross Profit
Or
= (Opening inventory + Purchases + Direct expenses) – Closing inventory

viii. Account Payables Period (APP)

This ratio calculates the link between an organization's average accounts payable and the number of days it takes to make credit purchases; the result provides insight into how long it takes the company to make payments to its account payables. This is how it is determined:

$$= \frac{\text{Accounts Payables}}{\text{Net credit purchases}} \quad \text{(measured in days)} \qquad \text{Equation -------------------3.8}$$

ix. Account Payables' Turnover Rate (APTR)

This ratio analyzes the link that exists between credit purchases and the average amount owed to account payables. The result of the calculation is used to determine whether or not the company is meeting its obligations to its account payables on schedule. This is how it is determined:

$$= \frac{\text{Net Credit Purchase}}{\text{Accounts Payables}} \quad \text{(measured in times)} \qquad \text{Equation ---------3.9}$$

Where accounts payables = account payables+ bills payable

3.10 Computation of Working Capital Requirements Based on Working Capital Ratios

The level of investment in working capital that a company needs to meet its working capital requirements in order to ensure that its business operations run smoothly and without interruptions is referred to as the working capital requirements. The amount of working capital that must be invested is mostly determined by the size of the company as well as the volume of its production and commerce.

Illustration 3.3
From the financial information extracted from the books of XYZ Company Ltd., compute the cash conversion cycle in days, assuming that the average period of credit allowed by suppliers is 26 days.

Table 3.1 Financial Information of XYZ Company Ltd.

	GHS
Average total of account receivables outstanding	480,000
Raw Materials consumption	2,500,000
Total Production cost	6,000,000
Total Cost of sales	8,000,000
Sales for the year	11,500,000
Value of average inventory maintained:	
Raw material	320,000
Work-in-Progress	350,000
Finished Goods	260,000

Solution: **Workings**

i. Raw materials Holding Period (in Days):

$$\frac{\text{Inventory of Raw Material}}{\text{Raw Material Consumption}} \times 365 = \frac{320{,}000 \times 365}{2{,}500{,}000}$$

= **46.72 days**

ii. Inventory of W.I.P Holding Period:

$$\frac{\text{Inventory of W.I.P}}{\text{Production Cost}} \times 365 = \frac{350{,}000 \times 365}{6{,}000{,}000}$$

= **21.29 days**

iii. Finished Goods Holding Period:

$$\frac{\text{Inventory of finished goods}}{\text{Cost of Sales}} \times 365 = \frac{260{,}000 \times 365}{8{,}000{,}000}$$

= **11.86 days**

iv. Receivables Holding Period:

$$\frac{\text{Account Receivable Outstanding}}{\text{Cost of Sales}} \times 365 = \frac{480{,}000 \times 365}{11{,}500{,}000}$$

= **15.23 days**

XYZ Company Ltd.
Statement Showing Operating Cycle

	(Days)
Raw materials Holding Period:	46.72
Inventory of W.I.P Holding Period:	21.29
Finished Goods Holding Period:	11.86
Account Receivables Period:	<u>15.23</u>
	95.10
Less: Average Payables Period Allowed	(26.00)
CCC =	**69.10 days**

Illustration 3.4

From the following financial data relating to Adom Company Ltd., you are required to compute the following:

i. Working capital cycle
ii. Number of operating cycles in a year assuming 360-day a year, and
iii. Average working capital required if the annual cash operating expenses are estimated as GHS10,200,000

Inventory Holding: Raw Materials : 30 days

                W.I.P : 15 days

                Finished Goods : 35 days

Average Receivables Period : 50 days

Average Payables Period : 40 days

Solution:

i. **Computation of Working Capital Cycle**
  = Raw materials (days) + WIP (days) + Finished goods (in days) + Receivables (in days) – Payables (days)

  = [30 + 15 + 35 + 50) – 40 = **90 days**

ii. **Number of Operating Cycles in a year:**
  = Number of days in a year / Operating Cycle (in days)

  = 360 / 90 = **4 cycles in a year**

iii. Computation of Average working capital required given operating expenses of GHS10,200,000.

  Average working capital required = Annual cash operating expenses / Number of operating cycles

  = GHS10,200,000 / 4 cycles

  = **GHS 2,550,000**

Illustration 3.5

From the following data, prepare a statement showing the estimated working capital requirements of OWAN Company Ltd. Budgeted sales: GHS 3,600,000 p.a.

Table 3.2: OWAM Co. Ltd. Analysis of Cost and Profit per each unit:

	GHS
Raw materials	6
Labour	8
Overheads	4
Profit	2
Selling price per unit	20

It is further estimated that:

i. Pending use, raw materials are carried in inventory for one (1) week and finished goods for two (2) weeks.
ii. Factory processing (conversion process) will take two (2) weeks
iii. Suppliers will give five (5) weeks credit to OWAN Company Ltd.
iv. Customers will require six (6) weeks credit from the company.
v. It is assumed that production overheads accrue evenly throughout the year.

Solution: - **Workings**

i. **Number of units sold:** Budgeted sales
Budgeted sales per unit

$$= \frac{3,600,000}{20} = \underline{\mathbf{180,000}} \text{ units}$$

ii. **Annual Expenditure:**

Raw materials: 180,000 x 6 = 1,080,000
Labour: 180,000 x 8 = 1,440,000
Overheads: 180,000 x 4 = 720,000
Cost of Sales = **2,520,000**

Table 3.3: OWAN Company Ltd. Statement of Working Capital Requirements

Particulars	GHS	GHS
Raw Materials: [1,080,000 x 1/52]	20,769.23	
Work-in-progress:		
Raw materials: [1,080,000 x1/52] = 20,769.23		
Labour: [1,440,000 x 2/52 x 50%] = 27,692.31		
Overheads: [720,000 x 2/52 x 50%] = 13,846.16	62,307.70	
Finished Goods: [2,520,000 x 2/52]	96,923.08	180,000.01
Account receivables: 2,520,000 x 6/52]		290,769.23
Total Current Assets		**470,769.24**
Less: Current Liabilities Account payables for raw materials: [1,080,000 x 5/52]		(103,846.15)
Net Working Capital Required		**366,923.09**

Illustration 3.6
Table 3.4: Cost Sheet of Adom Company Ltd. provides the following:

	Cost per unit (GHS)
Raw materials	100
Direct labour	60
Overheads (including GHS20 depreciation)	50
Total Cost	**210**
Profit	40
Selling price	**250**

Additional Information:
i. Raw materials in inventory are kept for an average of 30 days
ii. Average material in progress is for 15 days
iii. Credit allowed by suppliers is for 8 days
iv. Credit allowed to account receivables is for 30 days
v. Average time lag in payment of wages is 12 days
vi. Average time lag in payment of overheads is 30 days
vii. Finished goods lie in the warehouse for 30 days before they are sold
viii. 35% of the sales are on-the-spot cash basis
ix. Cash balance is currently indicated as GHS 1,000,000
x. Assume there are 360 days in a year.

You are required to prepare a statement showing the working capital needed to finance a level of activity of 75,000 units of output. Production is carried out on evenly basis throughout the year, with wages and overheads accruing in the same way.

Solution: Workings

Annual Expenditure:

Raw materials:	750,000 x 100 = 75,000,000
Direct labour:	750,000 x 50 = 37,500,000
Overheads (Excluding depreciation):	750,000 x 30 = 2,250,000
Cost of Sales	**= 114,750,000**

Adom Company Ltd.
Table 3.5: Statement of Working Capital Requirements

Particulars	GHS	GHS
Raw Materials: [75,000,000 x 30/360]	6,250,000	
Work-in-progress:		
Raw materials: [75,000,000 x 15/360] = 3,125,000		
Direct Labour: [37,500,000 x 15/360 x 50%] = 781,250		
Overheads: [2,250,000 x 15/360 x 50%] = 46,875	3,953,125	
Finished Goods: [114,750,000 x 30/360]	9,562,500	19,765,625
Account receivables: [114,750,000 x 65% x 30/360]		6,215,625
Cash		1,000,000
Total Current Assets required		**26,981,250.00**
Less: Current Liabilities		
Account payables for raw materials: [750,000,000 x 10/360]	20,833,333.33	
Account payables-wages: [37,500,000 x 12/360]	1,250,000.00	
Account payables-Overheads: [2,250,000 x 30/360]	187,500.00	(22,270,833.33)
Net Working Capital Required		**4,710,416.67**

Illustration 3.7

You are required to compute the working capital requirement of **ABC Company Ltd.** from the information provided below:

	(GHS)
Annual Sales	15,000,000
Cost of production (including depreciation of GHS 350,000)	13,000,000
Raw materials purchases	9,200,000
Overheads per month	50,000
Anticipated opening inventory of raw materials	2,000,000
Anticipated closing inventory of raw materials	1,800,000

Note:

i. Inventory Norms:

    Raw materials: 6 weeks
    Work-in-Progress: 3 weeks
    Finished goods: 3 weeks
    Credit allowed to account receivables: 5 weeks
    Credit allowed by account payables: 3 weeks
    Cash balance desired to be kept: GHS200,000

ii. The Company received an advance of GHS1,500,000 on sales order.

Solution: - Workings

Table 3.6: Calculation of Raw Materials Consumed:

	GHS
Opening inventory of raw materials	2,000,000
Add: Purchase of Raw materials	9,200,000
	11,200,000
Less: Closing inventory of Raw materials	1,800,000
Raw Materials Consumed	**9,400,000**

Calculation of Cash Cost of Production:

	GHS
Cost of Production:	13,000,000
Less Depreciation:	(350,000)
Cash Cost of Production	**12,650,000**

ABC Company Ltd.
Table 3.7: Statement of Working Capital Requirements

Particulars	GHS	GHS
Current Assets:		
Inventory:		
Inventory- Raw Materials: [9,400,000 x 6/52] = 1,084,615.38		
Inventory of Work-in-progress:		
Raw materials: [9,400,000 x 3/52] = 542,307.69	1,644,320.76	
Overheads: [600,000 x 3/52 x 50%] = 17,307.69		
Finished Goods: [12,650,000 x 3/52]	729,807.69	2,374,128.45
Account receivables: [12,650,000 x 5/52]		1,216,346.15
Cash		200,000
Total Current Assets required		3,790,474.60
Less: Current Liabilities		
Account payables for raw materials: [9,200,000 x 3/52]	530,769.23	
Advance from Account receivables	1,500,000	(2,030,769.23)
Net Working Capital Required		**1,759,705.37**

3.11 Chapter Review Questions

1. Define the term 'working capital management'
2. Examine the key components of working capital management.
3. What are the factors that account for the variations in working capital requirements?
4. Explain the following type of working capital:

    i. Gross working capital
    ii. Permanent working capital
    iii. Temporal working capital
    iv. Zero working capital
5. Explain the following working capital policies:

    i. Aggressive working capital policy
    ii. Conservative working capital policy
    iii. Moderate working capital policy
6. What are the main objectives of working capital?
7. To what extent can an efficient working capital management can affect the profitability of the firm?
8. Examine the concept of cash conversion cycle and it effect on liquidity.
9. Not all profitable firms are liquid. Evaluate this statement.
10. From the financial information extracted from the books of ADOM Company Ltd., compute the cash conversion cycle in days, assuming that the average period of credit allowed by suppliers is 30 days.

Details	GHS
Average total of account receivables outstanding	480,000
Raw Materials consumption	2,500,000
Total Production cost	6,000,000
Total Cost of sales	8,000,000
Sales for the year	11,500,000
Value of Average inventory maintained:	
Raw material	320,000
Work-in-Progress	350,000
Finished Goods	260,000

11. From the following financial data relating to ABAM Company Ltd., you are required to compute the following:
   i. Working capital cycle
   ii. Number of operating cycles in a year assuming 365-day a year, and
   iii. Average working capital required if the annual cash operating expenses are estimated as GHS15,000,000

Inventory Holding: Raw Materials : 15 days

                W.I.P : 10 days

                Finished Goods : 25 days

Average Receivables Period : 40 days

Average Payables Period : 30 days

12. From the following data, prepare a statement showing the estimated working capital requirements of BLESS Company Ltd. Budgeted sales: GHS 5,600,000 p.a.

Analysis of cost and profit per each unit:

Details	GHS
Raw materials	8
Labour	12
Overheads	5
Profit	5
Selling price per unit	30

It is further estimated that:

a. Pending use, raw materials are carried in inventory for two (2) week and finished goods for three (3) weeks.
b. Factory processing (conversion process) will take one (1) week
c. Suppliers will give four (4) weeks credit to BLESS Company Ltd.
d. Customers will require three (3) weeks credit from the company.
e. It is assumed that production overheads accrue evenly throughout the year.

13. The cost sheet of XYZ Company Ltd. Provides the following data:

	Cost per unit (GHS)
Raw Materials	200
Direct Labour	70
Overheads (including GHS20 depreciation)	60
Total Cost	**330**
Profit	70
Selling price	**400**

Additional Information:

1. Raw materials in inventory are kept for an average of 15 days
2. Average material in progress is for 25 days
3. Credit allowed by suppliers is for 10 days

4. Credit allowed to account receivables is for 40 days
5. Average time lag in payment of wages is 10 days
6. Average time lag in payment of overheads is 20 days
7. Finished goods lie in the warehouse for 45 days before they are sold
8. 30% of the sales are on-the-spot cash basis
9. Cash balance is currently indicated as GHS 1,500,000
10. Assume there are 360 days in a year.

You are required to prepare a statement showing the working capital needed to finance a level of activity of 85,000 units of output. Production is carried out on evenly basis throughout the year, with wages and overheads accruing in the same way.

14. You are required to compute the working capital requirement of ABC Company Ltd. from the information provided below:

	(GHS)
Annual Sales	14,000,000
Cost of Production (including depreciation of GHS 250,000)	10,000,000
Raw Materials purchases	8,200,000
Overheads per month	60,000
Anticipated opening inventory of raw materials	1,000,000
Anticipated closing inventory of raw materials	800,000

Note:

i. Inventory Norms:

    Raw materials: 8 weeks

    Work-in-Progress: 4 weeks

    Finished Goods: 5 weeks

    Credit allowed to account receivables: 6 weeks

    Credit allowed by Account payables: 5 weeks

    Cash Balance desired to be kept: GHS500,000

iii. The Company received an advance of GHS 2,500,000 on sales order

3.12 Chapter References and Bibliography

[1] Abdou, H. A., & Pointon, J. (2011). Credit Scoring, Statistical Techniques and Evaluation Criteria: A Review of the Literature. *Intelligent Systems in Accounting, Finance and Management*, 18(2–3), 59–88. https://doi.org/10.1002/isaf.325.

[2] Attom, B. E. & Afzalur, R. (2022). Empirical study of the relationship between working capital policies and firm performance (profitability and firm value): evidence from the manufacturing firm listed on the Ghana Stock Exchange (GSE), *Journal of Statistics and Management Systems*, 25(4), 983-1000. https://doi:10.1080/09720510.2022.2058220.

[3] Brigham, E. F., & Houston, J. F. (1999). *Fundamentals of Financial Management*, 2nd ed. Harcourt Bruce and Company.

[4] Cangoz, M. C., & Secunho, L. (2020). *Cash Management*: How do countries perform sound practices?

[5] Kontuš, E. (2013). Management of accounts receivable in a company. *Ekonomska misao i praksa*, 22(1), 21-38.

[6] Mandal, N., & Goswami, S. (2010). Impact of working capital management on liquidity, profitability and non-insurable risk and uncertainty bearing: A case study of Oil and Natural Gas Commission (ONGC). *Great Lakes Herald*, 4(2), 21–42.

[7] Mansoori, D. E., Elyasi, M., & Mohammadi, R. (2019). Investigating the relationship between working capital management and stock price crash risk. *UKH Journal of Social Sciences*, 3(1).

[8] Mian, S. L., & Smith Jr, C. W. (1992). Accounts receivable management policy: Theory and evidence. *The Journal of Finance*, 47(1), 169-200.

[9] Ross SA, Westerfield R, Jordan BD (2002) Fundamentals of corporate finance, sixth edn. McGraw-Hill.

[10] Salas-Molina, F., Pla-Santamaria, D., & Rodriguez-Aguilar, J. A. (2018). A multi-objective approach to the cash management problem. *Annals of Operations Research*, *267*(1), 515-529.

[11] Samuels, J. M., Wilkes, F. M., & Brayshaw. (1990). *Management of Company Finance.* 5th ed., Chapman and Hall.

[12] Sohail, S., Rasul, F., & Fatima, U. (2016). Effect of aggressive & conservative working capital management policy on performance of scheduled commercial banks of Pakistan. *European Journal of Business and Management*, *8*(10), 40–48.

[13] Sousa, M. R., Gama, J., & Brandão, E. (2016). A new dynamic modeling framework for credit risk assessment. *Expert Systems with Applications*, 45(C), 341-351.

[14] Ukaegbu, B. (2014). The significance of working capital management in determining firm profitability: Evidence from developing economies in Africa. *Research in International Business and Finance*, *31*, 1–16.

[15] Zhang, T., Zhang, W., Xu, W., & Hao, H. (2018). *Multiple instance learning for credit risk assessment with transaction data. Knowledge-Based Systems.* doi:10.1016/j.knosys.2018.07.030.

3.13 Recommended Reading List

[1] Gao, H., Harford, J., & Li, K. (2013). Determinants of corporate cash policy: Insights from private firms. *Journal of Financial Economics* 109(3), 623–639

[2] Girgis, N. M. (1968). Optimal cash balance levels. *Management Science* 15(3), 130–140.

[3] Ross, S. A., Westerfield, R., & Jordan, B. D. (2002). *Fundamentals of corporate finance,* 6th ed. McGraw-Hill.

CHAPTER 4

DIVIDEND POLICY

4.1 Overview

Generally, companies distribute dividends to their shareholders in the form of a return on the investments they have made as firm proprietors. In instances of financial prosperity, it is not uncommon for a corporation to distribute dividends to its shareholders in the form of cash compensation. Although dividend payments are typically made quarterly, corporations have the option to distribute their funds on a monthly, semi-annual, or annual cycle as opposed to quarterly. A corporation that generates a profit and maintains a positive cash flow is faced with the decision of whether to reinvest those funds in the company's operations or distribute a portion of the earnings as dividends to its shareholders. The Board of Directors possesses the authority to determine whether the company will distribute dividends, and if so, how frequently and at what rate they will be done so, contingent upon the present dividend policy.

Objectives of the Chapter

This chapter seeks to achieve the following objectives:

- To explain the term dividend policy;
- To evaluate the factors that influence the size of dividend payout;
- To explain the types of dividend payments;
- To evaluate the types of dividend policies; and
- To examine Walter's theory on dividend policy.

> **Key Words Used in the Chapter**
>
> - ✓ Dividend policy
> - ✓ Interim dividend
> - ✓ Irregular dividend policy
> - ✓ Liquidating dividend
> - ✓ No-dividend policy
> - ✓ Regular dividend policy
> - ✓ Scrip dividend
> - ✓ Stable dividend policy

4.2 Definition of Dividend Policy

A dividend, which is frequently in the form of a distribution of earnings, denotes a payment made by the company to its shareholders as a return on their investment through share ownership. A corporation's dividend policy comprises a set of governing principles that must be followed with regards to the distribution of dividends to shareholders. It is necessary to establish the criteria for earnings distribution, the dividend issuance rate, and the methodology for payment (cash or inventory content).

In publicly traded corporations, dividends are customary. Establishing a dividend policy, which regulates the manner in which dividends are to be distributed, is a customary procedure undertaken by the Board of Directors of a corporation. Lease et al. (1999) define the dividend policy of a company as the approach adopted by management when determining dividend payouts, or, alternatively, the frequency and magnitude of cash disbursements to shareholders throughout the year.

By doing so, the organization guarantees its continued adherence to relevant legislation and regulatory frameworks. The policy specifies the parameters that ought to be applied in practice when determining the allocation of earnings to shareholders. It also contains detailed information regarding the procedure, size, nature, and timetable governing the distribution of dividends.

The quantity of dividends that a company distributes is determined by its dividend policy. A dividend policy comprises several key elements, namely the dividend distribution frequency, the dividend payout ratio, and the determination of whether to pay dividends. This document, which shall function as a directive for the distribution of dividends among different constituents of the organization, will be formulated by the Board of Directors.

4.3 Factors Influencing Size of Dividend Payout

The primary determinants of a company's dividend payment policy are its level of profitability, available investments, cash on hand, industry-wide dividend payment trends, and the company's past dividend payment performance. The dividend policy comprises two critical components: the initial consideration is whether to distribute dividends to shareholders, and the subsequent consideration is whether to retain the earnings for reinvestment in subsequent endeavors according to Kanakriyah (2020).

A company is thus confronted with a dual choice regarding the use of acquired funds: distribute a portion of the profit to shareholders (dividends) or retain a portion of the profit for future reinvestment in order to foster expansion and growth. Given the significant importance that owners place on the decision to distribute profits, the absence of a direct correlation between distribution and growth is a critical consideration. The dividend policy establishes the criteria for profit distribution, which can be ascertained via balance sheet analysis.

Cheung et al. (2018) posit that there is a positive correlation between firms' earnings ability and their propensity to distribute dividends, with the former likely to distribute greater amounts as dividends. Therefore, increased profitability may enable corporations to enhance their ability to distribute dividends and/or increase dividend payments. Dividend payout is therefore influenced by the following key factors:

1. **Legal requirements**

The authority to impose restrictions on the quantity of dividends that can be issued and to require corporations to retain their profits resides with the regulatory framework that supervises business operations. In Ghana, as stipulated in Act 179 of the Companies Code of 1963, dividend payments must not surpass the income surplus that existed prior to the dividend payment. Furthermore, the company must maintain the financial ability to meet its debt obligations in a timely manner following any dividend payment. Such a payment is considered illicit if it exceeds the income surplus that existed prior to the dividend disbursement. Directors will initially be held personally liable for the repercussions of any violations of this regulation; shareholders will soon follow suit.

2. **Control consideration**

The measure of control that an individual or entity exercises over a corporation is the ownership of its common shares. Potentially significantly influencing the degree to which an organization can retain control over itself is the manner in which it finances its operations. This could ultimately result in a dilution of control within the organization, for instance, if the firm's shares are to be issued to a new owner who is not presently a member of the group of shareholders. It is imperative that both shareholders and management continually exercise effective and consistent control over the degree of ownership in the company.

3. **Restrictions inherent in financial obligations**

The company may have an existing financial obligation that requires repayment; however, placing undue reliance on this possibility is not advisable. Business enterprises frequently make a determination regarding the establishment of a sinking fund account when they operate for the entire duration required to fulfill a specific debt obligation. Frequent remittances shall be deposited into this account to fulfill the obligation. Under the given conditions, a proportionate amount of the firm's after-tax profit is utilized, and this will impact the total amount of cash available to be distributed to shareholders as dividends. Constraints on the quantity of cash dividends that can be distributed to ordinary shareholders may apply to current borrowing even in specific situations. The terms of these covenants might be onerous.

These stipulations might be appended to the loan agreement. Covenants such as the one mentioned are implemented for the lender's protection and could potentially be utilized in the future to determine the maximum dividend amount.

4. Inflation

Assigned to a specific time period, typically one year, the rate of inflation quantifies the average price level throughout the economy. Percentages are the most prevalent format for showing inflation rates. Exorbitant financial resources would be required for management to arrive at any conclusion regarding the replacement of assets during inflationary periods. This would negatively impact the quantity of capital that the organization allocates towards its activities, given the impact that inflation has on average cost levels. This economic situation will certainly reduce how much money will be available for distribution as a dividend.

5. Current levels of profitability enjoyed by the company's activities

In most cases, a company's net earnings (also known as its current profit) will be reduced by the size of dividends that are owed to its shareholders. In the event that the company does not generate any profits, it will not be in a position to pay dividends to its shareholders. According to Ali (2022), in times of economic instability, it would be unexpected for companies to implement substantial dividend hikes. The only exception to this rule is if the company has sufficient funds in the income surplus account, from which transfers could be made to honor dividend payments. In the event that the firm is unable to earn any profits, the corporation will not be in a position to pay dividends to the shareholders who own it.

6. Availability of investment opportunities

If the company is working on capital investment projects that will result in the expansion and growth of the business, then it is in the company's best interest to keep some of its earnings for use in funding these new projects that will result in the growth of the business; this is a positive sign. If the company is not working on any capital projects that will result in the development and growth of the business, then it is not expedient to hold back some of the earnings. This will culminate in a higher dividend payout to shareholders.

7. Availability of various forms of financial support
When deciding whether or not to pay dividends, one of the most significant factors to take into account is the number of sources of capital that are accessible to the firm. For instance, when a company has sufficient retained earnings to fund new initiatives, that company has the financial means to distribute dividends from the profits of the current fiscal year. Retained earnings are also referred to as "accumulated earnings." An excellent illustration of this is the situation in which a company has sufficient retained earnings to finance new investment endeavors.

8. Recent trends and advancements in the field of dividend payouts
It is very vital for a company to have dividend payment rates that are comparable to those of the corporations with whom it is in direct competition in order for the company to achieve financial success. In such a situation, the shareholders have the option of selling the holdings they now hold in the firm and reinvesting the proceeds in the activities of other businesses that are in direct competition with their own.

9. History of dividend payments made by the company
If a company has a track record of regularly disbursing dividends, there is a greater likelihood that it will continue disbursing the same size of dividends over the entirety of its life. This is because a track record of reliable dividend disbursements builds investor confidence. Either the dividend amount or the dividend payment percentage is kept at the same level as a matter of practice, which is strictly adhered to at all times.

4.4 Types of Dividend Payments
When a company makes a profit, it is required to make a decision on what to do with that money: either it will retain it for re-investment or it will distribute it to the shareholders as a dividend. When it comes to determining whether or not to pay dividends, a corporation must take a variety of factors into account (guided by the dividend policy). The payment of dividends can take a number of different forms. The following is a list of the many different kinds of dividends that can be paid out:

- **Cash Dividend**

The great majority of dividends are paid out in the form of cash distributions to shareholders as a return on their investment. This method is the one that is used the most often and is the one that is recognized the most widely. The cash dividend amount is proportionately deposited into the shareholder's bank account based on the number of shares the shareholder has invested in the firm. This is done in accordance with the dividend policy of the company. Cash dividend payments are usually done twice a year, and these are the interim dividend payout and the final dividend payout.

- **Scrip Dividend or Stock Dividend**

This dividend-payout mode A dividend is a payment that is made by the firm and then distributed to each shareholder. This payment is known as a dividend. The cash dividend amount is sent to the shareholder's bank account in a manner that is proportional to the number of shares that the shareholder currently owns in the firm. This is done in line with the ownership stake that each shareholder has in the firm.

- **Property Dividend**

There are some scenarios in which a company may opt to deliver non-monetary benefits to its shareholders rather than distributing cash dividends to those who own shares of the company. The corporation keeps an eye on the property dividend and evaluates it in light of the asset's most recent valuation on the market in order to arrive at an estimate of how much it is worth. On the other hand, there is a possibility that the asset may sell at a price in today's market that is lower than its book value. As a result, the business needs to make a decision regarding whether or not to register a gain or a loss as a result of the transaction. This decision can either be positive or negative. If certain criteria are met, the Board of Directors of a company may make the decision to offer investors some kind of remuneration other than cash in exchange for their financial stake in the company. The asset in issue has to have a certain level of divisibility that makes it possible to divide it up into parts based on the number of shares that are actually held in the organization. Because of this restriction, the only sorts of assets that are normally capable of yielding property dividends are those that consist of inventory and security holdings. Other forms of assets, such as real estate, are not eligible for this type of payout.

- o **Liquidating Dividend**

This refers to the distribution of proceeds from liquidated businesses, and such proceeds (after payment of all liabilities) are paid to shareholders based on their shareholding capacity. A special dividend payment is made to shareholders during the process of liquidation, and it usually implies that part of the business or all of the business has been liquidated. If certain criteria are met, the Board of Directors of a company may elect to offer investors a type of remuneration that is not monetary in nature. This might be anything from inventory options to a vacation home. The asset in issue has to have a certain level of divisibility that makes it possible for it to be divided up into portions according to the number of shares that are actually held in the corporation. Because of this restriction, the only kinds of assets that are normally capable of yielding property dividends are those that consist of inventory and security holdings. Other sorts of assets, such as real estate, are not eligible for this form of payout.

4.5 Types of Dividend Policy

A company's dividend payment policy determines the total amount of dividends that will be disbursed among shareholders as well as the rate at which dividends will be paid out. This policy also decides how frequently dividends are handed out to shareholders. In regard to the dividend, the company is able to follow any one of a number of different strategies due to their flexibility. When the company achieves monetary success, it is the company's responsibility to decide how and where the profits will be invested as a result of that accomplishment. Either the company can choose to keep the profit it has created for itself, or it can choose to distribute the same amount of money to its shareholders in the form of dividends. Both of these options are available to the corporation.

Various patterns of dividend distribution are followed by different companies. The patterns are determined by the kind of dividend policy that they choose to implement. There are typically four distinct approaches to dividend policy that businesses use, and these are as follows:

- **Stable Dividend Policy**

The establishment of a predetermined number of dividend payments that are to be distributed on a regular basis to shareholders is an essential component of a dividend policy that is steady. This is done in order to keep everything on the same level. The amount of the dividend will not change regardless of whether the firm posts a profit or a loss for the period in question. This provision ensures that the dividend will be distributed to shareholders regardless of whether or not the company generates a profit. For instance, a company has the option of having a dividend distribution of GHS 12 per share for a period of four years in a row without interruption. When it comes to putting this strategy into action, businesses almost always rely on the income surplus account. If the company's income surplus is not sufficient to sustain the payment of dividends, it may instead choose to distribute bonuses or scrip dividends.

- **Regular Dividend Policy**

A "regular dividend policy" is a policy that mandates the payment of dividends to shareholders on a continuous and ongoing basis. In accordance with this policy, a predetermined share of the annual earnings of the business (for instance, 40% or 50%) must be distributed in the way described. When there is a big growth in the firm's earnings, the dividend distribution will also increase in a manner that is proportionate to the increase in profits. This will occur in a manner that is proportionate to the increase in earnings. This is due to the fact that dividends are paid as a proportion of earnings rather than a flat amount. It is not unheard of for knowledgeable individuals to have the viewpoint that this tactic is the one that is most suited for constructing goodwill and giving advantages to shareholders.

- **Irregular Dividend Policy**

In a firm that adheres to an irregular dividend policy, the choice of whether or not to pay dividends is left totally up to the discretion of the company's Board of Directors. In other words, the company may choose to pay dividends at any time it sees fit. When a company makes the decision to pay dividends to its shareholders, such payments are made to the shareholders in accordance with the criteria that the organization has set for the distribution of dividends. The priorities that have been defined for the organization will serve as the sole foundation for making a choice about what course of action to take. If the company is going to start a new venture in which they will need to make an investment, it is possible that they may choose to keep the earnings within the company rather than distribute them to the shareholders.

- **No Dividend Policy**

If a company decides that it will not pay dividends as part of its standard practice, this is an indication that the company plans to keep all of its profits for its own use and has consciously decided not to distribute any of them to its shareholders. In other words, the company does not intend to pay dividends as part of its standard practice. Companies that have their sights set on expanding their operations typically adhere to the practice of deferring dividend payments. As a result, there is a retention rate of one hundred percent (100%) and a payout rate of zero percent (0%). This strategy has the potential to be beneficial for businesses that have their sights set on expanding the number of customers they serve. On the other hand, it might be discouraging for prospective investors who were banking on obtaining a stable income over the course of a longer period of time.

4.6 Firm's Life Cycle and Type of Dividend Payout

- **Start-up**
  A no-dividend policy: All cash was saved for future use in the company's internal investments and expansion efforts.

- **Growth stage**
  A no-dividend policy: The rate of expansion had not yet slowed down significantly. As the pace of growth slows, the management team may consider instituting an irregular payment or a continuous dividend at a low rate. Alternatively, they may contemplate a combination of the two. Management may consider an irregular or constant dividend at a low rate as growth slows.

- **Maturity stage**
  A regular dividend policy: The firm pays out a large portion of its income to its shareholders or investors in the form of dividends; this type of company is called a dividend payer.

- **Decline stage**
  Irregular dividend policy: A significant number of companies have the capacity to consistently innovate themselves. They have the capacity to continue existing in the mature phase indefinitely.

An Interim Dividend

A dividend known as an interim dividend is one that may be distributed to shareholders at any time throughout the course of a company's fiscal year. It is the practice of a firm to distribute dividends prior to a yearly audit of the company's financial reports. The amount of the yearly dividend distribution is substantially more than that of the interim dividends, which are often given out on a regular basis, such as once a month (paid more than once). In addition, dividends are often paid out of the portion of earnings that are retained by the company. "Retained earnings" are the profits that a corporation continues to use in operations after the closing of one fiscal year, and the term "retained earnings" was coined to describe this practice.

The Board of Directors of the company is responsible for all aspects of declaring an interim dividend, including voting on whether or not to do so and securing approval for the distribution of the dividend once it has been declared. The shareholders have the opportunity to vote against receiving any interim dividends if they disagree with the decision that was taken by the Board of Directors. Companies will often make statements concerning dividend payments throughout the time period in between their quarterly and yearly reporting periods. Owners of shares in a firm have the potential to receive dividend payments in the form of interim dividends, which are disbursed at periods that are more frequently spaced apart. As a direct result of this, the total quantity of dividends that they earn is less than the dividend rate that they get. On the other hand, some businesses choose to award their shareholders a share of the company's inventory rather than distribute dividends in the form of cash.

Final Dividend
After the annual financial reports of the company have been made public, the board of directors of the company may make the decision to announce a final dividend to the company's shareholders. It is common practice in companies for the annual dividend to be much larger than any dividends that are given out over the various stages of the development of the financial year. This is because the annual dividend is paid out at the conclusion of the fiscal year. The sum is determined by looking at both the annual income of the company and the dividend policy that the company has in place.

The final dividend is chosen by the shareholders by a vote on an ordinary resolution that was presented at the annual meeting and was proposed by the Board of Directors. In order for the resolutions to be passed on by the shareholders, they need to have support from at least 51% of the total number of shares.

4.7 Advantages of Paying Regular Dividend
1. A firm that does not pay dividends to its shareholders is viewed as less trustworthy by those shareholders in comparison to companies that pay dividends to their shareholders on a consistent basis.

2. Investors who want to put their money into great firms and earn a reliable income through dividends are drawn to stocks or shares that pay dividends consistently.

3. These stocks and shares therefore provide the best value to both existing and potential investors. It is to everyone's advantage if the firm is transparent about its financial situation by paying out dividends on a consistent basis.

4. The dividend policy explains, in an open and transparent manner, the parameters of the dividend distribution that takes place between the company and its shareholders. Investors who hold stocks or shares that pay

dividends have the potential to generate two incomes (dividends and capital gains) from their investments.

5. The consistent payment of dividends to shareholders provides those individuals with financial stakes in a firm with reassurance regarding the health of the business's finances.

4.8 Walter's Theory on Dividend Policy

In terms of dividend policy, Walter's model adheres to the idea that dividends are an essential concept. It is believed that the value of a company will be affected when a determination is made regarding the percentage of a company's profits that will be distributed to shareholders in the form of dividends. This concept is elaborated upon even further by the mathematical model that Walter suggests, which may be found in the following sentence:

$$P = D/k + \{r \times (E-D)/k\}/k \qquad \text{Equation-----------------4.1}$$

where;
$\quad$ P = market price per share
$\quad$ D = dividend per share
$\quad$ E = earnings per share
$\quad$ r = internal rate of return of the firm
$\quad$ k = cost of capital of the firm

According to Walter's model, the dividend policy of the company is contingent not only on the availability of investment possibilities but also on the connection between the company's internal rate of return (r) and its cost of capital (k).

4.8.1 Ideas That Led to the Creation of Walter's Model

According to the dividend model that was established by Walter (1956), it has an influence on the valuation of the company's shares. This was the main proposal of this model. The results of this model led researchers to the conclusion that the dividend policy of a company in fact has an impact on its valuation. The two factors that have an impact on the price of the share were organized by him according to the following categories:

- The proportion of a company's profits that are paid out to shareholders in the form of dividends.; and
- The connection between an organization's internal rate of return and the cost of the capital it uses.

4.8.2 Relationship between Dividend Decision and Value of a Firm

As shown in Table 4.1, the dividend distribution, the internal rate of return (r), and the cost of capital (k) are all factors that, according to Walter's hypothesis, will have an effect on the value of the company in the following ways:

Table 4.1: Relationship between Dividend Decision and Value of a Firm

Relationship between r and k	Increase in Dividend Payout	Decrease in Dividend Payout
r>k	Value of the firm decreases	Value of the firm increases
r<k	Value of the firm increases	Value of the firm decreases
r=k	No change in the value of the firm	No change in the value of the firm

4.8.3 Key Assumptions Under the Walter's Model

The following presumptions serve as the foundation for Walter's model:

i. **Internal Financing**

   All of the investments made by the firm are paid for with the portion of the company's income that is kept and invested back into the company. For the same reason, there will not be any additional equity issued, and there are currently no plans to do so either.

ii. **IRR and Cost of Capital are Held Constant**

   All of the investments made by the firm are provided with financing, whose costs are constant. Additionally, there will not be any new equity shares issued, and there are no plans to do so either.

iii. **Earnings Per Share (EPS) and Dividends Per Share (DPS) Remain Constant or Stable**
The original earnings of the corporation as well as the dividends have been continuously steady throughout the course of the years. During the process of producing a value, it is anticipated that the EPS and DPS will continue to be the same even if the model is run with a range of different values for those variables. This is despite the fact that it is possible that those values might change. This is the case regardless of whether or not it is anticipated that they will alter their behavior.

iv. **Indefinite Existence of the Business (Going-Concern Concept)**
It is possible that the company has an infinite lifespan, but more likely it has a very long one. Given this information, it is possible to draw the conclusion that the company has no intention of ever ceasing to participate in the market in any way. As a direct consequence of this, it will continue to exist well into the foreseeable future.

v. **There are No Costs Associated with the Transaction or the Floatation, and No Taxes on Corporation Dividends.**
It is assumed by the theory that there are costs associated with the processes involved in raising capital from the capital market, and the company also pays no corporate tax. Hence, the financial market is expected to be frictionless.

vi. **The Company does not Utilize any Other Forms of Financing, Except Equity Financing**
When it comes to funding, a firm has just one choice: equity financing. In addition to the surplus, it includes the equity share capital as well as any reserves that may have been established. It is not possible to get finance in the form of preferred shares or debentures since there is no capital available in such forms. The hybrid type of financing known as preference share capital has elements of both debt and equity in a single financial instrument. To be more specific, preference share capital possesses some of the characteristics of equity.

vii. **There is a Perfect Capital Market**
What this indicates is that information on any and all securities is made available to any and all investors in an equal proportion. This is true for individual investors as well as investors from institutions. As a direct consequence of adopting this assumption, the price of the security does not reflect an overpricing or an underpricing of it. Instead, it is priced appropriately based on all available information. In addition to this, it creates the sense that every investor is an intelligent (rational) actor. It gives the impression that the goal of each and every investor is the same, which is to raise the amount of money they make while simultaneously lowering the amount of risk they take on.

Formula:
Walter's formula (Equation 4.1) to calculate the market price per share (P) is:

$$P = D/k + \{r \times (E-D)/k\}/k, \qquad \text{Equation ----------4.1}$$

where;

P = Market price per share
D = Dividend per share
E = Earnings per share
r = Internal rate of return of the firm
k = Cost of capital of the firm

In Walter's model, the dividend policy of the firm depends on the availability of investment opportunities and the relationship between the firm's internal rate of return (r) and its cost of capital (k).

Dividend Policy Options:
- Retain all earnings where r>k (i.e., optimum payout ratio of 0%)
- Distribute all earnings where r<k (i.e., optimum payout ratio of 100%)
- Dividend payout or retention (i.e., Dividend policy) has no effect on the value of the firm where r=k

Explanation

The mathematical equation indicates that the market price of the company's share is the sum of the present values of:
- An infinite flow of dividends; and
- An infinite flow of gains on investments from retained earnings.

The formula can be used to calculate the share price if the values of other variables are available.

Illustration 4.1

You are required to find the effect of different dividend policies on the value of shares (market price) for Growth firm; Normal firm; and Declining firm, given the following information:

Cost of capital (k) = 10%
Earnings per share (EPS) = 100
Rate of return (r) = 5%; 10%; and 15%

Find out the effect of dividend payouts on the market value of a firm when the payout ratio is:
    i.   Scenario 1: 0% Dividend payout;
    ii. Scenario 2: 40% Dividend payout;
    iii. Scenario 3: 80% Dividend payout;
    iv. Scenario 4: 100% Dividend payout;

Solution:

i. 0% Dividend payout (i.e., r > k: = Retain all the earnings)

P = D/k + {r x (E-D)/k}
                     k

Cost of capital (k) = 10%
Earnings per share (EPS) = 100
Rate of return (r) = 15%;

P= 0/0.10 + {0.15 x (100-0)/0.10}
                    0.10

= 0 + {0.15x (1,000)}
         0.10
= 0 + 0.15 (10,000)
= 0+ 1,500
P= 1,500

ii. Normal Growth Firm: 40% Dividend payout (i.e., r = k: Pay 40% of the earnings as Dividend)

Cost of capital (k)   = 10%
Earnings per share (EPS) = 100
Rate of return (r)   = 10%;

P= 40/0.10 + {0.10 x (100-40)/0.10}/ 0.10
   = 400 + {0.10x (600)/0.10
   = 400 + 0.10 (6,000)
   = 400+ 600

P= 1,000

iii. 80% Dividend payout (i.e., r < k: Pay 80% of the earnings as Dividend)

Cost of capital (k)   = 10%
Earnings per share (EPS) = 100
Rate of return (r)   = 5%;

P= 80/0.10 + {0.05 x (100-80)/0.10}/ 0.10
   = 800 + {0.05x (200)/0.10
   = 800 + 0.05(2,000)

= 800 + 100

P = 900

Table 4.2: Detailed Analysis of the Four Different Scenarios with Earnings Per Share = 100

	Growth Firm [r>k]	Normal Firm [r=k]	Declining Firm [r<k]
	P= Div. + (r/k)(EPS-Div.) / K Cost of capital (k) = 10% Earnings per share = 100 Rate of return (r) = 15%;	**P= Div. + (r/k)(EPS-Div.)** / K Cost of capital (k) = 10% Earnings per share = 100 Rate of return (r) = 10%;	**P= Div. + (r/k)(EPS-Div.)** / K Cost of capital (k) = 10% Earnings per share = 100 Rate of return (r) = 5%;
Scenario 1: 0% Payout	P = 0 + (0.15/0.10)(100-0.) 0.10 **P = 1,500**	P = 0 + (0.10/0.10)(100-0) 0.10 **P = 1,000**	P = 0 + (0.05/0.10)(100-0.) 0.10 **P = 500**
Scenario 2: 40% Payout	P = 40 + (0.15/0.10)(100-40) 0.10 **P = 1,300**	P = 40 + (0.10/0.10)(100-40) 0.10 **P = 1,000**	P = 40 + (0.05/0.10)(100-40) 0.10 **P = 700**
Scenario 3: 80% Payout	P = 80 + (0.15/0.10)(100-80) 0.10 **P = 1,100**	P = 80 + (0.10/0.10)(100-80) 0.10 **P = 1,000**	P = 80 + (0.05/0.10)(100-80) 0.10 **P = 900**
Scenario 3: 100% Payout	P = 100+(0.15/0.10)(100-100) 0.10 **P = 1,000**	P = 100 + (0.10/0.10)(100-100) 0.10 **P = 1,000**	P = 100 + (0.05/0.10)(100-100) 0.10 **P = 1,000**

Illustration 4.2

A company has an EPS of GHS 100. The market rate of discount applicable to the company is 12.5%. Retained earnings can be reinvested at an IRR of 10%. The company is paying out as follows: Year 1 = 10%; Year 2 = 50%; Year 3 = 100%, as a dividend. Calculate the market price of the share using Walter's model for the respective years.

Here:

D = Year 1= 10% = GHS 10
E = 25
k = 12.5%
r = 10%

Year 1: When there is 10% Payout:

Market price of the share: P = 10/0.125 + {0.10 x (100-10)/0.125}
                                                        0.125
      =   80 + {0.10 x (720)}
            0.125
      =   80 + (72/0.125)
      =   80 + 576

    P =   **GHS 656.00**

Year 2: When there is 50% Payout:

Market price of the share: P = 50/0.125 + {0.10 x (100-50)/0.125}}
                                                        0.125
      =   400 + {0.10 x (400)}
            0.125
      =   400 + (40/0.125)
      =   400 + 320

    P =   **GHS 720**

Year 2: When there is 100% Payout:

Market price of the share: P = 100/0.125 + {0.10 x (100-90)/0.125}
$$ 0.125$$

$$= \quad 800 + \{0.10 \times (0)\}$$
$$ 0.125$$

$$= \quad 800 + (0)$$

P = **GHS 800**

4.8.4 Walter's Model - Implications

The following are some of the significant ramifications that the model developed by Walter has for companies operating at different stages of development:

- **Growth Firm**

  One of the distinguishing characteristics of growing firms is an internal rate of return that is greater than the cost of capital, which is denoted as r > k. These businesses will have a plethora of other opportunities to invest in that will be rewarding. Because of this, companies that are still in the growth phase have the ability to provide a higher return for their shareholders than the return that those owners might get elsewhere, even if they reinvest the dividends. This is because businesses that are still in the growth phase have the ability to provide a higher return for their customers. As a consequence of this, the ideal payout ratio for firms that are expanding is zero percent of their entire earnings.

- **Normal Firm**

  The normal firm is where R = k is an abbreviation for the relationship between a typical company's rate of return on invested capital and the cost of that capital. When a company has reached the usual phase, it will begin to create returns that are analogous to those of a shareholder. As a result, the dividend policy is totally pointless when considered in the context of these particular circumstances. This will have no effect whatsoever on the price that the share is selling for on the market at the present time. Therefore, there is no payout ratio that is best for firms when they are in the normal period. This is because organizations go through cycles. Any reward is preferable to having none at all.

- **Declining Firm**
  Companies that are in the process of liquidating their assets often have an internal rate of return that is lower than the cost of the capital, which is mathematically expressed as r < k. In other words, the cost of the capital is higher than the rate of return on the investment. Additionally, the returns that shareholders are able to accomplish on their investments are greater than the profits that these corporations are able to earn for themselves. This is because shareholders have more control over their assets. As a result, the corporation should not consider reinvesting its profits back into the business itself because doing so would be a waste of money. In fact, the circumstance that results in the greatest possible increase in share price is one in which the company provides all of its earnings to its owners. This is the case in the condition that results in the largest possible gain in share price. This is due to the fact that taking this course of action will result in the most significant increase in share price that is feasible. Under these circumstances, the dividend payment ratio that would be considered ideal would be one that is equivalent to one hundred percent (100% payout) of the total dividends.

4.8.5 Criticisms of Walter's Model

In Walter's model, he makes the following excessively idealistic presumptions, which leads to criticism of his theory:

- **No External Financing**
  It is difficult to stick to Walter's premise that the firm would totally finance itself internally through retained earnings in the real world because of the challenges presented by the real world. It is necessary for businesses to find additional funding outside of the firm in order to support new projects.

- **Constant (r) and (k)**
  Due to the difficulties that are present in the actual world, it is impossible to adhere to Walter's premise that the company would completely finance itself internally through retained revenues. This is because of the competition that exists in the real world. In order for businesses to be able to finance new projects, it is vital for them to raise more money.

- **Assumption of 100% Retention of Earnings**
  The conclusion of the Walter Model is that it is impossible to keep one hundred percent of one's earnings if (r) is greater than (ke). It is essential for the firm to make equity dividend payments in light of the dividend payments made by other companies; failing to do so would cause the inventory of the company to fall out of favor. In terms of psychological gratification, a cash return will provide more than a change in the price of the security.

- **Other Unrealistic Assumptions**
  All of the unrealistic assumptions, such as assuming that there is no debt financing or funding through preferred shares, that there are no floatation costs or transaction costs, and that the capital market is flawless, are applicable here.

4.9 Chapter Review Questions

1. Define the term 'Dividend policy'
2. Evaluate the affect the size of dividend payout by firms.
3. Explain the various types of dividend policy that a firm can adopt.
4. Examine Walter's theory on dividend policy.
5. You are required to find the effect of different dividend policies on the value of shares (market price) for Growth firm; Normal firm; and Declining firm, given the following information:

Cost of capital (k) = 12%
Earnings per share (EPS) = 150
Rate of return (r) = 6% 15%; and 20%

Find out the effect of dividend payout on the market value of a firm when the payout ratio is:
   v. Scenario 1: 0% Dividend payout;
   vi. Scenario 2: 30% Dividend payout;

vii. Scenario 3: 80% Dividend payout;
viii. Scenario 4: 100% Dividend payout;

6. A company has an EPS of GHS 200. The market rate of discount applicable to the company is 10.5%. Retained earnings can be reinvested at an IRR of 10%. The company is paying out as follows: Year 1= 15%; Year 2 = 55%; Year 3 = 100%, as dividend.

Calculate the market price of the share using Walter's model for the respective years.

4.10 Chapter References and Bibliography

[1] Ali, H. (2022). Corporate dividend policy in the time of COVID-19: Evidence from the G-12 countries. *Finance Research Letters*, *46*, 102493.

[2] Cheung, A., Hu, M., & Schwiebert, J. (2018). Corporate social responsibility and dividend policy. *Accounting & Finance*, *58*(3), 787-816.

[3] Driver, C., Grosman, A., & Scaramozzino, P. (2020). Dividend policy and investor pressure. *Economic Modelling*, *89*, 559-576.

[4] Kanakriyah, R. (2020). Dividend policy and companies' financial performance. *The Journal of Asian Finance, Economics and Business*, *7*(10), 531-541.

[5] Lease R.C., John, K., Kalay, A., Loewenstein, U. & Sarig, O.H. (1999). Dividend Policy: Its Impact on Firm Value. *OUP Catalogue*.

[6] Pattiruhu, J. R., & Paais, M. (2020). Effect of liquidity, profitability, leverage, and firm size on dividend policy. *The Journal of Asian Finance, Economics and Business*, *7*(10), 35-42.

[7] Walter, J. E. (1956). Dividend policies and common inventory prices. *Journal of Finance*, *11*(1), 29-41.

4.11 Recommended Reading List

[1] Dewasiri, N. J., Koralalage, W. B. Y., Azeez, A. A., Jayarathne, P. G. S. A., Kuruppuarachchi, D., & Weerasinghe, V. A. (2019). Determinants of dividend policy: evidence from an emerging and developing market. *Managerial Finance*, *45*(3), 413-429.

[2] Masulis, R. W., & Trueman, B. (1988). Corporate investment and dividend decisions under differential personal taxation. *Journal of Financial and Quantitative Analysis*, 23(4), 369-385.https:// doi.org/10.2307/2331077

[3] Nguyen, T. N. L., & Nguyen, V. C. (2020). The Determinants of profitability in listed enterprises: A Study from Vietnamese Stock Exchange. *Journal of Asian Finance, Economics and Business*, 7(1), 47-58. https://doi.org/10.13106/jafeb.2020. vol7.no1.47.

CHAPTER 5

CAPITALIZATION

5.1 Overview

Companies rely on various sources of capital to finance their total assets and operations. The capital of the company may be made up of a wide variety of sources, such as common and preferred inventory, debentures, bonds, and long-term loans. The total amount of the company's capital is recorded in the capital account of the balance sheet. Capitalization encompasses a wide variety of financial instruments, including but not limited to share capital, debentures, loans, free reserves, and other financial instruments.

Objectives of the Chapter

This chapter seeks to achieve the following objectives:

- To explain the meaning of the concept of capitalization;
- To examine the concept of overcapitalization;
- To evaluate the concept of undercapitalization; and
- To explain what is meaning of fair capitalization.

Key Words Used in the Chapter

- ✓ Capitalization
- ✓ Fair capitalization
- ✓ Overcapitalization
- ✓ Undercapitalization

5.2 Definition of 'Capitalization'

The total amount of money that has been invested in an organization is referred to as its "capitalization." The invested capital of a company is included in the calculation of its capitalization, along with the company's debt, which is typically of the long-term variety. A company's growth and the assets associated with that growth are supported by capitalization, which is a form of funding that is intended to be permanent and is used for that purpose.

5.3 Over- Capitalization

A situation known as overcapitalization occurs when a company raises more money than is required for the level of business activity and requirements it currently satisfies. The term "business activity" refers to the typical operations that are carried out by the company. If a company's total owned and borrowed capital is greater than its fixed and current assets, then the company is said to be overcapitalized. This means that the company is making use of more capital than is actually required, and the funds are not being used in a prudent manner, which usually results in inefficiency. Since the excess capital is not being utilized to its full potential, the only solution is for the company to either grow or reduce its share capital.

When a business enterprise persistently fails to earn an amount of income on the capital employed that is sufficient to give dividends to its shareholders at a rate that is considered to be reasonable, this is unquestionably a case of overcapitalization.

It was determined by Bonneville et al. (1959) that an organization is considered to have an excessive amount of capital "when it is unable to earn a fair rate of return on its outstanding securities." When a company's earnings are not sufficient to generate a satisfactory return on the number of shares and bonds it has issued, the company is said to have excessive levels of capital. One thing that must be made abundantly clear is that a business can only be considered overcapitalized if it has not been able to generate a sufficient amount of revenue over an extended period of time (Langley & Leyshon, 2017). If something like this were to occur, the real value of an organization's total assets would be lower than their book value at the time of the event.

When a company's actual profits are not sufficient to meet the company's financial obligations, including the payment of interest on debentures and loans as well as the distribution of dividends on shares of inventory over a specified amount of time, this situation is referred to as "over-capitalization," and it is one of the situations that falls under the purview of the term "over-capitalization." This problematic situation arises when a company is able to successfully raise more capital than it requires for its operations. There is always some portion of capital that is sitting idle and doing nothing. The rate of return shows a pattern of decreasing returns as a direct consequence of this fact, which exhibits the pattern of decreasing returns.

5.3.1 Causes of Over- Capitalization
The following are some of the primary reasons for excessive capitalization:

- **A high price to pay for promotion**
  In circumstances in which a company incurs high promotional expenses, such as making contracts, canvassing, underwriting commissions, drafting documents, and the like, but the actual returns do not suffice in proportion to the high expenses, the company is said to be overcapitalized.

- **Acquisition of assets at more expensive prices**
  When a company buys assets at a price that has been artificially inflated, the end result is that the book value of the assets ends up being higher than the actual returns on the assets. This is referred to as the "value mismatch." As a result of this situation, the company has an excessive amount of capital that is readily available.

- **A company's floatation in boom period**
  When economic conditions are favorable, the company is responsible for ensuring its financial stability so that it can continue to operate normally. When something of this nature occurs, it indicates that the rate of return on the capital being utilized is lower than average. The company's actual earnings and earnings per share have fallen as a direct result of this factor.

- **Inadequate depreciation provision**
  In the event that the finance manager is unable to provide an accurate rate of depreciation, the end result will be that insufficient funds will be available for use in the event that the assets need to be replaced or become obsolete. When new assets are needed, it is necessary to purchase them at high prices, which ultimately ends up being quite costly.

- **Conservative dividend policy**
  If the Board of Directors of a company chooses to pay all of its earnings after interest and tax (EBIT) to shareholders in the form of dividends, the company will have insufficient retained profits. Sufficient retained profits are necessary for a company to continue to have high earnings. This has a negative impact on the company, which is a direct consequence of the situation. The company decides to go out and raise new capital in order to make up for the shortfall; this not only makes the company's operations more expensive, but it also results in the company having more capital on hand than it actually requires.

- **Over-estimation of earnings**
  If inadequate financial planning causes the promoters of a company to overestimate the company's earnings, the company will seek out borrowings that are difficult to meet and will not invest capital in a way that will generate a profit. Both of these outcomes are bad for the company. This ultimately leads to a decrease in the total earnings per share achieved.

5.3.2 Effects of Overcapitalization

1. **On the Shareholders-**

The following is the list of the challenges that shareholders face when dealing with companies that have an excessive amount of available capital:
- Because of the decline in profitability, the rate at which shareholders earn money has also slowed down. This is a direct consequence of the decline in profitability.
- The low profitability of the company contributes to a fall in the market price of the shares as a result of the decline.

- As a consequence of the deteriorating profitability, the shareholders are being adversely affected. The amount of money they make now raises some eyebrows.
- The decline in the company's goodwill results in a corresponding drop in the value of the shares in the company. Because of this specific circumstance, it is currently impossible to sell shares on the capital market.

2. **On the Company-**
   - The low profitability of the business has had a negative impact directly on the reputation of the company.

   - The market makes it difficult to dispose of the company's shares in a timely manner.

   - When a company's profits decrease, the goodwill that consumers have for that company also decreases. When something like this occurs, it is much more challenging to acquire new loans for the company because the company's credibility has been damaged.

   - The company engages in unethical business practices, such as manipulating its financial statements to give the appearance of high profits, in order to safeguard its good name and preserve its good standing in the industry.

3. **On the Public-**
   The general public suffers from a number of negative effects as a result of an over-capitalized company, including the following:
   - The management of the company implements various strategies in order to cover up their earning capacity, such as increasing the prices of their products or decreasing the quality of those products.

   - The rate of return on the capital that is put to use is not particularly high. Because of this, the general public might get the impression that their cash resources are not being utilized in an efficient manner.

- The company's credibility takes a hit as a result of its low earnings because the company is unable to make timely payments to its account payables as a result of the company's financial situation.

- It also has an effect on the working conditions and the payment of wages and salaries, both of which are reduced as a result of this.

5.4 Undercapitalization

If a company generates unusually high profits in comparison to other companies operating within the same industry, then that company is regarded as being under-capitalized. In other words, an under-capitalized company does not have sufficient cash on hand to carry out its functions and, in most cases, is unable to qualify for loans from financial institutions due to the unacceptably high debt-to-equity ratio that the company carries.

Under-capitalization is simply the opposite of over-capitalization, but it should never be misunderstood to mean that there is a lack of capital or that there is not enough capital. When a company begins earning at a rate that is higher than its current rate, the company in question has entered the stage of undercapitalization. In fact, it is an indicator of appropriate and efficient utilization of the capital that is employed in the concern.

A company is said to be "under-capitalized" when either the rate of profits that it is making on the total capital is exceptionally high in relation to the return enjoyed by similar companies in the same industry or when it has too little capital with which to conduct its business (Story, 2017). As a consequence of this, additional funds are raised, additional profits are made, high levels of goodwill and earnings are achieved, and the rate of return on capital shows an upward trend.

5.4.1 Causes of Undercapitalization

The following are some of the possible causes:
- During the depths of the Great Depression, the company went public;
- Ability on the part of the directors to be effective;
- A provision for depreciation that is adequate in terms of its amount;

- The purchase of assets at prices that are lower than their current value;
- When the company adopts a more conservative approach to its dividend policy; and
- There is a widespread belief that there are substantial hidden reserves.

5.4.2 Effects of Undercapitalization

1. **On the Shareholders**
   - The company's profitability has been on the rise. As a direct consequence of this, the rate of earnings would increase.
   - The value of the share on the market increases leading to maximization of shareholders' wealth.
   - A sizeable dividend payment is promised to the shareholders.
   - Additionally, the firm's financial reputation improves.

2. **On the Company**
   - When a company's earnings are higher, their reputation grows stronger.
   - The market tends to become more competitive when earnings rates are higher.
   - Consumers may lose interest in a business if they believe that it is exploiting a situation in which it is highly profitable to charge excessive prices for its goods.
   - The high profits may cause an increase in the demand for workers, leading to increased staff agitations.

3. **On the Society**
   - There is a potential for unhealthy speculation in the Stock market when earnings are high, profitability is high, and the market price of shares is high.
   - The company keeps secret reserves, which may result in the company paying lower taxes to the government.
   - Because these businesses are able to import innovations, advanced technology, and, as a result, products of the highest quality, the general public has extremely high expectations for these organizations.

5.5 Fair Capitalization

In essence, there should not be either an excessive amount of capital or an inadequate amount of capital. A reasonable amount of capitalization is something that an entity that does business absolutely needs to have. The stage of capitalization known as "fair capitalization" refers to the situation in which the total amount of capitalization equals the earnings that are warranted by those earnings. At this point in the process of fair capitalization, the situation is very close to perfect. This can be accomplished through the incorporation of both debt and equity into the capitalization structure.

5.6 Chapter Review Questions

1. Define the term 'capitalization'
2. Examine the concept of 'overcapitalization'
3. Explain the main causes and effects of overcapitalization.
4. Distinguish between overcapitalization and undercapitalization.
5. What are the main causes and effect of undercapitalization?

5.7 Chapter References and Bibliography

[1] Bonneville, J. H., Dewey, L. E., & Kelly, H. M. (1959). *Organizing and Financing Business. [By] JH Bonneville... LE Dewey... Harry M. Kelly*. Englewood Cliffs.

[2] Langley, P., & Leyshon, A. (2017). Platform capitalism: The intermediation and capitalization of digital economic circulation. *Finance and Society*, 3(1), 11-31.

[3] Story, M. (2017). Mergers and Acquisitions: A Panacea to under Capitalization Challenges Faced by Zimbabwe Non-Life Insurance Companies in the Multicurency Era. *The International Journal of Business & Management*.

5.8 Recommended Reading List

[1] Abrahams, T., & Sidhu, B. K. (1998). The role of R&D capitalizations in firm valuation and performance measurement. *Australian Journal of Management*, *23*(2), 169-183.

[2] Johnman, L., & Murphy, H. (1999). A very British institution! A study in undercapitalization: the role of the Ship Mortgage Finance Company in post-delivery credit financing within shipbuilding, 1951–671. *Financial History Review*, *6*(2), 203-221.

CHAPTER 6

CAPITAL STRUCTURE

6.1 Overview

Capital is the single most important factor in getting a business off the ground. It serves as the basis upon which the company is built. The two primary kinds of capital that can be obtained by a company are known as debt and equity, respectively. The ownership stakes in a company, as well as claims on the company's future cash flows and profits, are the sources of equity capital. Equity can be created through the issuance of shares, preferred inventory, or retained earnings, whereas debt can take the form of loan obligations or bond issues.

Objectives of the Chapter

- To explain the meaning if capital structure;
- To explain the factors that determine capital structure;
- To outline the importance of capital structure;
- To ascertain the key principles underlying the theory of capital structure;
- To evaluate capital structure point of indifference;
- To examine the theories underlying capital structure; and
- To evaluate the impact of changing capital structure on key financial ratios.

> **Key Words Used in the Chapter**
>
> ✓ Capital structure
> ✓ Point of indifference
> ✓ Net Income (NI) approach
> ✓ Trade-off theory
> ✓ Pecking order theory
> ✓ Capitalization rate

6.2 Definition of Capital Structure

A company's capital structure refers to the specific mix of debt and equity financing that it employs in order to finance its day-to-day operations as well as its future expansion. The term "capital structure" refers to the way in which a company finances its day-to-day operations as well as its expansion (investments) through a combination of equity and debt capital sources. This combination is used by the company to ensure that it can continue to exist and grow.

6.3 Understanding Capital Structure

A company's capital structure can be defined as the ratio of the various types of securities it issues to the total amount of money it raises to finance its assets. There are two primary choices involved in the capital structure:

- Equity shares, preference shares, and long-term borrowings are the three types of securities that are going to be issued (Corporate bonds or Debentures).
- The procedure known as capital gearing can be utilized to ascertain relative ratios of securities.

On the basis of this criterion, the businesses are split into two categories:

a. High-Geared Firm
Companies that have a high level of debt in relation to their equity capitalization are said to have a high level of debt. Thus, debt constitute more than 50% of the total capitalization.

b. Low-Geared Firms
companies whose equity capital constitutes a significant portion of their total capitalization. Hence, equity constitutes more than 50% of the total capitalization.

Take, for example, the fact that there are two different companies, A and B. The total amount of capitalization for each of these cases comes to GHS 200,000. In company A, the proportion of equity capital to total capitalization is GHS 50,000, while in company B, the proportion of equity capital to total capitalization is GHS 150,000. This means that the proportion of equity capital in company A is 25 percent, while the proportion of equity capital in company B is 75 percent. In this scenario, company A is considered to have a high degree of gearing, while company B is considered to have a low degree of gearing.

On the balance sheet, you will find entries for debt as well as equity. The assets of a company, which are also listed on the balance sheet, can be acquired by using either debt or equity. The long-term debt, short-term debt, common stock (equity shares), and preferred stocks (shares) that make up a company's capital structure can all be combined in a variety of ways. When conducting an analysis of a company's capital structure, one of the factors that is taken into consideration is the ratio of the company's short-term debt to its long-term debt.

When financial analysts talk about a company's capital structure, they are almost always talking about a company's debt-to-equity (D/E) ratio. A company that has a capital structure that is more aggressive and, as a result, presents a greater risk to investors is typically one that is heavily financed by debt. Despite this, the possibility exists that this risk is the primary driver of the company's expansion.

One of the two primary ways that a company can raise money through the capital markets is by taking on debt. It is possible to deduct the interest payments that are made as a result of borrowing funds, which is one of the tax advantages that debt provides to companies. In contrast to equity, debt enables a company or business to keep its existing control and ownership structure. In addition, when interest rates are low, there is a plentiful supply of debt that is not difficult to obtain.

External investors are able to acquire a stake in the company through the purchase of equity. When interest rates are relatively low, equity typically carries a higher price tag than debt does. However, unlike debt, equity does not need to be paid back. In the event that earnings continue to decrease, the company will benefit from this. On the other hand, equity is the owner's claim to a portion of the company's future earnings and reflects the owner's ownership stake in the business.

A high leverage ratio and an aggressive capital structure are both characteristics of businesses that finance their assets and their operating activities with a greater proportion of debt (debentures or bonds) than equity. A company with a low leverage ratio (an unleveraged firm) and a conservative capital structure is one that purchases its assets with a greater proportion of equity than debt. That being said, a high leverage ratio as well as an aggressive capital structure can also lead to higher growth rates, whereas a conservative capital structure can lead to lower growth rates. Both of these factors are potentially advantageous for businesses.

Finding the optimal ratio of debt to equity, also referred to as the optimal capital structure, is the objective of the management team of a company. This ratio is used to finance business operations. Investors are able to keep an eye on the capital structure of a company by tracking the D/E ratio and comparing it to the company's competitors in the same industry.

6.4 Factors that Determine Capital Structure Composition

- **Trading on Equity**

  The concept of ownership of a company is denoted by the term "equity." Trading on equity refers to the practice of using equity share capital as collateral to secure reasonable amounts of borrowed money. It is predicated on the idea that equity shareholders will be in the driver's seat if the rate of dividend on preference capital and the rate of interest on borrowed capital are both lower than the overall rate of the company's earnings. As a result, it is recommended that a company opt for a balanced combination of preference shares, equity shares, and debentures in its capital structure. When shareholder expectations are high, trading on equity becomes a more important aspect of the business.

- **Degree of Control**

  In a company, the individuals who are referred to as the "elected representatives of equity shareholders" are the company's Board of Directors. The voting rights of preference shareholders are significantly less than those of debenture holders, who have no voting rights at all. If the policies of the company's management are such that they want to keep their voting rights in their own hands, then the capital structure of the company should be comprised of debenture holders and loans rather than equity share investors.

- **Flexibility of Financial Plan**

  It is important for an organization's capital structure to be designed in such a way that it allows for both tightening and loosening of plan parameters. Debentures and loans are both able to be paid back when the time comes to do so. While equity capital is not eligible for a refund at any time, this restriction lends a degree of rigidity to the plans. As a result, in order to realize the desired capital structure, the company ought to pursue the issuance of debentures in addition to other types of loans.

- **Firm's Corporate Tax Position**

  One of the most fundamental reasons for utilizing debt is that interest paid by the company is tax deductible. Because of this, the effective cost of debt

is reduced, which is especially beneficial in situations in which the corporate tax rate increases over time. When there is an increase in corporate tax, the after-tax cost of debt decreases, and there is no question that the company will use a greater proportion of debt in its capital structure compositions. However, when there is a decrease in the corporate tax rate, the after-tax cost of debt rises, which makes it unattractive for the company to use debt in this round of financing. Instead, the company may choose to increase the amount of equity capital that is included in the capital structure.

Illustration 6.1
Assume that Jack Company Ltd. is financed by debenture inventory at an 8 percent rate and that the company is subject to a corporate tax rate of 40 percent on an annual basis. The cost of capital, after taxes, will be significantly lower than the compound rate of 8 percent that has been assigned to the debenture.

Solution:

Since debenture interest is tax deductible, the after-tax cost of debt will be:

After-tax cost of debt = $K_d (1-t)$ Equation ------------------6.1

Where K_d = Cost of debt
        t = Corporate tax rate
        1 = Constant

Given that:
    t = 40%
    K_d = 8%
    = 8% (1 – 0.40)
    = 0.08 (0.60)
    = 0.048

After-tax cost of debt = **4.8%**

Assume the corporate tax rate is revised upwards to 50% per annum. The after-tax cost of debt would be computed as:

= 8% x (1-0.50)

= 8% x (0.50)

= 4%

Due to the increase in the corporate tax rate, the after-tax cost of debt has decreased, which has allowed the company to use more debt if its gearing would allow it. If, on the other hand, the corporate tax rate was to be reduced to 20 percent per year, the after-tax cost of capital would be greater than the after-tax cost of debt, which had been calculated previously to be 4.8 percent. Hence, the new after-tax cost of debt will be:

= K_d x (1- 0.20)

= 8% x (1- 0.20)

= 8% x (80%)

= 6.4%

- **Financial Flexibility**

The objective of financial managers is to preserve a certain degree of financial flexibility. It is always preferable to have a steady supply of capital, as this is necessary to ensure stability in operations, which ultimately leads to long-term success for a business. The more financially flexible a firm is, the greater its ability to switch from one source of capital to another. Thus, this will certainly facilitate the ease of switching from equity sources to debt sources.

- **Attitude of Management**

The decisions made by management have a significant impact on the various components that make up the capital structure. The perspective of management is extremely important with regard to the decision of whether or not to issue new shares or to raise additional capital through the issue of debt stock. It should come as no surprise that some managers are significantly more aggressive than others. To this end, some companies would rather try to improve their profitability by taking on additional debt as opposed to issuing new shares of stock. This makes perfect sense when you consider the context.

- **Attitude of Investors/ Lenders**

In general, the company's policy is to separate investors into various categories for each type of security they offer. As a result, a capital structure ought to provide sufficient investment options to accommodate any and all types of investors. Equity shares are typically purchased by investors who are bold and adventurous, while loans and debentures are typically raised with the consideration of investors who are conscious.

- **Capital Market Condition**

The current price of the company's shares on the market will have a significant impact over the course of the company's existence. Debentures and loans make up the majority of the company's capital structure while the country is experiencing the Great Depression. When the economy is doing well and inflation is on the rise, a good portion of a company's capital should be made up of equity shares and share capital.

- **Cost of Capital or Financing**

When deciding on a capital structure, a company must take into consideration the cost of raising capital through the sale of securities. It has been observed that, when a company is earning a profit, debentures prove to be a more cost-effective source of financing when compared to equity shares, which require equity shareholders to receive an additional portion of company profits.

- **Government Policies**

The regulations and policies that are established by the government can also have an effect on the capital structure. The decisions regarding the structure of capital are subject to change whenever there is a shift in either monetary or fiscal policy.

- **Stability in Sales**

The company is able to fulfill its fixed commitments because it is an established business that operates in a market that is expanding and has a high sales turnover. Regardless of whether or not there is a profit, interest on debentures must be paid. As a result, when sales are high, profits are high as well, and the company is in a better position to meet its fixed commitments, such as interest on debentures and dividends on preference shares, when sales are high. If a company is experiencing unstable sales, then it is not in a position to meet the obligations that have been fixed. Therefore, equity capital is a prudent choice in this circumstance.

- **Sizes of the Company**

The capital structure of medium- and small-sized businesses typically consists of retained profits and loans from financial institutions. On the other hand, large corporations that have a solid reputation, a consistent revenue stream, and an established profit can more readily issue shares and debentures, as well as take out loans and other forms of financial assistance from financial institutions. The total capitalization is increased proportionally to the size of the company.

6.5 Capital Structure Decision

Assuming that a company has the ability to obtain capital (for example, from investors or lenders), that company will likely work to keep its cost of capital as low as possible. The calculation known as weighted average cost of capital (WACC) can be used to accomplish this goal. In order to determine the weighted average cost of capital (WACC), the manager or analyst will multiply the cost of each capital component by its proportional weight. A company that has accumulated an excessive amount of debt is considered to be facing a credit risk as a result of its inability to fulfill its debt obligations by way of excessive interest payments. However, having an excessive amount of equity might indicate that the company is missing out on potential growth avenues or is overpaying for the cost of the capital it needs (as equity tends to be more costly than debt).

Unfortunately, there is no "magic ratio" of debt to equity that can be used as a guide to arrive at the optimal capital structure for the real world. The definition of a debt-to-equity ratio that is considered to be healthy shifts depending on the industry in which a company operates, the stage of development the company is currently in, and it can even shift over the course of time due to changes in the external environment, such as changes in interest rates and regulations. For example, a company that operates in the retail sector will have a different definition than a company that operates in the technology sector.

6.6 Components of Capital Structure

The term "capital structure" refers to the combination of a company's financial resources in a way that makes the most efficient use of a variety of long-term funding options, the most general of which are equity and debt. A company can acquire a variety of funds by selling preference shares, equity shares, retained earnings, long-term loans, and so on.

1. Equity Capital

Money that is owned by the company's shareholders or owners is referred to as equity capital. There are two distinct varieties included in it.

- **Retained Earnings**

    The portion of a company's profit that is set aside in a separate account (the income surplus account) by the organization and used for the purpose of further investment by the company is referred to as retained earnings. Reserves are the funds that have been set aside for a particular objective and that the organization plans to use in the foreseeable future. The portion of profits or gains that have been set aside for a particular objective is known as a reserve. It is common practice to establish reserves in order to purchase fixed assets, pay bonuses, pay an anticipated legal settlement, pay for repairs and maintenance, and pay off debt.

    When a business makes a profit at the end of the year, a portion of that profit is put back into the trading concern so that it can better prepare for future challenges and opportunities for growth. These opportunities may include making stable dividend payments, being prepared for unanticipated events or legal mandates, making investments, or improving the financial situation. For example, there is a reserve for paying stable dividends, a general reserve, a reserve for increased costs associated with replacement, a reserve for expansion, etc.

- **Contributed Capital**
  Contributed capital can refer to either the sum of money that the owners of the company invested in the company when it was first launched or the sum of money that the company received from shareholders in exchange for ownership of the company. This is typically referred to as the fully paid-up share capital that the shareholders have contributed in order to indicate their ownership stake in the company.

2. Debt Capital
The money that is obtained through loans and used in commercial enterprises is referred to as "debt capital." There are numerous varieties of debt capital to choose from.

- **Long-term Bonds (Corporate bonds)**

Because of the extended repayment period and the fact that only interest is required to be repaid during this time, these kinds of bonds are regarded as the most secure form of debt. The principal is only due upon the bonds' maturation.

- **Commercial Paper**

Companies will often turn to this form of short-term debt instrument in order to raise capital for a period of time that is only a few years away.

6.7 Optimal Capital Structure
The perfect balance of debt and equity financing is what we mean when we talk about optimal capital structure. This balance is what helps a company achieve its goal of maximizing its value in the market while at the same time minimizing its cost of capital. The capital structure varies across industries. A high debt ratio is not appropriate for a company that is involved in mining or the extraction of petroleum and oil; however, certain industries, such as insurance and banking, have a significant amount of debt as part of their capital structure.

6.8 Benefits of Capital Structure
Because it determines the overall stability of a company, capital structure is an essential component of any business. The following are some of the additional considerations that bring to light the significance of capital structure:

1. If a company has a healthy capital structure, then there is a greater possibility that it will be able to raise the market price of the shares and securities that it possesses. Because of this, the market's valuation of the asset will increase;

2. A sound capital structure ensures that the available resources are put to good use by the organization. It prevents either excessive or insufficient capitalization;

3. It is beneficial to the company in terms of increasing its profits, which in turn results in higher returns to the company's stakeholders;

4. A well-designed capital structure will help a company get the most out of its shareholders' investments while keeping the overall cost of capital to a minimum; and

5. A strong capital structure gives companies the ability to adapt to changing market conditions by either increasing or decreasing the amount of debt capital they hold.

6.9 Principles Underlying the Theory of Capital Structure

In order to optimize returns, a manager of finances needs to choose the appropriate mix of capital based on particular rules and the many sources of money that are accessible. The following is a list of guiding principles for capital structure:
- Cost principle;
- Risk principle;
- Control principle;
- Flexibility principle; and
- Timing principle.

Cost Principle
- ✓ The primary focus of this strategy is to maximize earnings per share while minimizing the amount of money spent on funding the business.

- ✓ The cost of borrowing is controlled by the interest rate as well as the tax rate.
- ✓ The idea that the cost of capital may be reduced by using debt.

Risk Principle
- ✓ The most important aspect of this philosophy is that it will not tolerate taking significant risks.
- ✓ Liquidity traps can be caused by high interest rates on loans relative to profits.
- ✓ It is not required that shareholders declare dividends.

Control Principle
- ✓ The issuance of preferred shares in order to maintain ownership of the company is the primary focus of this idea.
- ✓ It helps maintain a reasonable ratio of inventory to debt in the company's capital structure.

Flexibility Principle
- ✓ The accumulation of surplus capital for use in meeting future requirements is the primary focus of this guiding concept.
- ✓ Long-term financing demands management to make effective use of the resources they have at their disposal (if needed).

Timing Principle
- ✓ Keeping to this advice means that you should always be on the lookout for opportunities given by dynamic markets and seize those opportunities when you find them.
- ✓ The costs associated with soliciting cash are kept to a minimum.

6.10 Capital Structure and Point of Indifference Determination

The point of indifference under capital structure refers to the level of earnings before interest and taxes (EBIT) at which earnings per share (EPS) remain the same regardless of the debt-equity mix or the composition of the capital structure. This level can be reached when EBIT reaches a certain level. This stage might also be referred to as the point at which you are profitable again. In general, it refers to the point at which the EPS of two distinct alternative financial plans needs to be equal to any amount of EBIT analysis. This threshold might vary depending on the specific situation.

According to Besley & Brigham (2008), "the point of indifference refers to the EPS indifference point, which is the number of sales at which EPS will be the same, regardless of whether the corporation employs debt or common inventory financing."

The level of EBIT that, when contrasted with two different types of capital structure, results in the same amount of earnings per share is referred to as the point of indifference (Van Horn, 2002).

6.11 Calculation of Point of Indifference under Capital Structure

The 'equivalency point' or 'point of indifference' refers to the level of EBIT, or profits before interest and tax, at which EPS remains the same regardless of the many possibilities of the debt-equity mix. EPS stands for earnings per share. The point at which the rate of return on capital employed is equal to the cost of debt is known as the break-even level of EBIT for alternative financial plans. This level of EBIT is known as the break-even level of EBIT since it is the point at which the alternative financial plan is profitable.

The Equivalency or Point of Indifference can be Calculated Algebraically, as below:

$$X = \frac{(X-I_1)(1-T) - PD_1}{S_1} = \frac{(X-I_2)(1-T) - PD_2}{S_2} \quad \text{Equation------6.2}$$

Where:

X = Equivalency Point or Point of Indifference or Break-Even EBIT Level.
I_1 = Interest under alternative financial plan 1.
I_2 = Interest under alternative financial plan 2.
T = Tax Rate
PD = Preference Dividend
S_1 = Number of equity shares or amount of equity share capital under alternative 1.
S_2 = Number of equity shares or amount of equity share capital under alternative 2.

The point of indifference can also be determined by preparing the EBIT chart or range of earnings chart. This chart shows the expected earnings per share (EPS) at various levels of earnings before interest and tax (EBIT), which may be plotted on a graph, and a straight line representing the EPS at various levels of EBIT may be drawn. The point where this line intersects is known as the point of indifference or break-even point.

Illustration 6.2

A project under consideration by your company requires a capital investment of GHS 6,000,000.00. Interest on a term loan is 15% p.a. with a corporate tax rate of 50%. Calculate the point of indifference for the project if the debt-equity ratio insisted on by the financing agencies is 2:1. The share price is quoted at GHS 100 per share. As the debt-equity ratio insisted on by the financing agencies is 1:2, the company has two alternative financial plans:

(i) Raising the entire amount of GHS 6,000,000 by the issue of equity shares, thereby using no debt, and

(ii) Raising GHS 2,000,000 by way of debt and GHS 4,000,000.00 by issue of equity share capital.

Solution:

Calculation of point of Indifference:

$$= \frac{(X-I_1)(1-T) - PD_1}{S_1} = \frac{(X-I_2)(1-T) - PD_2}{S_2}$$

Where, X = Point Indifference

I_1 = Interest under alternative 1; i.e., Zero (0)
I_2 = Interest under alternative 2, i.e., 15/100 = 0.15 x 2,000,000 = GHS 300,000
T = Tax rate, i.e., 50% or 0.5

PD = Preference Divided, i.e., zero (o) as there are no preference shares.
S_1 = Amount of equity capital under alternative 1, i.e., 6,000,000.
S_2 = Amount of equity capital under alternative 2, i.e., 4,000,000.

$$= \frac{(X-0)(1-0.50) - 0}{6,000,000} = \frac{(X-300,000)(1-0.50) - 0}{4,000,000}$$

Substituting the values:

$$= \frac{0.5X}{6,000,000} = \frac{X-300,000 (0.5)}{4,000,000}$$

$$= \frac{0.5X}{6,000,000} = \frac{0.5X - 150,000}{4,000,000}$$

$$= \frac{0.5X}{1.50} = 0.5X - 150,000$$

0.5X = 1.5 (0.5X-150,000)

0.5X = 0.75X - 225,000)

0.5X -0.75X = - 225,000

$$-0.25X = -225{,}000$$

$$X = \frac{-225{,}000}{-0.25}$$

X = GHS 900,000

Point of Indifference (X) = **GHS 900,000**

Thus, EBIT, at point of indifference is **GHS 900,000**.

Table 6.1: Point of Indifference Confirmation

Details	Option 1 [GHS]	Option 2 [GHS]
Earnings before interest and tax (EBIT)	900,000	900,000
Interest @ 15%	-	(300,000)
EAIBT	**900,000**	**600,000**
Corporate Tax @ 50%	(450,000)	(300,000)
EAIT	**450,000**	**300,000**
Preference Dividend – PD	0	0
Equity Earnings	**450,000**	**300,000**
No. of Shares	60,000	40,000
Earnings per share	7.50	7.50

Illustration 6.3

A new project under consideration requires a capital outlay of GHS 1,000,000 for which the funds can either be raised by:

i. Issue of equity shares of GHS 1,000,000 with share price quoted as GHS100 each; **OR** by the issue of equity shares of the value of GHS 500,000, issue of 15% loan of GHS 300,000, and 13% Preference shares of GHS 200, 000. Find out the indifference level of EBIT given the tax rate at 50%.

ii. Issue ordinary share capital of GHS 600,000 and 15% debentures of GHS400,000; **OR** by issuing ordinary share capital of GHS 400,000, 13% Preference share capital of GHS 200,000 and 15% debentures of GHS400,000.

Solution i: Calculation of point of Indifference:

$$\frac{(X - I_1)(1-T) - PD_1}{S_1} = \frac{(X - I_2)(1-T) - PD_2}{S_2}$$

$$= \frac{(X-0)(1-0.50) - 0}{1,000,000} = \frac{(X - 45,000)(1-0.50) - 26,000}{500,000}$$

Substituting the values:

$$= \frac{0.5X}{1,000,000} = \frac{0.5X - 22,500 - 26,000}{500,000}$$

$$= \frac{0.5X}{2} = 0.5X - 22,500 - 26,000$$

$$= 0.5X = 2(0.5X - 22,500 - 26,000)$$

$$= 0.5X = 2(X - 48,500)$$

$$= 0.5X = X - 97,000$$

$$0.5X - X = -97,000$$

$$-0.5X = -97,000$$

$$X = 194,000$$

Point of Indifference (X) = **GHS 194,000**

Thus, EBIT, at point of indifference is **GHS 194,000**.

Table 6.2: Point of Indifference Confirmation

Details	Option 1 [GHS]	Option 2 [GHS]
Earnings before interest and tax (EBIT)	194,000	194,000
Interest @ 15%	-	45,000
EAIBT	**194,000**	**149,000**
Corporate Tax @ 50%	(97,000)	(74,500)
EAIT	**97,000**	**74,500**
Preference Dividend – PD	0	(26,000)
Equity Earnings	**97,000**	**48,500**
No. of Shares	10,000	5,000
Earnings per share	**9.70**	**9.70**

Solution ii: Calculation of Point of Indifference:

$$= \frac{(X - I_1)(1-T) - PD_1}{S_1} = \frac{(X - I_2)(1-T) - PD_2}{S_2}$$

$$= \frac{(X - 60{,}000)(1 - 0.50) - 0}{600{,}000} = \frac{(X - 60{,}000)(1 - 0.5) - 26{,}000}{400{,}000}$$

Substituting the values:

$$= \frac{0.5X - 30{,}000}{600{,}000} = \frac{0.5X - 30{,}000 - 26{,}000}{400{,}000}$$

$$= \frac{0.5X - 30{,}000}{1.5} = 0.5X - 22{,}500 - 26{,}000$$

$$= 0.5X - 30{,}000 = 0.75X - 84{,}000)$$

$$= 0.5X - 0.75X = -84{,}000 + 30{,}000$$

=	- 0.25X = - 54,000	

$$X = 216{,}000$$

Point of Indifference (X) = **GHS 216,000**

Thus, EBIT, at point of indifference is **GHS 216,000**.

Table 6.3: Point of Indifference Confirmation

Details	Option 1 [GHS]	Option 2 [GHS]
Earnings before interest and tax (EBIT)	216,000	216,000
Interest @ 15%	(60,000)	(60,000)
EAIBT	**156,000**	**156,000**
Corporate Tax @ 50%	(78,000)	(78,000)
EAIT	**78,000**	**78,000**
Preference Dividend – PD	0	(26,000)
Equity Earnings	**78,000**	**52,000**
No. of Shares	60,000	40,000
Earnings per share	**1.30**	**1.30**

6.12 Theories Underlying Capital Structure

The value of a firm is significantly impacted by the capital structure of the business. Some businesses have capital structures that are based on debt, while others have capital structures that are based on equity, and yet others have capital structures that are a combination of debt and equity in their financial mix.

The net income technique was given by Durand, and he claims that if there is a change in financial leverage, there will also be a change in the cost of capital as well as a change in the valuation of the firm. When valuing a company, its capital structure is an important consideration. The value of the company will go up in response to an increase in the weighted average cost of capital (WACC), which is caused by an increase in financial debt.

6.12.1 Net Income (NI) Approach

The amount of money left over after interest payments is a significant factor in determining the market value of equity shares. The market value is assumed to be contingent on the size of capital that is made accessible to equity owners by this strategy. The use of debt in the capital structure has an effect on the market value of the company's equity shares, which in turn has an effect on the net income and cost of capital.

The net operating income (NI) approach to capital structure indicates that "a higher debt content in the capital structure (i.e., higher financial leverage) will result in a decline in the overall or weighted average cost of capital, and this will incidentally cause an increase in the value of the firm."

$NI = NOI - I$ Equation --------------------6.3

Where, NI = net income,

NOI = net operating income and

I = interest on debt.

$NI = EBIT - I$ Equation --------------------6.4

6.12.1.1 Assumptions Underlying Net Income Approach

- There are no corporate taxes;
- Cost of equity is more than cost of debt. Hence, dividend rate is more than interest rate;
- Both debt and equity capitalization are constant;
- Debt proportion is independent of investors risk. Hence, debt content does not change the risk perception of the investors; and
- Dividend pay-out ratio is 1.

Formula:

$$V = E + D \quad \text{Equation 6.5}$$

Where;

V = Market value (Firm)

E = Market value (Equity)

D = Market value (Debt)

E = Net income/ cost of equity

D = interest rate on debt/ cost of Debt

$$V = \frac{NI}{K_e} \quad \text{Equation 6.6}$$

$$\text{Cost of Capital (K)} = \frac{EBIT}{V} \quad \text{Equation 6.7}$$

Or:

$$\text{Cost of Capital (K)} = \frac{NOI}{V}$$

$$\text{Degree of Financial leverage} = \frac{D}{V}$$

Note: in this approach, 'Ke' is kept as constant.

Illustration 6.4

i. Adom Company Limited is expecting an annual net operating income of GHS 1,000,000. The Company has GHS 4,000,000 in 10% Debentures and the cost of equity is 12.5% p.a. You are required to calculate the total value of the firm and the overall cost of capital.

ii. The company desires to raise an additional GHS 1,000,000 by issuing 10% debentures and used the proceeds to redeem equity shares. Find the value of the firm and the overall cost of capital of the Company.

iii. The Company further decides to redeem debentures of GHS 1,000,000 from the original capital structure by issuing additional equity shares of GHS 1,000,000. Calculate the value on the firm and the overall cost of capital. You are required to provide your conclusions pertaining to the net income (NI) approach to capital structure.

Solution:

i. EBIT   = GHS 1,000,000
    Debt   = GHS 4,000,000
    Cost of Debt   = 10%
    Cost of Equity = 12.5%

EBIT   = 1,000,000
Less Int. (10%)   = (400,000)
Net Income (NI) = GHS **600,000**

Market Value of Equity = $\dfrac{NI}{K_e}$

$= \dfrac{600{,}000}{0.125}$

= **GHS 4, 800,000**

V = E + D

V = 4,800,000 + 4,000,000

V = GHS 8,800, 000

Market Value of the Company (V) = **GHS 8,800, 000**

Hence, overall cost of capital (K) = $\dfrac{\text{EBIT}}{\text{V}}$

$$= \dfrac{1,000,000}{8,800,000}$$

K = 11.36%

ii. Where the Company issues an addition capital of GHS 1,000,000 by way of 10% debentures to redeem equity.

    EBIT = GHS 1,000,000
    Debt = GHS 4,000,000 + GHS 1,000,000 = **GHS 5,000,000**
    Interest (10%) = GHS 500,000

EBIT = 1,000,000

Less Int. (10%) = (500,000)

Net Income (NI) = GHS **500,000**

Market Value of Equity = NI ÷ Ke

$$= \dfrac{500,000}{0.125}$$

= GHS 4, 000,000

V = E + D

V = 4,000,000 + 5,000,000

V = GHS 9,000, 000

Market Value of the Company (V) = **GHS 9,000, 000**

Hence, overall cost of capital (K) = $\dfrac{\text{EBIT}}{\text{V}}$

$$= \dfrac{1,000,000}{9,000,000}$$

K = 11.11%

iii. Where the Company issues an addition capital of GHS 1,000,000 by way of Equity to redeem 10% debentures worth GHS 1,000,000

EBIT = GHS 1,000,000

Debt = GHS 4,000,000 - GHS 1,000,000 = **GHS 3,000,000**

Interest (10%) = GHS 300,000

EBIT = GHS 1,000,000

Less Int. (10%) = GHS (300,000)

Net Income (NI) = GHS **700,000**

Market Value of Equity = $\dfrac{\text{NI}}{\text{Ke}}$

$$= \dfrac{700,000}{0.125}$$

= GHS 5, 600,000

$V = E + D$

$V = 5,600,000 + 3,000,000$

V = GHS 8,600, 000

Market Value of the Company (V) = **GHS 8,600, 000**

Hence, overall cost of capital (K) = $\dfrac{EBIT}{V}$

$$= \dfrac{1,000,000}{8,600,000}$$

K = 11.62%

Overall Conclusions of the net income (NI) approach

Value of Debt Capital (D)	Value of the Firm (V)	Overall cost of Capital (K)
Increase in "D"	Increase in "V"	Decrease in "K"
Decrease in "D"	Decrease in "V"	Increase in "K"

6.12.1.2 Criticisms/ Disadvantages of Net Income (NI) Approach

1. The assumption does not take into account the payment of corporate taxes.
2. This is not achievable in reality, despite the fact that it has a fixed cost of loan (the interest rate is determined by the fund providers).
3. However, according to the NI method, the financial risk does not rise in proportion to the amount of debt held.
4. The ratio of financial leverage to equity capital grows as equity capitalization rises.

6.12.2 Net Operating Income Approach (NOI): Irrelevance Approach

The mix or ratio of debt to equity that a company chooses to use in their manner of financing determines the firm's capital structure. Although the ultimate objective is to maximize both their market value and their profitability, different companies may choose to finance their assets with a greater proportion of debt or of equity depending on their preferences.

Durand (1959) coined the phrase "net operating income" (NOI). According to the net operating income technique, changes in the debt components of a company or firm have no effect on the company's or firm's value. The NOI approach upholds the following guidelines:

- This hypothesis is predicated on the premise that changes to a company's capital structure have no effect on the company's market value;
- The market value of a firm may be established by capitalizing the company's net operating income (NOI) at an assumed constant cost of capital (K). This will provide the company's market worth;
- Additionally, the market value of equity may be computed by deducting the market value of the company's debt from its market value. This is done in order to determine the equity's market value; and
- According to the idea of net operating income, a company's worth is defined by a mix of its operational income and the associated business risk. The change in debt components will have no effect on the company's value.

6.12.2.1 Assumptions Under the Net Operating Income Approach

1. The company does not make any payments toward the corporation tax burden.
2. It is assumed that the total cost of capital, denoted by "K," remains the same regardless of the degree of debt-to-equity ratio or leverage.
3. The value of the company as a whole is capitalized by the market; as a result, the proportion of the company's assets that are debt and equity is unimportant.
4. Because the use of debt that has a low cost increases the risk of equity owners, the benefit of capitalization is exactly compensated by an increase in the amount of equity capitalization.
5. There are no earnings that have been kept.
6. The cost of investments in equity is higher than the cost of investments in debt when compared to the same time period.

Market value of a firm (V) is ratio of earnings before income taxes (EBIT) and weighted average cost of capital or overall cost of capital (K) or (WACC).

Hence, $V = \dfrac{EBIT}{K}$ Equation --------------------6.8

Total equity (E) is difference of market value of a firm (V) and market value of Debt (D).

Hence, **E = V – D** Equation --------------------6.9

Cost of equity (Ke) is ratio of difference between Earnings per share (EBIT) and interest (I) to market value of equity shareholder's (E).

Hence, $Ke = \dfrac{NI}{E}$ Equation --------------------6.10

Verification: $K = Kd (D/V) + Ke (E/V)$ Equation --------------------6.11

Where:

V = Market Value of firm.

E = Market value of equity.

D = Market value of debt.

K = Overall cost of capital (WACC).

Kd = Cost of debt.

Ke = Cost of equity.

"K" is kept constant.

Illustration 6.5

i. ABC Company Ltd. has EBIT of GHS1,000,000. Cost of debt is 10% and the ordinary share capital. Debt amounts to GHS 4,000,000 with the overall capitalization rate being 12.5%. calculate the total value of the firm and equity capitalization.

ii. The Company decides to an additional sum of GHS 1,000,000 through debt at 10% and uses the proceeds to pay off the equity shareholders. Calculate the value of the firm and the equity capitalization rate.

Solution:

i.

V = Market Value of firm = (E+D)
E = Market value of Equity
D = Market Value of Debt

V = E - D

Therefore:

V = E+D

E = V - D

EBIT = GHS1,000,000

K = 12.5%

Value of the firm (V) = $\dfrac{EBIT}{K}$

$$V = \dfrac{GHS\ 1,000,000}{0.125}$$

V = **GHS 8,000,000**

Value of the Firm (V) = GHS 8,000,000

Less Value of Debt (D) = (GHS 4,000,000)

Value of Equity (E) = **GHS 4,000,000**

$$Ke = \dfrac{NI}{E} = \dfrac{EBIT - Interest}{E}$$

Equity capitalization rate (Ke) = $\dfrac{GHS1,000,000 - GHS400,000}{4,000,000}$

$$K_e = \frac{GHS\ 600,000}{GHS\ 4,000,000}$$

$K_e = 15\%$

ii. When Debt is increased by GHS 1,000,000

Value of the firm $(V) = \frac{EBIT}{K}$

$$V = \frac{GHS\ 1,000,000}{0.125}$$

V = GHS 8,000,000

Value of the Firm (V) = GHS 8,000,000

Less Value of Debt (D) = (GHS 5,000,000)

Value of Equity (E) = **GHS 3,000,000**

$K_e = \frac{NI}{E} = \frac{EBIT - Interest}{E}$

Equity capitalization rate $[K_e] = \frac{GHS\ 1,000,000 - GHS\ 500,000}{GHS\ 3,000,000}$

$$K_e = \frac{GHS\ 500,000}{GHS\ 3,000,000}$$

Cost of Equity **$K_e = 16.67\%$**

Overall Conclusions pertaining to the Net Operating Income (NOI) Approach to Capital Structure.

Value of Equity (E)	Value of Debt (D)	Cost of Equity (Ke)
Decreases	Increases	Increases

6.12.2.2 Criticisms/ Disadvantages of NOI
- It is a fallacy to assume that there are no taxes levied against businesses; this is not the case.
- There will be a proportional rise in financial leverage if the cost of debt goes up, which will ultimately lead to an increase in the cost of capital as a result of the domino effect.
- When a considerable amount of debt is included in a company's capital structure, investors will have a different view of the firm as a whole when making their investment decisions.

6.12.3 Traditional Approach to Capital Structure Theory
The traditional approach to analyzing a company's capital structure places an emphasis on the idea that there is an optimal proportion of equity to debt within a company's capital structure. At this point, the market value of the company is at its highest point, and this is the point at which the market value of the company is optimal.

- Regarding the composition of a firm's capital, this strategy stipulates that the amount of debt that a company can lawfully be compelled to bear at any given moment must never exceed a certain maximum. Once this threshold is exceeded, any further increase in the company's leverage will result in a decrease in its value. This will be the case regardless of the firm's current debt.

- To rephrase, this indicates that there exists a sweet spot for the debt-to-equity ratio at which the WACC is minimum and the market value of the business is maximum. That is to say, there is an optimum debt-to-equity ratio.

- After a certain debt-to-equity ratio, the cost of equity increases, which has a negative effect on the weighted average cost of capital (WACC). If the debt-to-equity ratio is more than the threshold, the weighted average cost of capital (WACC) will increase and the firm's market value will begin to decline.

6.12.3.1 Key Assumptions Under the Traditional Approach

When applying the Traditional Approach, the following are the assumptions that are taken into consideration:

1. After a certain amount of time, the interest rate on the debt remains the same; but, after that point, it begins to rise in tandem with an increase in leverage.

2. The rate of return on investment that is expected to be generated by equity investors either stays the same or gradually becomes higher. As soon as the threshold is exceeded, equity shareholders will become aware of a potential financial risk; at this point, which is the optimal moment, the anticipated rate of interest will begin to rapidly increase.

3. As a direct result of the interplay between the cost of capital and the expected rate of return, the weighted average cost of capital (WACC) decreases at the outset and later increases. The lowest possible point on a graph of capital structure is the optimal ratio.

The traditional approach of a firm's capital structure *indicates that the average cost of capital is not based on the level of gearing.* In this argument, it follows that there is an individual firm ideal level of gearing of which the cost of capital will be minimized whilst the value of the firm maximized.

Where a firm has both debt and equity components in its capital structure, the cost of capital can be computed as the weighted average cost of capital; whereas, the cost of each type of capital in the firm is weighted by percentage value in terms proportional value in the total value of the firm.

6.12.4 Trade-Off Theory

The trade-off strategy considers the potentiality that initiating bankruptcy proceedings would incur a financial obligation. Based on this theoretical framework, it is posited that there exists a benefit to depending on debt financing, specifically the tax deduction of interest expenses prior to the payment of corporate tax: $k_d(1-t)$, which is also referred to as "interest-tax shield". More precisely, the tax advantage associated with debt and the consequence of interest expenses being tax deductible prior to the payment of corporate tax, as represented by kd (1-t).

The optimal level of debt, according to the trade-off theory is determined by balancing the marginal benefit (interest payment tax deductibility) of one dollar of debt with the marginal cost (increased default risk) of an additional dollar of debt. (Abel, 2018).

Likewise, as an organization employs an increasing number of loans, the marginal benefit of additional debt increases diminishes while the marginal cost of additional debt escalates. This is due to the increasing number of loans utilized by the company. This phenomenon occurs due to the diminishing marginal benefit of increased debt, which occurs as the organization increasingly employs its debts. Due to this, it is critical that the organization implement the requisite measures to ensure that the marginal advantages of augmented debt and the marginal disadvantages of escalating expenses remain in a state of balance (trade-off).

The trade-off theory provides a company with the ability to determine the optimal level of debt utilization during a specific time period so as to maximize the company's benefit in light of changes in its capital structure. The company obtains this information through the measure of debt that ought to be utilized. The idea's capacity to flexibly accommodate various eras and time periods renders this occurrence plausible. This framework posits that variations in leverage among firms or changes in leverage over time may be ascribed to disparities in the marginal cost of default and/or the marginal interest tax shield.

6.12.5 Pecking Order Theory

The notion that distinct avian species adhere to a predetermined hierarchy was first proposed by Myers in 1984. When the expense of asymmetric information is considered, this notion is completely and logical. This suggests that organizations prioritize their capital sources, such that, in accordance with the principle of least efforts, internal financing is utilized prior to external financing, and equity financing is considered a last resort. Chen & Chen (2011) posit that the pecking order theory operates under the assumption that no target capital structure exists. The firms establish a hierarchy of capital preferences as follows: internal financing, debt, and equity.

Companies ought to strive for entirely debt financing, as said by Modigliani & Miller (1963), on account of the tax deductions that are linked to interest payments on debt. This effect motivates businesses to utilize debt, as increased debt results in greater after-tax profits for the proprietor.

The precedence order theory posits that organizations possess a distinct hierarchy of preferences regarding the capital they utilize to fund their operations (Myers & Majluf, 1984). As a result of information asymmetry between the firm and potential investors, retained earnings are preferred over debt, short-term debt is preferred over long-term debt, and debt is preferred over equity.

The fact that equity financing is considered a final option signifies that organizations assign greater importance to their capital sources. The preference of corporations for alternative capital sources over equity financing indicates that they hold this form of financing in lower regard. Due to the fact that financing via shares entails the greatest degree of risk among all available alternatives, this is the case.

With this regard, retained earnings would be utilized prior to initial reliance on internal loans; external obligations (such as bonds) would be issued as replacement financing if retained earnings were depleted. This is because retained earnings are considered to be more readily convertible than the internal debts of the company. This is due to the perception that retained earnings are a more readily convertible asset of a company than its internal debts. In situations where the continued utilization of debt is deemed illogical and not in the best interest of the organization, equity shares would be allocated.

The pecking-order theory, according to Myers (1984), indicates that shares are less desirable method of generating new capital due to its lesser position in relation to equity on the pecking order. This is due to the fact that debt is ranked higher than other forms of financial obligations by the theory.

6.13 Chapter Review Questions

1. Explain the term capital structure with an illustration.
2. Examine the main factors that determine a firm's capital structure.
3. Explain the importance of capital structure theory
4. Examine the principles underlying the theory of capital structure
5. define the term 'Point of indifference' in the capital structure theory
6. Explain the following capital structure theories
   i. Pecking order theory
   ii. Trade-off theory

7. A project under consideration by your company requires a capital investment of GHS5,000,000.00. Interest on term loan is 25% p.a. with a corporate tax rate of 40%. Calculate the point of indifference for the project, if the debt-equity ratio insisted by the financing agencies is 2:1. The share price is quoted at GHS90 per share. As the debt-equity ratio insisted by the financing agencies is 1:2; the company has two alternative financial plans:

(i) Raising the entire amount of GHS5,000,000 by the issue of equity shares, thereby using no debt, and

(ii) Raising GHS2,000,000 by way of debt and GHS3,000,000.00 by issue of equity share capital.

8. A new project under consideration requires a capital outlay of GHS 2,000,000 for which the funds can either be raised by:

iii. Issue of equity shares of GHS 2,000,000 with share price quoted as GHS100 each; **OR** by the issue of equity shares of the value of GHS 800,000, issue of 20% loan of GHS 700,000, and 13% Preference shares of GHS 500, 000. Find out the indifference level of EBIT given the tax rate at 50%.

iv. Issue ordinary share capital of GHS 1,600,000 and 15% debentures of GHS400,000; **OR** by issuing ordinary share capital of GHS 600,000, 13% Preference share capital of GHS 800,000 and 15% debentures of GHS600,000.

9. Adom Company Limited is expecting an annual net operating income of GHS 3,000,000. The Company has GHS 2,000,000 in 10% Debentures and the cost of equity is 12.5% p.a. You are required to calculate the total value of the firm and the overall cost of capital.

i. The company desires to raise an additional GHS 1,500,000 by issuing 12% debentures and used the proceeds to redeem equity shares. Find the value of the firm and the overall cost of capital of the Company.

ii. The Company further decides to redeem debentures of GHS 1,500,000 from the original capital structure by issuing additional equity shares of GHS 1,500,000. Calculate the value on the firm and the overall cost of capital.

10. ABC Company Ltd. has EBIT of GHS1,000,000. Cost of debt is 10% and the ordinary share capital. Debt amounts to GHS 4,000,000 with the overall capitalization rate being 12.5%. calculate the total value of the firm and equity capitalization.

i. The Company decides to an additional sum of GHS 1,000,000 through debt at 10% and uses the proceeds to pay off the equity shareholders. Calculate the value of the firm and the equity capitalization rate.

6.14 Chapter References and Bibliography

[1] Abel, A. B. (2018). Optimal debt and profitability in the trade-off theory. *The Journal of Finance, 73*(1), 95-143.

[2] Besley, S., & Brigham, E. F. (2008). *Essentials of managerial finance*. Cengage learning.

[3] Chen, L. J., & Chen, S. Y. (2011). How the pecking-order theory explain capital structure. *Journal of International Management Studies*, 6(3), 92-100.

[4] Modigliani F. and Miller M.H. (1958). The cost of capital, corporation finance and the theory of investment", American economic Review, 48(3), 261-297.

[5] Modigliani F. and Miller M.H. (1963). Corporate income taxes and the cost of capital: a correction", American economic Review, 53,.433-443.

[6] Myers S.C. (1977). Determinants of capital borrowing, Journal of Finance Economics, 5, 5147-5175.

[7] Myers S.C. and Majluf N. (1984). Corporate financing and investment decisions when firms have information that investors do not have, Journal of Financial Economics, 13, 187-221.

[8] Van Horne James, C. (2002). *Financial management & policy, 12/E.* Pearson Education India.

6.15 Recommended Reading List

[1] Jarallah, S., Saleh, A. S., & Salim, R. (2019). Examining pecking order versus trade-off theories of capital structure: New evidence from Japanese firms. *International Journal of Finance & Economics*, 24(1), 204-211.

[2] Sutomo, S., Wahyudi, S., Pangestuti, I., & Muharam, H. (2020). The determinants of capital structure in coal mining industry on the Indonesia Stock Exchange. *Investment Management and Financial Innovations*, 17(1), 165-174.

CHAPTER 7

CAPITAL BUDGETING: RISK ANALYSIS, INFLATION AND TAXATION

7.1 Overview

The process of identifying, analyzing, and selecting investments for the purpose of determining a company's expenditures on assets with cash flows that are anticipated to extend beyond a single year is known as capital budgeting. It is an important process because capital expenditures require a large investment but are limited by the availability of funds (also known as capital rationing), greatly influences a company's ability to achieve its financial objectives, and can become a tool of control.

> **Objectives of the Chapter**
>
> This chapter is designed to achieve the following key objectives:
> - To explain the capital budgeting and risk consideration;
> - To justify the need to take into consideration risk assessment in capital budgeting decisions;
> - To explain the term risk and examine types of risks
> - To examine risk-adjusted discount rate in capital budgeting decisions;
> - To examine the certainty equivalent method in capital budgeting decisions;
> - To evaluate sensitivity analysis in capital budgeting decisions;
> - To examine the probability technique in capital budgeting decisions;
> - To evaluate the use of decision trees in capital budgeting decisions; and
> - To examine the use of simulation technique in capital budgeting decisions.

> **Key Words Used in the Chapter**
>
> - Capital budgeting
> - Certainty coefficients
> - Certainty equivalent
> - Counterparty risk
> - Decision trees
> - Default risk
> - Risk-adjusted discount rate
> - Sensitivity analysis
> - Simulation technique

7.2 Capital Budgeting and Risk Consideration

When the results of an event cannot be predicted with absolute certainty, this can give rise to the possibility of uncertainty. When dealing with assets whose cash flows are anticipated to continue for more than one year, there is undeniably an element of risk involved in the situation. Therefore, the evaluation of risk is contingent upon the decision maker's capacity to recognize and comprehend the nature of the uncertainty that surrounds the key variables, as well as upon their possession of the tools and methodology necessary to process the implications of that uncertainty.

7.3 Importance of Ascertaining Risk in Capital Budgeting

It is of the utmost importance to identify and make preparations for potentially risky or detrimental events that could have an impact on fundamental projects or business initiatives.

1. Risk analysis gives companies knowledge and information regarding unexpected turn of event (undesirous happening) that may affect their investment which they have to put to use in making important decisions

about certain long-term investments. This information and knowledge can be obtained from rigorous risk analysis.

2. An in-depth risk assessment performed by a qualified professional is required before one can determine whether or not investments with a long-term horizon are worthwhile. The process of capital budgeting can be fraught with uncertainty, but companies can protect themselves in every possible way by commissioning a professional risk assessment.

3. Companies will be in a better position to accurately weigh their investment opportunities if they have knowledge of the expected outcomes, and they will be able to move forward with a solid understanding of all of the risks that may be involved.

Therefore, before your company invests in new projects, equipment, machinery, research development, or expands existing products or replaces non-current assets of whatever kind, equip yourself with critical insight and conduct a professional risk analysis to evaluate your capital budgeting forecast. This should be done before you make any of these investments.

In order to make these risk adjustments when making financial decisions about capital budgeting, various methods regarding risk assessment are frequently used. They include:
- Risk-adjusted discount rate (RADR);
- Certainty equivalent method (CEM);
- Sensitivity analysis;
- Probabilities;
- Decision tree technique; and
- Simulation technique.

7.4 Factors Influencing Strategic Investment Decision

It is not simple to make decisions regarding capital investments because of the substantial amount of initial capital that is required, as well as the degree to which such decisions affect the future cash flows. Therefore, the investment problem is not simply one of replacing old equipment with new equipment;

rather, it is concerned with replacing an existing process in a system with another process that makes the effectiveness of the entire system greater.

7.4.1 Company Factors

- **Management Viewpoint**

When the management is forward-thinking and has an aggressive marketing and growth outlook, it will encourage innovation and favor capital proposals that ensure better productivity. In certain sectors of the economy, where the product that is being manufactured is a straightforward and easily standardized one, innovation can be challenging, and management may be highly cost conscious. On the other hand, businesses that try to "make do" with the equipment they already have are doomed to fail in certain fields, such as the chemical and electronic manufacturing industries. In situations like this, management needs to be forward-thinking, and a culture of innovation needs to be fostered.

- **Cash Flow Budget**

The evaluation of a cash-flow budget, which depicts the flow of cash into and out of the company, may influence the decision to invest in capital in two different ways.

1. The analysis may indicate that a company may acquire the necessary cash to purchase the equipment not immediately but after a certain period of time, say after one year, or it may show that the purchase of capital assets now may generate the demand for major capital additions after two years and that such expenditure might conflict with anticipated expenditures that cannot be postponed.

2. The cash flow budget illustrates the timing of cash flows for alternative investments, which assists management in choosing the investment project that best meets their needs.

- **SWOT Analysis**

The acronym SWOT refers to a company's "Strengths, Weaknesses, Opportunities, and Threats" analysis. A framework that can assist in assessing and gaining a better understanding of the internal and external forces that may present opportunities or risks for an organization is known as a SWOT analysis.

Internal factors can be broken down into strengths and weaknesses. They are aspects of a company that, when compared to other businesses in its industry, place it in a position of relative advantage (or disadvantage, depending on the context). These factors do affect capital budgeting decisions.

- **Market Forecast**

When making decisions regarding the investment of capital, it is important to consider both short-term and long-term market forecasts. In order to take part in the long-term forecast for the market's potential, it is necessary to make crucial decisions regarding the investment of capital.

7.4.2 Industry Factors

An industry's overall environment can be better understood through the use of a tool called a PESTEL analysis. The acronym PESTEL refers to the following categories of considerations: political, economic, social, technological, environmental, and legal. It enables a company to form an opinion regarding the factors that may have an effect on a new business or industry. PESTEL analysis is a framework or tool that marketers use to analyze and monitor the macro-environmental (external marketing environment) factors that have an impact on an organization, company, or industry. A PESTLE analysis enables a strategic and systematic evaluation of a business's prospects, risks, and opportunities in a new environment.

- **Competitor's Strategy**

The approach taken by competitors with regards to the investment of capital is a significant factor that affects a company's choice to make investments. The existence of the company that does not follow suit in installing more equipment and succeeding in producing better products could be in grave danger if competitors continue to install more equipment and make these improvements. In many cases, a company is forced to make a decision because of its reaction to the policy that a competitor has regarding capital investment.

- **Opportunities Created by Technological Changes**

Since advancement in technology results in the production of new pieces of machinery that may signify significant shifts in procedure, businesses often find themselves in a position where they need to reevaluate the capital equipment they already possess. New investments might be warranted in light of certain changes. Because of advances in technology, older pieces of machinery that have to be retired in favor of more modern alternatives may occasionally be repurposed for use in different kinds of businesses. A correct evaluation of this facet is required, but it is frequently not given the due consideration that it deserves. When making decisions regarding investments, one crucial consideration is the amount of money that must be spent on brand-new machinery.

- **General Economic Conditions**

Since these factors have a direct effect on how much capital the company can raise, general economic conditions such as inflationary rate, foreign exchange volatility, and interest rate can greatly influence the investment decision made by the company.

7.4.3 Fiscal Incentives and Non-Economic Factors

The method for allowing depreciation deduction allowance as well as tax concessions either on new investment incomes or investment allowance allowed on new investment decisions are all factors that influence new investment decisions. Additionally, the new equipment might make the workshop a more pleasant place to be, which would allow for increased opportunities for socialization while working. Absenteeism would go down, while productivity would go up as a result of this change.

7.5 Definition of Risk

In the field of finance, "risk" refers to the chance that actual profit from an event or return from an investment may differ from the anticipated outcome or return. The danger of losing a portion or the entirety of an original investment falls under the notion of risk. It is usual practice to examine prior behavior and its outcomes when assessing risk. The standard deviation is a frequent measure connected with risk in the world of finance. The standard deviation is a statistical metric that may be used to assess the extent to which current asset prices depart from their long-term norms during a certain time period.

Understanding the principles of risk and the elements that contribute to its size is essential for properly managing the risks connected with financial investments. All sorts of investors and company managers will be aided in averting unnecessary and costly losses by gaining an understanding of the risks that might apply to a number of circumstances and some of the techniques to manage them holistically.

Typically, risk is measured quantitatively by examining prior behaviors and the outcomes those behaviors created.

7.6 Types of Risk that Affect Capital Budgeting

Business Risk
The term "business risk" refers to the question of whether or not a company will be able to make sufficient sales and generate sufficient revenues to cover its operational expenses and turn a profit. This is the question that determines whether or not a business will be viable. While financial risk is concerned with the costs of financing, business risk is concerned with all of the other expenses an organization needs to cover in order to continue to be operational and function properly. These costs include wages and salaries, as well as production expenses, facility rent, office rent, and administrative costs. The cost of goods, changes in output prices, profit margins, the level of competition, and the overall level of demand for the products or services that a company sells are all factors that can have an effect on the level of business risk that a company faces.

Credit or Default Risk
Credit risk is the probability that a person or business may be unable to make contractual interest or principal payments on the debt it owes. Bond-holding investors are the ones who should be the most concerned about this specific form of risk. Therefore, government bonds give the lowest rates of return. Corporate bonds, on the other hand, are recognized to pose a bigger risk of default than the majority of other forms of bonds, but they also often provide higher interest rates. Bonds with a reduced probability of default are referred to as investment grade those, whereas bonds with a greater probability are referred to as high yield or trash bonds.

Foreign Exchange Risk

When investing in other nations, it is vital to remember that the price of the asset may also be affected by fluctuations in the currency exchange rate. All financial instruments denominated in a currency other than the native currency of your nation are susceptible to foreign exchange risk, also known as exchange rate risk. Whenever the local currency (the cedi) depreciates, the possibility of exchange rate risk exists.

Interest Rate Risk

Interest rate risk is the possibility that the value of an investment may fluctuate owing to a change in the absolute level of interest rates, the spread between two rates, the yield curve's form, or any other interest rate connection. This form of risk has a greater impact on the value of bonds than on the value of equities and poses a substantial threat to all bondholders. As interest rates rise, secondary market bond prices fall, and vice versa.

Political Risk

Political risk is the possibility that an investment's returns will be negatively impacted by political instability or political changes in a nation. Changes to the administration, legislative bodies, other actors in the creation of foreign policy, or military control can all contribute to the emergence of this danger. This risk, also known as geopolitical risk, becomes a more important factor to consider as the time horizon of an investment increases.

Counterparty Risk

The potential or probability that one party to a transaction would fail to keep its contractual commitments is known as the counterparty risk. In financial transactions including lending, investments, and trading, especially those conducted on over-the-counter (OTC) marketplaces, counterparty risk is conceivable. Investment products, such as shares, options, bonds, and derivatives, are susceptible to the risk of dealing with a counterparty.

Liquidity Risk

The lack of capacity of an investor to swiftly turn their investment into cash is what "liquidity risk" refers to. In most instances, investors would demand a premium for illiquid assets as compensation for having to keep stocks or shares for a lengthy period of time that cannot be sold quickly.

7.7 Risk-Adjusted Discount Rate (RADR)

A risk-adjusted discount rate is the rate achieved when evaluating the present value of a dangerous or risky investment by adding an estimated risk premium to the risk-free rate. The purchase of real estate or the launch of a new business are examples of hazardous investments since they involve greater degrees of risk than other investments. In spite of the fact that it is usual practice to utilize the current market rate as the discount rate for the vast majority of applications, there are circumstances in which the use of a risk-adjusted discount rate is required.

Risk-adjusted discount factor for instance, is asserted in fundamental finance text as the "best of all" methods, according to Sametz & Lindsey (1963). While employing a constant discount rate is frequently deemed acceptable as a general principle, it can lead to erroneous conclusions regarding capital budgeting (Weitzman, 2010). This is an intriguing implication for such decisions.

The risk-adjusted discount rate, often known as RADR, is composed of two components. The total consists of two components: the risk-free rate and the risk premium. When a professional or an investor has to compute or determine the present value of a risky investment, having access to this rate is of great assistance. Consequently, we may say that RADR is the return an investor expects obtaining in exchange for assuming a greater level of risk.

7.7.1 Reasons why Discount Rate Should take into Account Risk

In most cases, discount rates are adjusted to account for the unpredictability of cash flow value, timing, or length of time. In the event of projects having a lengthy duration, a broader variety of issues, such as future market circumstances, inflation, and profitability, must be considered.

Businesses modify discount rates to reflect the risks connected with their projected liquidity and the risks involved with the likelihood of defaults by third parties. If the project is located in a different nation than the company's headquarters, companies will need to consider additional concerns, such as currency risks and geographical hazards. It is vital to adjust discount rates appropriately if investments entail the prospect of future legal action, difficulties with regulatory bodies, or reputational harm to the organization. Alterations may also be required as a consequence of the expected presence of competitors and threats to the market advantages earned by businesses.

7.8 Determining Risk-adjusted Discount Rate with a Capital Asset Pricing Model (CAPM)

The goal of a capital asset pricing model, often known as a CAPM, is to determine the risk-adjusted discount rate for a particular investment. This model modifies the risk-free interest rate by combining it with a projected risk premium determined based on the project's beta.

Risk-adjusted discount rate = Risk-free interest rate + Expected risk premium

The risk premium can be calculated by first deducting the rate of return associated with the absence of risk from the rate of return associated with the market, and then multiplying the resulting number by the project's beta.

Risk premium = (Market rate of return - Risk free rate of return) x Beta

Whereas covariance is a measure of the asset's return in comparison to the market's return, and variance is a measure of the market's movement in comparison to its mean value.

To put it another way, the formula for calculating RADR is simply the addition of the "prevailing risk-free rate" and the "risk premium" appropriate for the type of risk that is being proposed or anticipated.

Illustration 7.1
Suppose Company Y is considering a project that requires an initial cash outflow of GHS 80,000. This project will result in a cash inflow of GHS 100,000

in three years' time. A similar project is offering a return of 5%. So, Company Y will use the same rate to discount the cash flow.

On this basis, the PV of the cash flow is GHS 86,384. Since PV is more than the initial investment, so Company Y should accept the project.

However, this project is in another country, hence, Company Y would like to include currency risk in the discount rate as well. Thus, Company Y determines a risk-adjusted discount rate of 8% (5%, the return available on another project, or the Risk-Free Rate plus 3% on account of currency risk). On this basis, the PV of the cash inflow is **GHS 79,383.**

After considering the currency risk, the PV of cash inflow is less than the initial cash outflow. This makes the project unacceptable since it is not worthwhile.

Illustration 7.2

Suppose ADOM Company Ltd. has an offer to invest in three projects – A, B, and C. However, The Company has funds to invest in only one project. So, it decides to use the NPV method to decide on the project that it should invest in given the mutual exclusiveness of the projects.

Project A – GHS 56,000 (Initial Investment), Cash flows for years 1, 2 and 3 are GHS 25,000; GHS 10,000; and GHS 15,000 respectively. The risk-free rate is 2%, while risk premium is 5%.

Project B – GHS 68,000 (Initial Investment), Cash flows for years 1, 2 and 3 are GHS 32,000; GHS 12,000; and GHS 41,000 respectively. Risk-free rate is 1.2%, while risk premium is 4%.

Project C – GHS 85,000 (Initial Investment), Cash flows for years 1,2 and 3 are GHS 12,000; GHS 30,000; and GHS 53,000). The Risk-free rate is 3%, while risk premium is 7%. From the illustration above the risk-adjusted discount rate (RADR) for each project will be estimated as follows:

Project A = 2% + 5%   = 7%

Project B = 1.2% + 4% = 5.2%
Project C = 3% + 7% = 10%

Now, we need to calculate the PV of cash flows for each project using the above RADR. Following is the NPV of the three projects:
Project A – GHS 53,103
Project B – GHS 71,400
Project C – GHS 75,522

Now, to make a decision on the most profitable project, there is the need to deduct the initial cash outflow from the PV to get the NPV as follow:
Project A = GHS 53,103 – GHS 56,000 = **GHS -2,897**
Project B = GHS 71,400 – GHS 68,000 = **GHS 3,400**
Project C = GHS 75,552 – GHS 85,000 = **GHS -9,448**
Since Project B has a positive NPV, ADOM Company Ltd. should invest in Project B.

Illustration 7.3

A firm has an investment that cost GHS 100,000 with projected associated cash inflows of:

Table 7.1: Investment Cash Flows:

Year	Cash Inflows GHS
0	(100,000)
1	50,000
2	25,000
3	20,000
4	20,000
5	10,000

Other details about the investment:

- The investment will have no residual value after the fifth year.
- Consider risk-free rate of 10%

- Risk premium rate of 5%

Required: Find the net present value (NPV) of the investment using risk-adjusted discount rate method and indicate whether the investment is worthwhile or not.

Solution:
Risk-adjusted discount rate (RADR) = Risk-free rate + Risk premium rate

RADR = 10% + 5%

RADR= **15%**

Table 7.2: Risk-Adjusted NPV Computation

Years	Cash Flow GHS	RADR (15%)	PV GHS
0	(100,000)	1.000	(100,000)
1	50,000	0.870	43,500
2	25,000	0.756	18,900
3	20,000	0.658	13,160
4	20,000	0.572	11,440
5	10,000	0.497	4,970
NPV			**(8,030)**

Decision: The investment is not worthwhile and should be rejected since it has negative NPV.

7.8.1 Advantages Using Risk-Adjusted Rates
- The risk-adjusted discount rates (RADR) are simple to comprehend and put into practice.
- It is attractive to an investor who is unwilling to take risks.
- This strategy helps to reduce the amount of uncertainty and volatility that is associated with the expected return.
- It also helps to bring out the risk level in an investment or project by appealing to investors and institutions, especially any investor who is risk-averse. This is especially helpful for bringing out the risk level in high-risk investments.

7.8.2 Disadvantages of Using RADR

1. The process of obtaining an accurate risk premium is a difficult one. Consequently, if the risk premium is not accurate, then the final result (the net present value) may also not be accurate.

2. This strategy is predicated on the assumption that investors shun taking risks. Having said that, this is not always the case. There are investors who would only be willing to take on additional risk if they were confident that the cash flows would also be increased.

7.9 Certainty Equivalent Method (CEM)

CEM addresses the risk aspects associated with capital budgeting, in which potentially dangerous future cash flows are stated in terms of specific cash flows that investors are ready to accept now. Using certainty equivalents is essential when doing risk assessments. It is common knowledge that investors anticipate a rate of return on their investments that is proportionate to the degree of risk they are prepared to assume; this suggests that the larger the level of risk, the higher the expected rate of return.

The lower rate of return or cash flow that an investor would choose to accept now over a greater but less assured rate of return in the future is known as the certainty equivalent. Or, we may argue that an investor prefers assured or guaranteed cash over taking a chance for a higher sum than he may receive in the future.

An uncertain cash flow may be transformed into a definite cash flow by multiplying it with a certainty coefficient, also known as a probability of occurrence. The range of the certainty coefficient is between 0 and 1.
To put it more simply, it is the amount of money that an individual would refuse in return for the chance to forego participation in an activity in which he or she has the potential to win an even bigger quantity of money.

In one form of game, for instance, participants must pick a card at random from an entire deck of playing cards. One hundred Ghanaian cedis are offered to everyone who brings a red card to the game. In this scenario, the chances of winning or losing are almost the same. Alternatively, if the individual decides to accept GHS 80 in return for not selecting the card, this GHS 80 is comparable to the certainty equivalent. In this circumstance, the individual is certain to earn GHS 80, and there is a chance that he will also win GHS 100. If he chooses to take the card, though, there is still a chance that he will receive nothing.

This idea is quite helpful when it comes to doing risk assessments. It is vital to remember that the level of risk tolerance of a particular investor is what defines the certainty equivalent; thus, it might vary from person to person. It is crucial that you remember this, since it is a vital aspect. For instance, a person who is approaching retirement would be viewed as having a high certainty equivalent since it is less probable that they will put their retirement money in peril.

The estimate for certainty equivalent can be described in terms of the investment's resulting cash flow. A cash flow with no risk is referred to as a certainty-equivalent cash flow. This sort of cash flow is considered to have the same value as a greater planned cash flow with a higher risk level.

Formula is:
CEM rate = Expected Cash Flow / (1 + Risk Premium)   Equation ------7.1
CEM rate is between 0 and 1

The term "Risk Premium" refers to the risk-adjusted rate that is higher than the risk-free rate in this context. The required rate of return on investment is the rate of return that takes risk into account. This rate is also utilized when we discount the cash flow of a company to arrive at its present value.

Illustration 7.4

Let us understand how to calculate certainty equivalent with the help of an illustration. Assume that an investor has a choice to accept (Option A) GHS 25,500 cash flow now. Or, choose the other option (Option B) that has the following expectations:
- A 30% probability of getting GHS 20,000
- A 50% probability of getting GHS 30,000
- A 20% probability of getting GHS 5,000

The expected outflow in this case will be = (30% x GHS 20,000) + (50% x GHS 30,000) + (20% x GHS 5,000)

= GHS 6,000 + GHS 15,000 + GHS1,000 = **GHS22,000**

Now assume the risk-adjusted rate to be 12% and the risk-free rate to be 2%. The risk premium will be 10% (12% less than 2%). Putting the values in the above formula we get the equation.
= GHS 22,000 / (1 + 10%) = GHS 20,000.

It means that to avoid taking a risk, an investor should accept any option that guarantees them GHS 20,000 or more. So, in this case, an investor should accept Option A.

The process of making decisions is always focused on the future; that is, we always weigh our options and make decisions based on what we want to happen in the future. Every factor that we think about when making decisions for the future contains some degree of risk and uncertainty. The process of making decisions pertaining to finances involves looking into the future and dealing with a great deal of uncertainty. In addition, such choices always involve making a compromise between the amount of risk taken and the potential reward. The concept of certainty equivalent is an important one in capital budgeting, and using it properly is an essential step in the process of making prudent financial decisions.

Illustration 7.5

The following table presents 5 years cash inflows. The certainty coefficients for the cash flows are also given which presents the probability of the occurrence of cash flows.

Table 7.3: Cash Flows and Certainty Coefficient

Year	Cash Inflows (GHS)	Certainty Coefficient
1	150,000	0.9
2	250,000	0.7
3	90,000	0.5
4	120,000	0.6
5	50,000	0.2

The Initial cost of the investment is GHS 320,000 and the discount rate is 10% annually. With the help of a certainty equivalent method, find out the NPV and analyze it.

Solution:

Net Present Value (NPV) = Present Values of all the cash inflows- Initial cost of investment. Now, for the calculation of present value of the cash inflows considered.

Table 7.4: NPV Computation Using CEM

Year	Cash Inflows GHS	Certainty Coefficient	Certainty Equivalent Cash Flow (GHS)	DF@ 10%	Present Value (GHS)
1	150,000	0.9	135,000	0.9090	**122,715.00**
2	250,000	0.7	175,000	0.8264	**144,620.00**
3	90,000	0.5	45,000	0.7513	**33,808.50**
4	120,000	0.6	72,000	0.6830	**49,176.00**
5	50,000	0.2	10,000	0.6209	**6,209.21**
	Total				**356,528.71**

Net Present Value: Present Value of Cash Inflows – Initial cost of Investment.
NPV = [GHS 356,528.71 - GHS 320,000.00] = **GHS 36,528.71**

Here, NPV is positive which means the project is viable in terms of cash flow. Therefore, project should be accepted.

Illustration 7.6

ABC Company Ltd. is considering an investment proposal which requires an initial outlay of GHS 2,000,000. The expected cash inflow and the certainty coefficients have been indicated as follows:

Table 7.5: Projected Cash Flows and Certainty Coefficient

Year	Cash inflow (GHS)	Certainty coefficient
1	600,000	0.90
2	300,000	0.85
3	700,000	0.80
4	800,000	0.75
5	900,000	0.65
6	500,000	0.50

The risk-free interest is 6% and the risk premium rate is 5%. Determine the net present value (NPV) of the investment proposal using the certainty equivalent method and indicate whether the proposal is worth investing into.

Solution:
a. Computation of Certainty Cash Flows:

Table 7.6: Computation of Certainty Cash Flows for ABC Company Ltd.:

Years	Cash Flows (GHS)	Certainty Coefficient	Certainty Cash Flows (GHS)
1	600,000	0.90	540,000
2	300,000	0.85	255,000
3	700,000	0.80	560,000
4	800,000	0.75	600,000
5	900,000	0.65	600,000
6	500,000	0.50	250,000

b. NPV Computation

Table 7.7: Computation of NPV using CEM

Years	Cash Flows (GHS)	Certainty Cash Flows (GHS)	Risk-free @ 6%	PVCIF (GHS)
0	(2,000,000)	-	1	(2,000,000)
1	600,000	540,000	0.943	509,220
2	300,000	255,000	0.890	226,950
3	700,000	560,000	0.840	470,176
4	800,000	600,000	0.792	475,200
5	900,000	585,000	0.747	436,995
6	500,000	250,000	0.705	176,250
	NPV			**294,791**

Decision: The investment proposal is worthwhile since it has a positive NPV of GHS 294,791 under the certainty equivalent method (CEM).

7.9.1 Certainty Equivalent in Gambling

The term "certainty equivalent" is not only useful in the field of finance but is also a common term in the field of gambling. In gambling, the term refers to the payoff that a player would need to be indifferent between the payoff and the gamble.

7.10 Sensitivity Analysis in Capital Budgeting

The sensitivity analysis of a project is an all-encompassing evaluation of the likelihood that a project will be successful based on data-driven projections. In addition to this, it distinguishes between high-risk and low-risk tasks, identifies risks, and quantifies the impact of those risks. Sensitivity analysis thus measures how sensitive the net present values or the internal rate of return are in relation to changes in the variables that affect the cash flows.

Sensitivity analysis is a tool used in financial modeling to analyze how the different values of a set of independent variables affect a specific dependent variable under certain specific conditions. Sensitivity analysis serves a multitude of objectives, as stated by Saltelli et al. (2019). The main function of sensitivity analysis is to quantify the extent to which model inputs, or subsets of inputs, contribute to the uncertainty in the model output.

A financial sensitivity analysis, also known as a what-if analysis or a what-if simulation exercise, is most commonly used by financial analysts to predict the outcome of a specific action when performed under certain specific conditions. A technique that can be used to model risk in any given assignment is called a sensitivity analysis in project and investment management. When assessing the sensitivity of a project, one looks at the big picture to determine which of the many factors or variables involved in the endeavor could potentially prevent one from achieving one or more of its outcomes.

The goal of a sensitivity analysis is to establish how various ranges of values for an independent variable influence the behavior of a specific dependent variable, given a specific list of assumptions by way of options. The primary purpose of project sensitivity is to select the most appropriate strategy or approach to addressing the project's most pressing issues relating to changes in the variables that have a direct effect on the cash flows.

Notwithstanding the evident significance of sensitivity analysis, several challenges are encountered in its application, and uncertainty analysis transcends academic disciplines. Saltelli et al. (2019) identify a variety of issues, including terminological misunderstandings and statistically erroneous methods that may (possibly perilously) underestimate model uncertainty.

7.10.1 Understanding Sensitivity Analysis

Sensitivity analysis is a tool for quality assurance or to gain a deeper understanding of processes within models and, by extension, the natural systems on which they are constructed (Becker et al., 2011). Sensitivity analysis can be employed when processes within models are poorly understood.

- The goal of a sensitivity analysis is to establish how various ranges of values for an independent variable influence the behavior of a specific dependent variable, given a specific list of assumptions.
- This type of model is also known as a "what-if" analysis or a "simulation analysis."
- It is possible to use sensitivity analysis as a tool to assist in making predictions regarding the share prices of publicly traded companies or the manner in which interest rates influence bond prices.
- The use of actual, historical data in forecasting is made possible by sensitivity analysis.
- In contrast to sensitivity analysis, which examines how various factors influence a particular occurrence, scenario analysis examines a variety of possible outcomes for a wider range of predicaments and is therefore more useful.

Illustration 7.7

Ananse Company Ltd. is evaluating two investment projects A and B. The initial capital outlay for each project GHS 200,000. The annual cash flows from each of the project is estimated GHS 55,000 per annum for the next 10 years. The cost of capital for the project is estimated at 16% per annum. The Optimistic, Most-likely and Pessimistic estimate of the annual cash flows are given below:

Table 7.8: Ananse Company Ltd. Annual Cash Flows:

Nature of Outcome Estimate	Cash Flows (GHS)	
	Project A	Project B
Pessimistic (P)	45,000	45,000
Most-Likely (ML)	55,000	55,000
Optimistic (O)	65,000	62,000

Required: Which of the two projects should be accepted based on sensitivity analysis and why?

Solution:

Table 7.9 Sensitivity in Project A - Computation

Estimate	Cash Flow (CF)	PVIFA @16% 10yrs	PV CF (GHS)	PV CF Minus Initial Investment	Difference
P	45,000	4.833	217,485	17,485	
ML	55,000	4.833	265,815	65,815	48,330
O	65,000	4.833	314,145	114,145	<u>48,330</u>
Variation / Sensitivity					96,660

Table 7.10 Sensitivity in Project B – Computation

Estimate	Cash Flow (CF)	PVIFA @16% for 10yrs	PV CF (GHS)	PV CF Minus Initial Investment	Difference
P	45,000	4.833	217,485	17,485	
ML	55,000	4.833	265,815	65,815	48,330
O	62,000	4.833	299,646	99,646	<u>33,831</u>
Variation / Sensitivity					82,161

Note: Since the value for the estimate "P" and "ML" have the same outcome, one needs to find the sensitivity between "P" and "O" by striking the difference between the two outcomes. Then accept the one with the lower level of variation (less sensitivity).

Decision: Project B should be accepted based on the sensitivity analysis indicated above since, it has lower level of variation.

Illustration 7.8

Compute the net present value of two projects (X and Y) for each of the possible cash flow using sensitivity analysis and suggest which of the project should be selected and invested in. The required rate of return for the investment in these projects is 8%.

Table 7:11 Cash Flows of Project X and Project Y

Particulars	Project X (GHS)	Project Y (GHS)
Initial Outlay	400,000	500,000
Cash inflow estimate for Time (t) =1-12years:		
Pessimistic (P)	40,000	30,000
Most-Likely (ML)	70,000	80,000
Optimistic (O)	90,000	150,000

Solution:

Table 7.12: Sensitivity in Project X Computation

Estimate	Cash Flow (CF)	PVIFA @16% 10yrs	PV CF (GHS)	PV CF Minus Initial Investment	Difference (GHS)
P	40,000	7.536	301,440	-98,560	
ML	70,000	7.536	527,520	127,520	226,080
O	90,000	7.536	678,240	278,240	150,720
Variation / Sensitivity					75,360

Table 7.13: Sensitivity in Project Y Computation

Estimate	Cash Flow (CF)	PVIFA @16% 10yrs	PV CF (GHS)	PV CF Minus Initial Investment	Difference (GHS)
P	30,000	7.536	226,080	- 273,920	
ML	80,000	7.536	602,880	102,880	376,800
O	150,000	7.536	1,130,400	630,400	<u>525,520</u>
Variation / Sensitivity					148,720

Decision: Accept Project X based on the sensitivity analysis indicated above since, it has lower level of variation or sensitivity.

Illustration 7.9

Compute the net present value of two projects (C and D) for each of the possible cash flow using sensitivity analysis and suggest which of the project should be selected and invested in. The required rate of return for the investment in these projects is 10%.

Table 7.14: Cash Flows for Project C and D

Particulars	Project C	Project D
Initial Outlay	400,000	400,000
	(GHS)	(GHS)
Cash inflow estimate for Time (t) =1-15years:		
Pessimistic (P)	60,000	0
Most-Likely (ML)	80,000	80,000
Optimistic (O)	100,000	160,000

Solution:

Table 7.15: Sensitivity Computation of Project C:

Estimate	Cash Flow (CF)	PVIFA @10% 15yrs	PV CF (GHS)	PV CF Minus Initial Investment	Difference (GHS)
P	60,000	7.606	456,360	56,360	
ML	80,000	7.606	608,480	208,848	152,488
O	100,000	7.606	760,600	360,600	151,752
Variation / Sensitivity					304,240

Table 7.16: Sensitivity Computation of Project D:

Estimate	Cash Flow (CF)	PVIFA @10% 15yrs	PV CF (GHS)	PV CF Minus Initial Investment	Difference (GHS)
P	0	7.606	0	-400,000	
ML	80,000	7.606	608,480	208,848	608,848
O	60,000	7.606	1,216,960	816,960	608,112
Variation / Sensitivity					1,216,960

Decision: Accept Project C based on the sensitivity analysis indicated above since, it has lower level of variation or sensitivity than project D.

Importance/ Benefits of Sensitivity Analysis

1. Any kind of financial model can benefit from sensitivity analysis, which verifies the model using a variety of different scenarios to bolster its credibility.

2. The analyst is given the ability to be flexible with the boundaries within which to test the sensitivity of the dependent variables to the independent variables. This is made possible by financial sensitivity analysis.

3. The sensitivity analysis enables one to make more educated decisions. The model is utilized by decision-makers in order to gain an understanding of how sensitive the output is to changes in specific variables. As a result, the analyst can be helpful in deriving tangible conclusions and can play an instrumental role in making decisions that are optimal.

4. Users of complex sensitivity analysis models are educated on the various factors that have an impact on a project; as a result, members of the project are informed about what they should be on the lookout for or what they should prepare for in advance.

Disadvantages of Sensitivity Analysis
1. It depends a great deal on hypotheses that may or may not be proven correct in the future.

2. It may become excessively complicated, which distorts an analyst's ability to make investment decisions.

3. It can result in an inaccurate integration of the independent variables (as one variable may not accurately reflect the impact of another variable).

7.11 Probability Technique in Capital Budgeting

In statistics, the probability distribution is used to characterize the likelihood of each conceivable outcome of a random event or experiment. It provides probability for each of the conceivable outcomes.

Probability is a measure of uncertainty applicable to several phenomena, whether they are probabilistic or deterministic. For instance, the probabilities governing the results of throwing a die define the possible possibilities. This distribution might be defined for any capital budgeting decisions with uncertain or unpredictability cashflow outcomes. The distribution may have a single or many periods.

Illustration 7.10

The following are potential net cash flows for projects Y and Z, given the estimated probability shown below. It is determined that both projects have a 10% discount rate. You must calculate the projected NPV for each project, assuming an initial cash investment of GH 50,000 for each. Which project ought to be approved?

Table 7.17: Cash Flows and Probabilities for Project Y and Z

Probability Event	Project Y		Project Z	
	Cash Flow (GHS)	Probability (x)	Cash Flow (GHS)	Probability (x)
A	40,000	0.10	120,000	0.10
B	50,000	0.20	100,000	0.15
C	60,000	0.40	80,000	0.50
D	70,000	0.20	60,000	0.15
E	80,000	0.10	40,000	0.10

Solution: Project Y

Table 7.18: Computation of NPV Using Probability Technique

Probability Event	Cash Flow (GHS)	Probability (x)	Expected Cash Flow (GHS)
A	40,000	0.10	4,000
B	50,000	0.20	10,000
C	60,000	0.40	24,000
D	70,000	0.20	14,000
E	80,000	0.10	8,000
Total Expected Cash flow			**60,000**
Present Value (PV) of Expected cash inflow (CIF) @10%			54,540
NPV			**4,540**

Solution: Project Z

Table 7.19: Computation of NPV Using Probability Technique

Probability Event	Cash Flow (GHS)	Probability (x)	Expected Cash Flow (GHS)
A	120,000	0.10	12,000
B	100,000	0.15	15,000
C	80,000	0.50	40,000
D	60,000	0.15	9,000
E	40,000	0.10	4,000
Total Expected Cash flow			**80,000**
Present Value (PV) of Expected cash inflow (CIF) @10%			72,727.27
NPV			7,272.72

Decision: Accept the investment in project Z since it has the higher positive NPV

Illustration 7.11

A company has determined the following probabilities for net cash flows for three successive years in respect of an investment project X. The initial investment of the project is GHS 400,000. You are required to calculate the net present value (NPV) of the cash flows using 10% as the discount rate, and determine whether the project is worth the investment. The probabilities are as follows.

Table 7.20: Cash Flows and Probability Distribution for Project Y

Year 1		Year 2		Year 3	
Cash flow GHS	Probability	Cash Flow GHS	Probability	Cash flow GHS	Probability
100,000	0.10	100,000	0.20	100,000	0.30
200,000	0.20	200,000	0.30	200,000	0.40
300,000	0.30	300,000	0.40	300,000	0.20
50,000	0.40	50,000	0.10	50,000	0.10

Solution:

Table 7.21: Computation of Expected Cash Flows

Year 1	Year 2	Year 3
100,000 x 0.10 = 10,000	100,000 x 0.20 = 20,000	100,000 x 0.30 = 30,000
200,000 x 0.20 = 40,000	200,000 x 0.30 = 60,000	200,000 x 0.40 = 80,000
300,000 x 0.30 = 90,000	300,000 x 0.40 = 120,000	300,000 x 0.20 = 60,000
50,000 x 0.40 = 20,000	50,000 x 0.10 = 5,000	50,000 x 0.10 = 5,000
Total = 160,000	= 205,000	= 175,000

Table 7.22: Computation of NPV Using Probability Technique

Years	Expected Cash Flow	Discount Factor @10%	PV Cash Flow (GHS)
0	(500,000)	1.000	(400,000)
1	160,000	0.909	145,440
2	205,000	0.826	169,330
3	175,000	0.751	131,425
NPV			46,195

Decision: Accept the investment in project X since it has a positive NPV of **GHS46,195**.

7.12 Inflation and Capital Budgeting

Inflation is the continual increase in the overall level of prices, often measured monthly or yearly. Typically, money loses value, with the exception of occasional recessions in which it may gain value. Investors are currently making investments. There is a requirement to generate a return in addition to compensating for inflation. This merely implies that they want to enhance their value in real terms, which is vital information for generating our cash flow forecasts. This is due to the fact that projects seldom deliver all cash flows simultaneously. Typically, cash flows from projects are spread out over many years or decades.

Consequently, inflation becomes essentially critical for calculating the appropriate values for capital budgeting decisions. Changes in the inflation assumptions can significantly affect the expected return on a project. By only altering the inflation estimates, a feasible project may become untenable.

7.12.1 Different Components Uniquely Affected by Inflation

First, we must recognize that inflation never impacts all income statement components consistently. Therefore, assuming a consistent rate for all components may provide theoretically accurate results, but in practice it will be a mistake. Consider, for instance, that labour expenses will increase annually. Employees often anticipate annual salary increases. Also, the cost of raw materials is anticipated to increase annually. However, the price rise cannot parallel these improvements. Typically, it will either be more or smaller than the percentage change in other components. The sales price is determined by the market, and we cannot raise it without suffering a loss.

Finally, a skilled analyst will assess the historical performance of each of these variables in terms of their inflationary proclivity. He or she will next try to forecast future patterns that are likely to dominate. Each component should have its own inflation rate on this basis. In a more thorough review, inflation forecasts will vary from year to year depending on the analyst's economic expectations.

7.12.2 Follow the Golden Rule

Regarding capital budgeting and inflation, the golden rule is to approach inflation consistently. The key phrase is consistency. Authentic cash flows must be discounted at the real rate of interest. Alternatively, if we have nominal cash flows (which is often the case), we must discount them at a rate of nominal interest. Although it may seem obvious, it is a common mistake to use an improper discount rate. A formula for converting nominal to real interest rates and vice versa has already been investigated.

The following is the formula:
(1 + nominal rate) = (1 + real rate) x (1 + inflation rate)
Real cash flows and discount rates:

Assume that the discount rate 16% includes investor's inflation expectation of 5%. Hence, the 'real' discount rate, r is given by:

$$1+r = \frac{(1+m)}{(1+i)}$$

Where:
r = is the real discount rate
m = is the money discount rate
i = is the inflationary rate

$$1+r = \frac{(1+0.16)}{(1+0.05)}$$

= 10.48%

The accuracy of capital budgeting decisions depends on the accuracy of the data regarding cash inflows and outflows. For example, failure to incorporate price-level changes due to inflation in capital budgeting situations can result in errors in the prediction of cash flows and, thus, incorrect decisions.

Typically, the financial manager has two options in dealing with a capital budgeting situation with inflation.
- Restate the cash flows in nominal terms and discount them at a nominal cost of capital (minimum required rate of return).
- Restate both the cash flows and cost of capital in constant terms and discount the constant cash flows at a constant cost of capital.

The two methods are basically equivalent.

Illustration 7.12

A company has these projected cash flows estimated in real terms:

Table 7.23: Real Cash Flows

Real Cash Flows (GHS 000s)				
Period	0	1	2	3
Cash Flows	(200)	135	150	130

The nominal cost of capital is 15 percent. Assume that inflation is projected at 10 percent a year.

Then the first cash flow for year 1, which is GHS 135,000 will be:
GHS 135,000 × 1.10 = **GHS 148,500** in year 1

Similarly, the cash flow for year 2 will be:
GHS 150,000 × $(1.10)^2$ = **GHS 181,500** in year 2.

The cash flow for year 3 will be:
GHS 130,000 × $(1.10)^3$ = **GHS 173,300** in year 3.

By discounting these nominal cash flows at the 15 percent nominal cost of capital, you come up with this net present value indicated below:

Table 7.24: NPV Computation

Period	Cash Flows	Present Value @ Disc. Factor 15%	Present Values GHS
0	(200,000)	1.000	(200,000)
1	148,500	.870	129,195
2	181,500	.756	137,214
3	173,300	.658	114,031.4
		Net Present Value =	180,440.40

Illustration 7.13:

A machine cost **GHS** 25,000 to buy and the it is expected to yield the following cash flows (estimated in current prices):

Table 7.25: Cash Flow Estimates in Current Prices

Timings (Years)	Cash flow GHS
1	4,000
2	5,000
3	3,000
4	8,000
5	7,000
6	4,000

Note: We expect an inflationary (both general and specific to these returns) to be at the rate of 8% per annum, and the money cost of capital is 12% per annum. Calculate the Net Present Value of this investment to see if it is worthwhile or not.

Solution: NPV Computation

Table 7.26: Actual Cash Flows with Inflation

Years	Current Price GHS	Inflationary @ 8%	Actual Cash Flow GHS
0	**(25,000)**	1	(25,000.00)
1	4,000	1.08	4,320.00
2	5,000	1.1664	5,832.00
3	3,000	1.2597	3,779.10
4	8,000	1.3605	10,884.00
5	7,000	1.4693	10,285.10
6	4,000	1.5869	6,347.60

Table 7.27: Computation of NPV With Inflation

Years	Actual Cash Flow GHS	DF @ 12%	PV GHS
0	(30,000.00)	1	(25,000.00)
1	4,320.00	0.8929	3,857.14
2	5,832.00	0.7972	4,649.23
3	3,779.10	0.7118	2,689.88
4	10,884.00	0.6355	6,917.06
5	10,285.10	0.5674	5,836.18
6	6,347.60	0.5066	3,215.93
		NPV	**2,165.43**

Where there is variation in the Inflationary rate for Cost and Revenue items:

It is generally known that the rate of inflation does not affect all costs to the same extent as some costs may increase above and below the average rate of inflation. Plainly, in respect of a given investment project, such variations are very essential and thus must be accounted for.

Illustration 7.14:

ABC Company Ltd. Is seriously considering a cost-savings investment project, which involves acquiring a state-of-the-art equipment to replace an existing machine that has outlived its usefulness. The new machine which costs GHS 2.7m will result in annual savings on wages cost of GHS100,000 and material cost of GHS 400,000.

The following forecast are made in respect of rates of inflation each year for the next six years:

Wage Costs:	10%
Material Cost	7%
General Price	9%

The cost of capital of the company in money terms is 12%

Required: Evaluate the project, assuming that the machine has a lifespan of six years and no scrap value.

Solution:

Table 7.28 Computation of Cost Savings

Years	Labour Cost Savings		Material Cost Savings		Total Savings
1	100,000 x 1.1	110,000.00	400,000 x 1.07	428,000.00	**538,000.00**
2	100,000 x $(1.1)^2$	121,000.00	400000 x $(1.07)^2$	457,960.00	**578,960.00**
3	100,000 x $(1.1)^3$	133,100.00	400000 x $(1.07)^3$	490,017.00	**623,117.00**
4	100,000 x $(1.1)^4$	146,410.00	400,000 x 1.07^4	524,318.00	**670,728.00**
5	100,000 x $(1.1)^5$	161,051.00	400000 x $(1.07)^5$	561,021.00	**722,072.00**
6	100,000 x $(1.1)^6$	771,561.00	400000 x $(1.07)^6$	600,292.00	**1,371,853.00**

Table 7.29: NPV Computation

Years	Total Savings	DF @12%	PV
0	(2,700,000)	1	(2,700,000.00)
1	538,000.00	0.8929	480,380.20
2	578,960.00	0.7972	461,546.91
3	623,117.00	0.7118	443,534.68
4	670,728.00	0.6355	426,247.64
5	722,072.00	0.5674	409,703.65
6	1,371,853.00	0.5066	694,980.73
	NPV		**216,393.82**

Decision:
The NPV of the Project is positive and thus the project is worth investing into.

Illustration 7.15:

Adom Company has taken a decision to invest in a machine that will cost GHS 800,000 to buy. The machine will help to produce 12,000 units per annum for this new product line. A standard cost card has been produced as follows:

	GHS
Materials	12
Labour	8
Variable Overheads	5
Fixed Overheads (excluding depreciation)	2
Depreciation	5
	32

The company has fixed selling price for the year at GHS 40 per unit given a budgeted profit of GHS 8 per unit. It is the policy of the firm to increase the selling price by 10% per annum from the beginning of every year.

The machine is expected to last for five years and at the end of which period, the machine will be sold for a scrap proceeds of GHS 80,000 (this is an estimate of the actual cash to be received). It is established that with the exception of selling price and the scrap proceeds, all estimates are in current prices, and it is anticipated that the costs will inflate at the following rates:

Materials	5% per annum
Labour	10% per annum
Overheads	8% per annum (in line with Retail Price Index)

The Company's accounting year starts from 1st January to 31st December of each year and all flows are to be assumed to occur at the ends of each year except the purchase price on 1st January of the year of investment. The cost of capital is 14% per annum.

You are to compute the net present value of this investment and indicate whether the investment is worthwhile.

Solution:

Table 7.30: Computation of Cost Savings

Time/Years	Cost/Scrap GHS	Material GHS	Labour GHS	Variable GHS	Revenue GHS	Total GHS
Y0	(800,000)	-	-	-	-	**(800,000)**
Y1	-	(151,200)	(105,600)	(64,800)	480,000	**158,400**
Y2	-	(158,760)	(116,160)	(69,984)	528,000	**183,096**
Y3	-	(166,698)	(127,776)	(75,583)	580,800	**210,743**
Y4	-	(175,033)	(140,554)	(81,629)	638,880	**241,664**
Y5	-	(183,785)	(154,609)	(88,160)	702,768	**276,214**
Y6	80,000	(192,974)	(170,070)	(95,212)	773,045	**394,789**

Table 7.31: Computation of NPV

Years	C.F GHS	DF @14%	PV GHS
Y0	(800,000)	1.0000	(800,000)
Y1	158,400	0.8772	138,948
Y2	183,096	0.7695	140,892
Y3	210,743	0.6750	142,252
Y4	241,664	0.5921	143,089
Y5	276,214	0.5194	143,466
Y6	394,789	0.4556	179,866
NPV			**88,513**

Decision: The investment is worthwhile since it has a positive net present value.

7.13 Impact of Income Tax on Capital Budgeting Decisions

Typically, the income tax has a substantial influence on a company's cash flow. Consequently, it must be factored into capital budgeting considerations. An investment that appears favorable while income tax is not considered may become unsatisfactory when it is. Before we can illustrate the influence of income tax on capital budgeting decisions using a net present value (NPV) example, we must first grasp three key concepts. These principles include:
- ✓ After-tax benefit;
- ✓ After-tax expense; and
- ✓ Tax-shield for depreciation.

Let's discuss and illustrate them quickly before applying them to the NPV calculation of a project.

After-tax benefit or cash inflow:

Taxable revenues or cash inflows, when reduced by the income tax, are known as ***after-tax benefit*** or ***after-tax cash inflow***. When income tax is considered in capital budgeting decisions, we use after-tax cash inflow. An example of taxable cash inflow is cash generated by a company from its operations.

After tax benefit or after-tax cash inflow can be easily computed using the following formula:

After-tax benefit or after-tax cash inflow = (1 − Tax rate) × Taxable cash receipt

Illustration 7.16:

XYZ company generated GHS 500,000 cash from its operations. The tax rate of the company is 40%. Compute after-tax cash inflow.

Solution:

After-tax benefit or after-tax cash inflow = (1 – Tax rate) × Taxable cash receipt.
= (1 – 0.4) × GHS 500,000
= 0.6 × GHS 500,000
= GHS 300,000

After-tax cost:
A tax-deductible cost reduces taxable income of the entity and helps save its income tax. A cost net of its tax effect is known as *after-tax cost* and can be computed using the following formula:

After-tax cost or after-tax cash outflow = (1 – Tax rate) × Tax deductible cash expense.

Illustration 7.17:
A company wants to start a training program that will cost it GHS 70,000. The cost of training program is a tax-deductible cost for the company. Compute after-tax cost of training program if tax rate of the company is 40%.

Solution:
After-tax cost or after-tax cash outflow = (1 – Tax rate) × Tax deductible cash expense
= (1 – 0.4) × GHS 70,000
= 0.6 × GHS 70,000
= **GHS 42,000**

7.13.1 Capital Budgeting with Income Tax

Since we have learned the concept of after-tax cash inflow, after-tax cost and depreciation tax shield, now we can explain the impact of income tax on capital budgeting with the help of a comprehensive example.

Illustration 7.18:
A company is considering the purchase of an equipment to save its costs. The relevant data for net present value analysis of the equipment is given below:

- Cost of the equipment: GHS 240,000
- Expected annual cash savings before tax to be provided by the equipment: GHS 100,000
- Useful life of the equipment: 6 years
- Expected residual or salvage value of the equipment at the end of 6-year period: GHS 30,000
- Tax rate: 40%
- Discount rate: 12%

The equipment is to be depreciated using straight line method of depreciation. The company does not deduct salvage value from the cost of the equipment for computing depreciation for tax purpose. **Required:** Determine net present value of the investment.

Solution:
Depreciation = GHS 240,000/6 years
= GHS **40,000**

Residual value (salvage value) is taxable because it has not been considered while computing depreciation. At the end of the useful life, the equipment will have a book value of zero.

Table 7.32: Computation of NPV- After-tax Cash Flows

Item	Years	Cash Flow	Tax Effect	After-tax CF	DF @ 12%	PV
Cost	0	(270,000)	-	270,000	1	(270,000)
Annual Savings	1-6	100,000	0.6	60,000	4.111	246,660
Depreciation	1-6	40,000	0.4	16,000	4.111	65,776
Residual	6	30,000	0.6	18,000	0.507	9,126
NPV						**81,562**

Note:
Future Value Interest Factor of Annuity and Future Value interest Factor were used to extract the discount factors for years **1-6** and for year **6** respectively.

We can also present the solution in horizontal format as follows:
- GHS 240,000 x 1.000 + (GHS 100,000 x 0.6 x 4.111) + (GHS 40,000 x 0.4 x 4.111) + (GHS 30,000 x 0.6 x 0.507)
= (−GHS 240,000) + (GHS 246,660 + GHS 65,776 + GHS 9,126)

NPV = GHS 81,562

Illustration 7.19

A4, Inc. is considering setting up a new paper mill at a cost of **GHS** 100,000. It is expected to stay economical for 5 years after which the company expects to upgrade to a more efficient technology and sell it for **GHS** 30,000. Following is an extract from a report prepared by the marketing department and engineering department.

Year	1	2	3	4	5
Revenue inflows **(GHS)**	90,000	85,000	80,000	70,000	60,000
Costs outflows **(GHS)**	50,000	46,000	40,000	36,000	40,000
Net cash flows before tax	**40,000**	**39,000**	**40,000**	**34,000**	**20,000**

A tax rate of 30% is applicable to both income and gains and is not expected to change in 5 years. Tax code requires the company to depreciate the plant over 5 years with **GHS** 10,000 as salvage value. A discount rate of 8% is appropriate.

Calculate NPV. Consider tax implications.

Solution:
Table 7. 33: Calculate NPV with Tax Implications

Year	Effect	1	2	3	4	5
		GHS'000	GHS'000	GHS'000	GHS'000	GHS'000
Revenue inflows		90.0	85.0	80.0	70.0	60.0
Costs outflows– (Less)	Minus	(50.0)	(46.0)	(40.0)	(36.0)	(40.0)
Before-tax net cash flows		40.0	39.0	40.0	34.0	20.0
Depreciation (Less)	Minus	(18.0)	(18.0)	(18.0)	(18.0)	(18.0)
Income before taxes		22.0	21.0	22.0	16.0	2.0
Taxes @ 30%	Minus	(6.6)	(6.3)	(6.6)	(4.8)	(0.6)
After-tax net income		15.4	14.7	15.4	11.2	1.4
Depreciation	Plus	18.0	18.0	18.0	18.0	18.0
After-tax cash flows		33.4	32.7	33.4	29.2	19.4
After-tax salvage value	Plus					24.0
After-tax net cash flows		33.4	32.7	33.4	29.2	43.4
Discount rate @ 8%	×	0.926	0.857	0.794	0.735	0.681
Present value of cash flows		30.9	28.0	26.5	21.5	29.5
Total Present Value		\multicolumn{5}{c}{GHS 136,500}				

After-tax salvage value included in the schedule above

= **GHS** 30,000 – (**GHS** 30,000– **GHS** 10,000) × 30%

= **GHS 24,000**

Net Present Value

= present value of cash flows – initial outlay

= **GHS** 136,500 – **GHS** 100,000

= **GHS 36,500.**

Since the NPV is positive, the company should go ahead with the setup of paper mill. Please note that we will get the same after-tax total net cash flows if we subtract taxes from before-tax cash flows directly (instead of finding net income and then adding non-cash items to arrive at after-tax cash flows).

Calculation for Year 1 is illustrated below.

After-tax cash flows in Year 1

= before-tax cash flows – taxes

= **GHS** 40,000 – **GHS** 6,600

= **GHS 33,400**

Illustration 7.20:

ABA Company Ltd. is considering a new venture to manufacture rubber products. This requires machinery costing GHS 210,000, with a life-span of five years and a terminal value of GHS 10,000. Profits before depreciation from the project will be GHS 15,000 p.a. However, there will be cash flows which will differ from profits by the built-up of working capital during the first year of operations and its run-down during the fifth year, amounting to GHS 6,000.

Tax-allowance on the equipment is estimated at 20% p.a. on a reducing balance basis. At the end of the project's life a balancing charge or allowance will arise equal to the difference between the scrap proceeds and the tax written down value.

Tax is payable one year after the end of the accounting year on which it is based, at a rate of 40%. The start of the project is definitely, the start of the accounting year. Cost of Capital is 18%. You are required to examine the viability of this project.

Depreciation Tax-shield:
Depreciation is a non-cash tax deductible expense that saves income tax for business entities by reducing their taxable income. The amount of tax that the annual depreciation of an entity saves is known as ***depreciation tax shield***. The formula to compute depreciation tax shield is as follows:

Depreciation tax shield = Tax rate × Depreciation deduction

Illustration 7.21:
The annual tax-deductible depreciation expense of a company is GHS 50,000. Its tax rate is given as 40%. Compute tax savings from depreciation (i.e., depreciation tax shield).

Solution:
Depreciation tax shield = Tax rate × Depreciation deduction
= 0.4 × GHS 50,000
= GHS 20,000

7.14 Capital Allowances in Capital Budgeting

A company may claim capital allowances for capital expenditures it incurs on certain types of business assets and business premises. Capital allowances are akin to a tax-deductible expense and are available in respect of qualifying capital expenditure incurred on the provision of certain assets in use for the purposes of a trade or rental business. They effectively allow a taxpayer to write off the cost of an asset over a period of time. Capital allowances are a type of tax relief for businesses. They enable companies to deduct some or all of the value of an item from their profits before they pay tax.

Capital allowances are generally calculated based on the net cost of the business asset or premises. There are different rates available, depending on the type of asset. A company can claim capital allowances on:

- Plant and machinery;
- Motor vehicles;
- Industrial buildings;

- Transmission capacity rights; and
- Computer software.

7.14.1 Capital allowances- Benefits

- Claim an immediate tax / cash benefit.
- Reduce or completely shelter a tax liability.
- No restriction on high earners claiming wear and tear allowances and most industrial buildings allowances.
- Improve cash flow and keep cash in your business.
- Possible cash refund / repayment of taxes.

In capital budgeting capital allowances enable businesses or individuals to enjoy the full benefit of tax savings.

Illustration 7.22:

For instance, a machine is purchased for GHS 500,000 and has an expected life-span of five years. Assuming that the firm is required to calculate the cash flows based on 20% writing-down allowance, while the company pays corporate tax of 32%.

The tax position is as indicated below:

Year 1: Allowance = 20% x 500,000

= GHS 100,000

Thus, at the tax rate of 32% this will result in a tax savings (an inflow) of:

32% x GHS 100,000

= **GHS 32,000**

Year 2: Allowance 20% of reduced balance

= 20% (GHS 500,000 - GHS 100,000)

= 20% (GHS 400,000)

= **GHS 80,000**

Thus, at the tax rate of 32% this will result in a tax savings (an inflow) of:

32% x GHS 80,000

= **GHS 25,600**

Year 3: Allowance 20% of reduced balance
= 20% (GHS 500,000 − (GHS 100,000+180,000)
= 20% (GHS 320,000)
= GHS 64,000

Thus, at the tax rate of 32% this will result in a tax savings (an inflow) of:
32% x GHS 64,000
= **GHS 20,240**

Year 4: Allowance 20% of reduced balance

= 20% (GHS 500,000 − (GHS 100,000+80,000+ 64,000)

= 20% (GHS 256,000)

= **GHS 51,200**

Thus, at the tax rate of 32% this will result in a tax savings (an inflow) of:

32% x GHS 51,200

= **GHS 15,360**

Year 5: Allowance 20% of reduced balance

= 20% (GHS 500,000 − (GHS 100,000+80,000+ 64,000+51,200)

= 20% (GHS 204,800)

= **GHS 40,960**

Thus, at the tax rate of 32% this will result in a tax savings (an inflow) of:

32% x GHS 40,960

= **GHS 13,107.20**

Note: Assume that the equipment is sold at GHS 50,000 at the end of fifth year. Thus, given the written down value of GHS 40,960, a balancing charge for tax hence arises in the form of net liability of 32% (GHS 50,000 - GHS 40,960)

$$= 32\% \times \textbf{GHS } 9,040$$

Balancing charge = **GHS 2,712**

Table 7.34: Net Present Value Computation for Capital Allowance

Years	Allowance	Tax Savings	D.F @ 12%	PV
t_0	-	-	-	-
t_1	100,000	-	-	-
t_2	80,000	32,000	0.7972	25,510
t_3	64,000	25,600	0.7118	8,222
t_4	51,200	20,240	0.6355	12,863
t_5	40,960	15,360	0.5674	8,715
t_6	-	13,107	0.5066	6,640
t_6 [Balancing allowance] 9,040		2,712	0.5066	1,374
NPV				**GHS 73,324**

7.15 Decision Tree Analysis

7.15.1 Definition of Decision Tree

A decision tree is a graphical depiction of all the possible solutions or outcomes for resolving a specific problem or taking advantage of a prospective opportunity. It is a handy piece of financial modeling that visually simplifies the task of categorizing all of the probable outcomes for a specific situation.

It may also be viewed as a flowchart, with a primary concept at its base and numerous branches resulting from your actions. The model is referred to as a "decision tree" since its structure frequently resembles tree branches. These trees are the basis of the decision tree analysis technique, which is used to visually depict the alternative outcomes, costs, and repercussions of a difficult decision.

By employing decision trees, it is possible to compute the expected value of each outcome through an examination of the choices and results that contributed to that particular outcome. Then, upon comparing the results, you will possess the ability to promptly select the most effective subsequent action. Moreover, a decision tree can be employed to address challenges, reduce costs, and identify opportunities. Waters (2011) posits that decision trees function as a conceptual framework that aids in the recognition, understanding, and transmission of the underlying structure of these issues.

7.15.2 Steps in Decision Tree Analysis

1. The first thing that needs to be done is to gain an understanding of and then specifically define the problem area that calls for decision making.

2. The second step is to analyze the situation, write down all of the potential solutions to the problem, and then consider the repercussions of those solutions.

3. The presentation of the variables on a decision tree along with their associated probability values constitutes the third step in the process.

4. Finding out the results of all of the variables and specifying them in the decision tree constitutes the fourth step in the process.

5. The very last step is of the utmost importance and provides support for the overall analysis of this process. It requires one to calculate the end values for each of the possible chance nodes or options in order to determine the answer that will result in the highest expected value.

7.15.3 Decision Tree Symbols

A decision tree analysis includes a number of symbols with comments that describe your actions and results, as well as any pertinent values that explain your gains or losses. You have the choice of manually sketching your decision tree or digitally mapping it using a flowchart tool. The following symbols are utilized inside Decision Tree, which are regarded industry standards:

- **Alternative Branches**
  On a decision tree, alternate branches are depicted as two lines extending in opposite directions from a central option. Depending on the decision made at the tree's root, the tree's branching structure may result in two possible outcomes or lines of behavior. These outcomes, or behaviors, constitute courses of action.

- **Decision Nodes**
  Each of the multiple squares that comprise the decision nodes on the decision tree reflects a distinct decision made at some point throughout the process. At the beginning of the creation of every decision tree, a node referred to as a decision node will be formed.

- **Chance Nodes**
  Chance nodes are diagrams that take the shape of circular plots and indicate a variety of various potential outcomes if any of those potential outcomes is realized.

- **End Nodes**
  The triangles in a network that lead to a conclusion stand in for the terminal nodes of the network, as here is where the triangles' trips conclude.

7.15.4 Steps in Decision Tree Analysis

- **Start with Your Idea**
  Place the most important notion or choice at the center of your diagram to get started. Your decision tree will begin with a decision node, and from there, you will add single branches that correspond to each of the options under consideration. If you want to build a new digitally-enabled marketing infrastructure or expand an existing marketing strategy, for example, you can use a decision tree to analyze the potential outcomes of each option and determine the best course of action by choosing the option that will result in the best overall outcome.

- **Add Chance and Decision nodes**
  After you have contributed your main concept to the tree, you may continue to construct it by adding nodes that reflect chance or choice after each process decision you make. This will help you develop your central idea further. Because selecting this option might result in several alternative outcomes, the decision tree may require an additional branch after the chance node. This is required to take into account the scenario. This is necessary to take into consideration the situation. If you construct a new infrastructure for digitally-enabled marketing and it is well received by customers, there is a high likelihood that your sales revenue will increase considerably. This is due to the fact that clients will be more likely to purchase your stuff. If your decision to construct the new infrastructure was a wise one, you will find yourself in this situation.

  There is also a chance that the application may not be granted, which might result in a loss in revenue. The most important aspect of your decision tree will be the mapping of the two potential outcomes.

- **Expand until you reach end points**
  You are required to continue adding nodes to your decision tree that represent chance and decisions until you can no longer make modifications that would make the tree larger. When you reach this point in the process of constructing a tree, you will know that the tree-making process is

complete since you will have added end nodes. When you reach this stage, you will realize this to be true. After you have completed the construction of your tree, you may analyze each decision you made throughout its construction. This may be done whenever the tree has been completed.

- **Calculate the Decision Tree values**

    In a perfect world, each of your decision tree's nodes would correspond to a single piece of numerical information. The most often utilized piece of information in decision trees is a measure of monetary worth. Consider, for illustrative purposes, that the development of a new application or the upgrading of an existing one will cost your business a particular amount of money. It may be useful to record these values in your decision tree and file them under each decision as you progress through the decision-making process. You may also attempt to estimate the expected value that will be produced as a result of each decision, regardless of how large or small it is.

To compute the anticipated value of each conceivable result, the following data is required:
- ✓ The cost of each possible outcome; and
- ✓ The probability that it will occur.

You can use this information in conjunction with the following formula: The following is the formula that is used to determine the expected value (EV):

- ✓ Expected Value (EV) is computed by deducting the cost from (first potential result times probability of outcome) plus (+) (second possible outcome times likelihood of outcome) plus (+) (third possible outcome times likelihood of outcome) etc.

- ✓ Multiply each of the two potential outcomes by the probability (% chance) that it will actually occur, and then add the resulting numbers to obtain the expected value. This will provide you with the total cost you should anticipate. In addition, you must subtract any startup costs from the total amount of money you have accumulated.

5. Evaluate Outcomes

When you have an understanding of the outcomes that may be anticipated from each choice, you can determine which option is best for you by considering the degree of risk you are willing to accept. Once you have this information, you will be able to select the optimal alternative. Because taking the highest level of project or investment risk carries the possibility of the largest possible return on the project or investment, there is a probability that the alternative with the highest projected value should not necessarily be prioritized.

7.15.5 Advantages of Decision Tree Analysis

1. **It shows the most suitable project**

    After considering all of the various outcomes, it is an efficient way to choose the one that will produce the best results, whether it is a project or a solution.

2. **It facilitates easy data interpretation and classification**

    Making use of decision trees, the use of which does not call for any kind of sophisticated mathematical understanding to put into action, makes the process of classifying newly acquired data into various categories a great deal less complex.

3. **It assists in multiple decision-making tools**

    Another advantage for the person who is making the choice is that it gives information for other analytical approaches, such as the tree that nature has constructed. This is an example of a natural phenomenon.

4. **It considers the use of both categorial and numerical data**

    This approach takes into account the quantitative as well as the qualitative aspects of the variables in order to achieve more favorable results.

7.15.6 Disadvantages of Decision Tree Analysis

1. **It is inappropriate for excessive data**
   It is not acceptable to utilize this approach in circumstances in which a substantial amount of data needs to be categorized because it is a non-parametric method. Because of this, it cannot be applied in those specific circumstances.

2. **It is difficult to use numerous outcomes**
   When there are several possible outcomes for each option, creating a decision tree may be a hard and time-consuming procedure. This is especially true when there are multiple potential outcomes for each decision.

3. **There is the possibility of classification errors**
   Someone with less experience is more likely to make an error while developing a decision tree than someone with more experience since they are less likely to have the necessary experience.

4. **Expensive Data Gathering Process**
   Because they are resource-intensive procedures, the collection of appropriate data, the classification of said data, and the analysis of said data each require large financial input from the individual.

Illustration 7.23

In the decision tree analysis example below, you can see how you would map out your tree diagram to meet an anticipated high demand for a firm's products that has necessitated the need for extra space for storage. Hence, you were choosing between building a new warehouse or expanding an existing one.

Decision nodes from this example:
- Build new digitally-enabled market infrastructure: GHS 600,000
- Expand an existing market infrastructure: GHS 200,000

Chance nodes from this example:
- Large and Small revenue for decision one: 60% and 45%
- Large and Small revenue for decision two: 35% and 40%

End nodes from this example:
- Potential profits for decision one: GHS 350,000 or GHS210,000
- Potential profits for decision two: GHS 120,000 or GHS 90,00

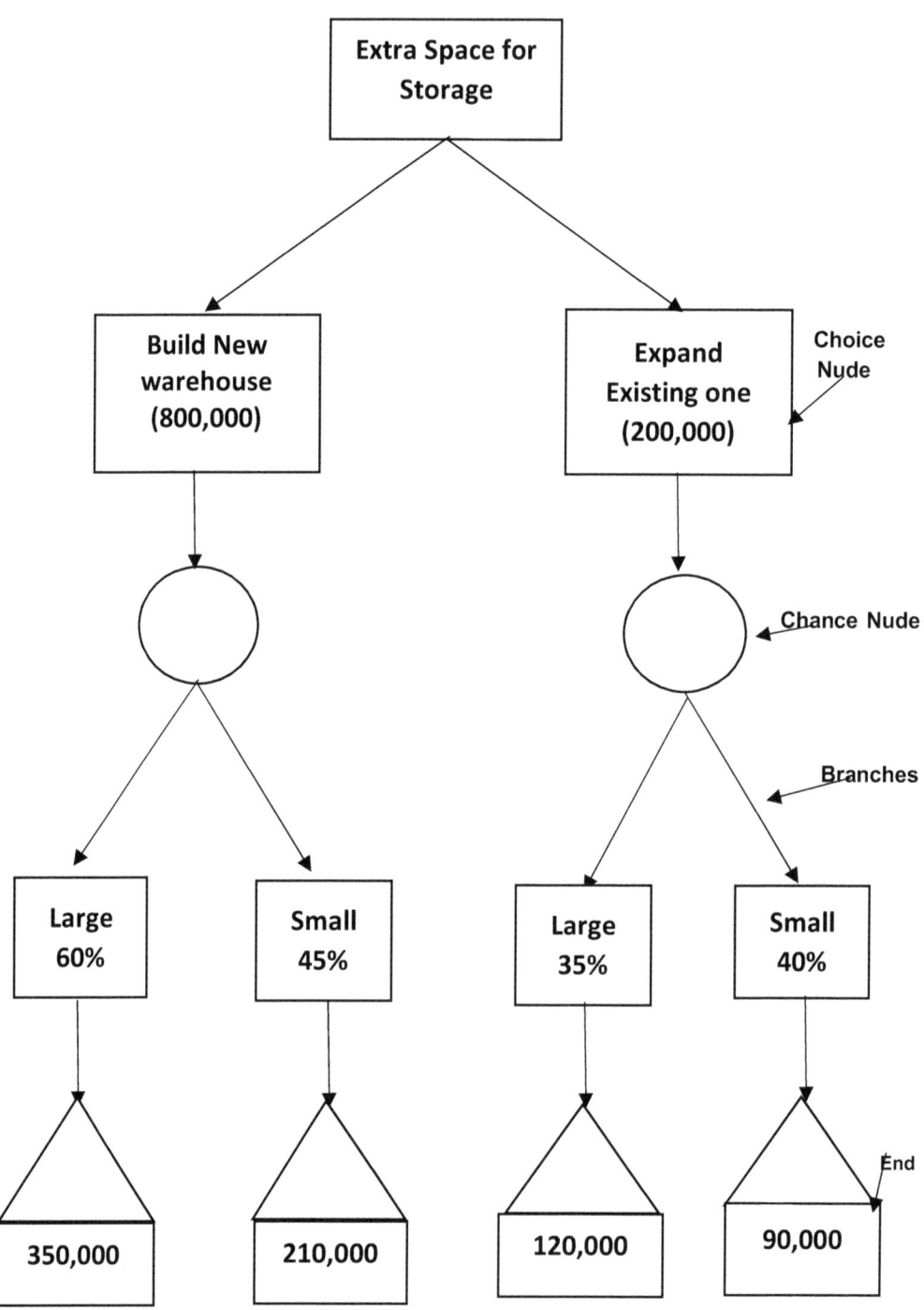

Option 1:

[750,000 x 0.6] + [410,000x 0.45]
    450,000 + 184.5 = **634,500**
                 (600,000) (cost)
Expected Values = **GHS 34,000**

Option 2:

[420,000 x 0.35] + [290,000 x 0.40]
   147,000 + 116,000 = **263,000**
                 (200,000) (cost)
Benefit   = **GHS 63,000**

Decision: Accept option 2 since it has more benefit (Expected values) savings.

Illustration 7.24

A company is considering to buy a new equipment. The net cash flows of the equipment have been estimated and indicated below. The life of the equipment is two years and the initial cost is GHS 50,000 with a cost of capital indicated as 12%. Use a decision tree technique to ascertain the NPV, recommend whether the equipment should be purchased or not.

	Year 1		Year 2	
	Cash flow	Probability	Cash Flow	Probability
I.	40,000	0.40	30,000	0.50
			20,000	0.50
II.	30,000	0.60	60,000	0.40
			20,000	0.60

Solution:

Table 7.35: Computation of NPV Using Decision Tree Technique

Options	Cash Flows		PV @ 12%		Total PV's CF	NPV of CF	Joint Prob	Expected NPV of CF x JP
	Year 1	Year 2	0.893	0.797				
I	40,000	30,000	35,720	23,910	59,630	9,630	0.4x0.5 = 0.20	1,926.00
	40,000	20,000	35,720	15,940	51,660	1,660	0.4x0.5 = 0.20	332.00
II	30,000	60,000	26,790	47,820	74,610	24,610	0.6x0.4 = 0.24	5,906.40
	30,000	20,000	26,790	15,940	42,730	(7,270)	0.6x0.6 = 0.36	(2,617.20)
Expected NPV (Joint Prob.)								**5,547.20**

Decision:
Since the expected NPV is positive **GHS 5,547.20**, the project is worthwhile and should be accepted.

Illustration 7.25
Using decision table approach, find the NPV for the following cash flows accruing to a project with an initial investment of GHS 12,000 and a cost of capital of 15%. Required:

i. Draw a decision table to represent the data; and
ii. Compute the NPV of the cash flows and suggest whether the intended project would be worthwhile and accepted based on the data table below:

Table 7.36: Cash Flows and Probability Distribution

Period 1			Period 2			Period 3		
Option	Prob.	CIF	Option	Prob.	CIF	Option	Prob.	CIF
			H	0.70	8,000	H	0.50	8,000
HIGH	0.60	6,000				L	0.50	5,000
			L	0.30	6,000	H	0.60	5,000
						L	0.40	4,000
			H	0.5	5,000	H	0.60	6,000
LOW	0.40	4,000				L	0.40	4,000
			L	0.5	4,000	H	0.70	6,000
						L	0.30	3,000

Decision Tree

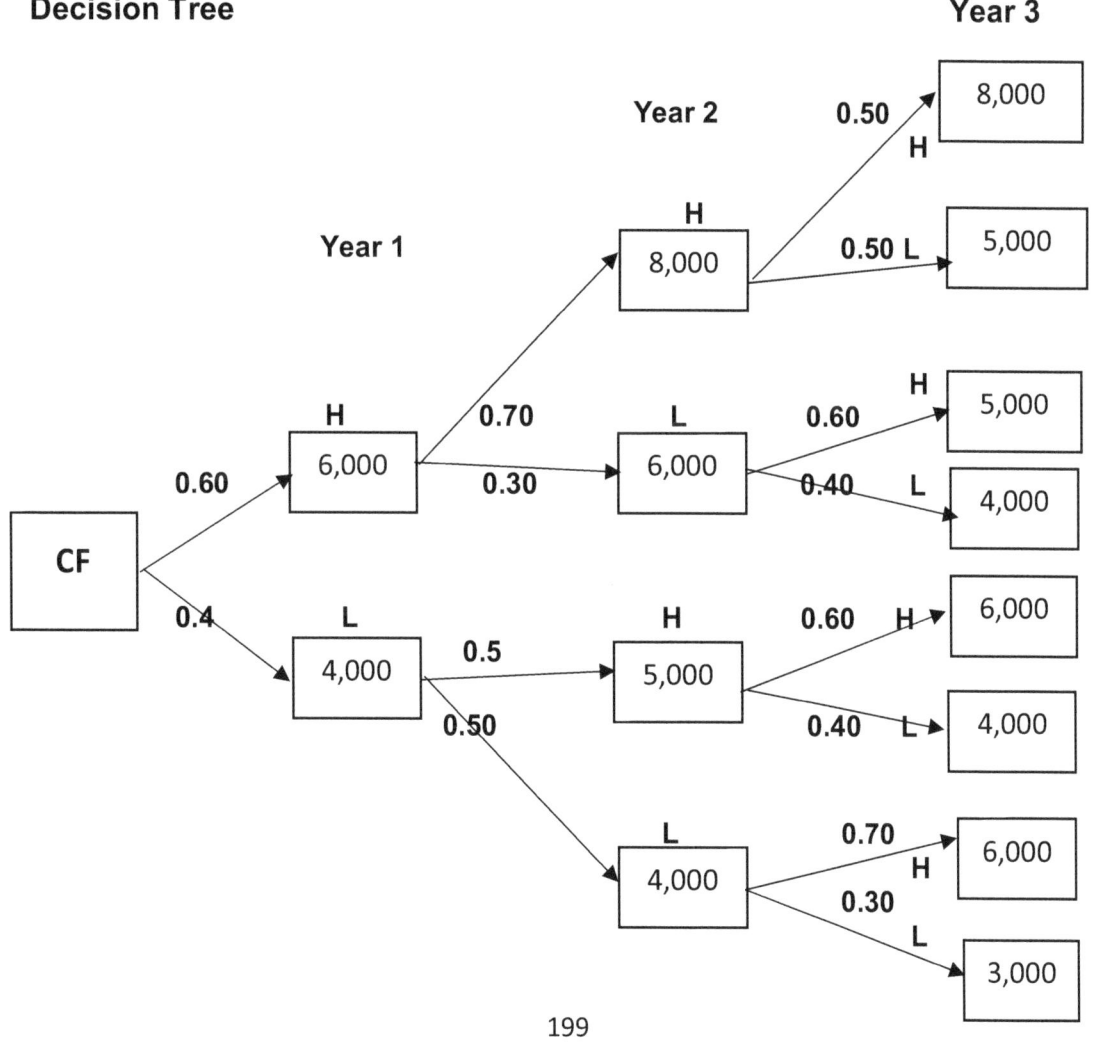

Solution ii:

Table 7.37: NPV Computation- Under Decision Tree

	Y_1	Y_2	Y_3	Y_1 0.87	Y_2 0.756	Y_3 0.658	Total PVCF
	GHS	GHS	GHS	GHS	GHS	GHS	GHS
	6,000	8,000	8,000	5,220	6,048	5,264	16,532
	6,000	8,000	5,000	5,220	6,048	3,290	14,558
HIGH	6,000	6,000	5,000	5,220	4,536	3,290	13,046
	6,000	6,000	4,000	5,220	4,536	2,632	12,388
	4,000	5,000	6,000	3,480	3,780	3,948	11,208
LOW	4,000	5,000	4,000	3,480	3,780	2,632	9,892
	4,000	4,000	6,000	3,480	3,024	3,948	10,452
	4,000	4,000	3,000	3,480	3,024	1,974	8,478

Table 7.38: NPV Computation- Under Decision Tree (Cont'd.)

	Initial Investment	NPV CIF	Joint Probability (JP)	(NPV CIF) x (JP) GHS
	12,000	4,532	0.5 x 0.7 x 0.6 = **0.21**	951.72
	12,000	2,558	0.5 x 0.7 x 0.6 = **0.21**	537.18
HIGH	12,000	1,046	0.6 x 0.3 x 0.6 = **0.11**	115.06
	12,000	388	0.4 x 0.3 x 0.6 = **0.07**	27.16
	12,000	-792	0.6 x 0.5 x 0.4 = **0.12**	(95.04)
LOW	12,000	-2,108	0.4 x 0.5 x 0.4 = **0.08**	(168.64)
	12,000	-1,548	0.7 x 0.5 x 0.4 = **0.14**	(20.72)
	12,000	-3,522	0.3 x 0.5 x 0.4 = **0.06**	(211.32)
NPV				**1,135.40**

7.16 Simulation Technique

The essence of a simulation is a computer model that seeks to recreate a real-world event. Simulation analysis is a methodology used in the field of finance to analyze big projects and discover how changes to input factors influence target variables. This type of model is called a simulation. The model performs simulations to create predictions on how the results of a choice would change based on how a set of input variables are tweaked within a specific range.

In contrast to scenario analysis and sensitivity analysis, simulation analysis does not give a single solution. In its place, it presents a spectrum of potential outcomes due to the variable's malleability. In reality, there is only a simulation of cash flows, but we make it look as though there is a real-world scenario.

Prior to initiating the simulation analysis, the statistical distribution of each input must be understood. In the majority of instances, simulations are conducted to examine the effect that continually changing inputs have on the ensuing outputs. The estimated output is computed by first averaging the actual outputs. When there are several inputs that are independent of one another and have the capacity to alter independently, simulation analysis is at its most effective.

7.16.1 General Steps in Simulation Analysis
Simulation Analysis contains the following steps –
- Identifying the various factors at play
- Developing the equations for use
- Providing an indication of the likelihood distribution
- Creating a software application for a computer

7.16.2 Specific Steps in Simulating Cash Flows - Capital Budgeting
- Assign to the cash flows appearance numbers starting from zero (0) to nine (9) in a systematic order. Some cash flows will have more probability value than others.
- Assign the Set numbers systematically for each year of the cash flows.
- Simulate the cash flow and find the present values.

- Construct the row additions of the present values for the number of years in question.
- Find the NPV for each row by deducting the initial cost from the row total PV's
- Sum up the row NPV's to obtain the overall NPV for all the cash flows.
- Make a decision based on:
    - the overall value of NPV (whether positive or negative) and
    - the probability score of positive NPV's.

Illustration 7.26

Ebeyeyie Company Limited is evaluating the installation of new automatic machine with the intention of reducing labour cost. The new machine can also effectively meet the demand for greater capacity needed to meet increased in demand for their products and thus, resulting in increasing profit for at least three (3) consecutive years.

However, due to the uncertainty in the expected demand for the product of the firm, cash flows cannot be accurately estimated. Hence, probabilities have been assigned in this respect for the estimated cash flows as follows:

Table 7.39: Estimated Cash Flows and Probabilities

Year 1		Year 2		Year 3	
Cash flow	Probability	Cash flow	Probability	Cash flow	Probability
80,000	0.20	60,000	0.10	50,000	0.30
45,000	0.60	40,000	0.20	80,000	0.50
50,000	0.20	50,000	0.30	60,000	0.20
		90,000	0.40		

The initial outlay for the new machine is GHS 150,000 and a scrap value of GHS 20,000.

i. Evaluate the proposal at a discount rate of 10%.

ii. Analyze the risk inherent in this situation by simulating the cash flow values, given the following five set of random numbers of the cash flows. Find out the expected net present value (NPV) and the probability of the NPV of the proposal.

Table 7.40: Appearance Numbers

Year	Set 1	Set 2	Set 3	Set 4	Set 5
1	4	7	6	5	0
2	3	6	9	0	2
3	8	9	7	3	5

Solution:

Table 7.41: Computation of Expected or Probable Cash Flows

Year 1			Year 2			Year 3		
CF	Prob.	Expected CF (GHS)	CF	Prob.	Expected CF (GHS)	CF	Prob.	Expected CF (GHS)
80,000	0.20	16,000	60,000	0.10	6,000	50,000	0.30	15,000
45,000	0.60	27,000	40,000	0.20	8,000	80,000	0.50	40,000
50,000	0.20	10,000	50,000	0.30	15,000	60,000	0.20	12,000
			90,000	0.40	36,000			
Total Expected CF		53,000			65,000			67,000

Table 7.42: Computation of NPV of Expected Cash Flow

Year	Expected Cash Flow GHS	DF @ 10%	PV of CF GHS
0	(130,000)*	1.000	(130,000)
1	53,000	0.909	48,177
2	65,000	0.826	53,690
3	67,000	0.751	50,317
NPV of Expected Cash Flows			**22,184**

NB: Cash flow at year 0 = Initial investment - Residual
150,000 - 20,000 = GHS **130,000***

ii. Simulation of Cash Flows:

Table 7.43: Assignment of Appearance Numbers

	Year 1			Year 2			Year 3	
CIF	Prob.	App. Num.	CIF	Prob.	App. Num.	CIF	Prob.	App. Num.
80,000	0.20	0,1	60,000	0.10	0	50,000	0.30	0,1,2
45,000	0.60	2,3,4,5,6,7	40,000	0.20	1,2	80,000	0.50	3,4,5,6,7
50,000	0.20	8,9	50,000	0.30	3,4,5	60,000	0.20	8,9
			90,000	0.40	6,7,8,9			

Table 7.44: Simulation of Cash Flows

	Year 1			Year 2			Year 3	
Set No.	CIF	PV CIF @10% 0.909	Set No.	CIF	PV CIF @10% 0.826	Set No.	CIF	PV CIF @10% 0.751
4	45,000	**40,905**	3	50,000	**41,300**	8	60,000	**45,060**
7	45,000	**40,905**	6	90,000	**74,340**	9	60,000	**45,060**
6	45,000	**40,905**	9	90,000	**74,340**	7	80,000	**60,080**
5	45,000	**40,905**	0	60,000	**49,560**	3	80,000	**60,080**
0	80,000	**72,720**	2	40,000	**33,040**	5	80,000	**60,080**

Table 7.45: Addition of PVCIF in Rows

Year 1	Year 2	Year 3	Total PVCIF (ROWS)	Initial Inv.- Res.	Simulated End NPV
40,905	41,300	45,060	**127,265**	130,000	- 2, 735
40,905	74,340	45,060	**160,305**	130,000	30,305
40,905	74,340	60,080	**175,325**	130,000	45,325
40,905	49,560	60,080	**150,545**	130,000	20,545
72,720	33,040	60,080	**165,840**	130,000	35,840
Sum of Simulated NPV					129,280

NB: Find the Average Simulated NPV:

= $\dfrac{129,280}{5}$

= **GHS 25,856**

Probability:
From the computation above the probability of NPV= 0 is 0.20 (i.e., 1/5) since only one of the simulated NPVs was negative.

Decision: Accept the project since it is worthwhile.

Illustration 7.27
Adom Company Limited is planning to purchase a new machine but the cash flows attached cannot be correctly estimated due to the high uncertainty associated with them. The following probabilities have been assigned to the cash flow:

Table 7.46: Cash Flows and Probability Distribution

Year 1		Year 2		Year 3	
Cash flow	Probability	Cash flow	Probability	Cash flow	Probability
15,000	0.30	10,000	0.20	15,000	0.35
25,000	0.40	20,000	0.10	10,000	0.25
50,000	0.20	25,000	0.25	30,000	0.25
40,000	0.10	30,000	0.45	25,000	0.15

The cost of the new machine is GHS 60,000 and a scrap value of GHS 8,000. Consider a discount factor of 12% and thereby simulate the net present values (NPVs) using the random numbers provided, to establish the viability of this investment proposal.

Table 7.46: Appearance Numbers

Year	Set 1	Set 2	Set 3	Set 4	Set 5
1	2	3	1	4	6
2	8	2	0	2	9
3	4	7	6	8	1

Solution: Simulation of Cash Flows:

Table 7.47: Assignment of Appearance Numbers

Year 1			Year 2			Year 3		
CIF	Prob.	App. Num.	CIF	Prob.	App. Num.	CIF	Prob.	App. Num.
15,000	0.30	**0,1,2**	10,000	0.20	**0,1**	15,000	0.30	**0,1,2**
25,000	0.40	**3,4,5,6,**	20,000	0.10	**2**	10,000	0.20	**3,4**
50,000	0.20	**7,8**	25,000	0.30	**3,4,5**	30,000	0.10	**5**
40,000	0.10	**9**	30,000	0.40	**6,7,8,9**	25,000	0.40	**6,7,8,9**

Table 7.48: Simulation of Cash Flows

Year 1			Year 2			Year 3		
Set No.	CIF	PV CIF @12% 0.893	Set No.	CIF	PV CIF @12% 0.797	Set No.	CIF	PV CIF @12% 0.712
2	15,000	**13,395**	8	30,000	**23,910**	4	10,000	**7,120**
3	25,000	**22,325**	2	20,000	**15,940**	7	25,000	**17,800**
1	15,000	**13,395**	0	10,000	**7,970**	6	25,000	**17,800**
4	25,000	**22,325**	2	20,000	**15,940**	8	25,000	**17,800**
6	25,000	**22,325**	9	30,000	**23,910**	1	15,000	**10,680**

Table 7.49: Addition of PVCIF in Rows

Year 1	Year 2	Year 3	Total PVCIF (Rows)	Initial Inv.- Res.	Simulated End NPV
13,395	23,910	7,120	**44,425**	52,000	**(7,575)**
22,325	15,940	17,800	**56,065**	52,000	**4,065**
13,395	7,970	17,800	**39,165**	52,000	**(12,835)**
22,325	15,940	17,800	**56,065**	52,000	**4,065**
22,325	23,910	10,680	**56,915**	52,000	**4,915**
Sum of Simulated NPV					**(7,365)**

NB: Find the average simulated NPV

= (7,365)
   ———
     5

= **GHS (1,473)**

Probability:
From the computation above the probability of NPV= 0 is 0.40 (i.e., 2/5) since only two of the simulated NPVs were negative.

Decision:
Based on NPV acceptance criteria, the project is not worthwhile and it should be rejected since it has a negative average NPV (i.e., GHS **-1,473**). However, since there is a 60% chance of securing a positive NPV, the firm can reconsider its earlier decision of outright rejection of the project.

7.17 Chapter Review Questions

1. What are the key factors that affect a firm's capital budgeting decision?

2. Define the term 'risk-adjusted discount rate' (RADR)?

3. Explain the key types of risk that affect a firm's capital investment decision

4. The following table presents 4 years cash inflows. The certainty coefficients for the cash flows are also given which presents the probability of the occurrence of cash flows.

Year	Cash Inflows (GHS)	Certainty Coefficient
1	170,000	0.7
2	150,000	0.9
3	60,000	0.7
4	180,000	0.2

The Initial cost of the investment is GHS 250,000 and the discount rate is 12% annually. With the help of a certainty equivalent method, find out the NPV and analyze it.

5. Adom Company Ltd. Is seriously considering a cost-savings investment project, which involves acquiring a state-of-the-art equipment to replace an existing machine that has outlived its usefulness. The new machine which costs **GHS** 2.1m will result in annual savings on wages cost of **GHS 9**0,000 and material cost of **GHS** 200,000. The following forecast are made in respect of rates of inflation each year for the next five years:

- Wage Costs: 12%
- Material Cost   8%
- General Price   10%

The cost of capital of the company in money terms is 15%

Required: Evaluate the project, assuming that the machine has a lifespan of five years and no scrap value.

6. Adom Company has taken a decision to invest in a machine that will cost GHS 1,000,000 to buy. The machine will help to produce 10,000 units per annum for this new product line. A standard cost card has been produced as follows:

	GHS
Materials	15
Labour	9
Variable Overheads	8
Fixed Overheads (excluding depreciation)	5
Depreciation	3
	40

The Company has fixed selling price for the year at GHS 50 per unit given a budgeted profit of GHS 10 per unit. It is the policy of the firm to increase the selling price by 10% per annum from the beginning of every year.

The machine is expected to last for five years and at the end of which period, the machine will be sold for a scrap proceeds of GHS 50,000 (this is an estimate of the actual cash to be received). It is established that with the exception of selling price and the scrap proceeds, all estimates are in current prices, and it is anticipated that the costs will inflate at the following rates:

- Materials 6% per annum
- Labour 8% per annum
- Overheads 6% per annum (in line with Retail Price Index)

The Company's accounting year starts from 1st January to 31st December of each year and all flows are to be assumed to occur at the ends of each year except the purchase price on 1st January of the year of investment. The cost of capital is 15% per annum. You are to compute the net present value of this investment and indicate whether the investment is worthwhile.

7. A company is considering the purchase of an equipment to save its costs. The relevant data for net present value analysis of the equipment is given below:
- Cost of the equipment: GHS 440,000
- Expected annual cash savings before tax to be provided by the equipment: GHS 150,000
- Useful life of the equipment: 5 years
- Expected residual or salvage value of the equipment at the end of 5-year period: GHS 20,000
- Tax rate: 50%
- Discount rate: 15%

The equipment is to be depreciated using straight line method of depreciation. The company does not deduct salvage value from the cost of the equipment for computing depreciation for tax purpose. Determine net present value of the investment.

8. ABA Company Ltd. is considering a new venture to manufacture rubber products. This requires machinery costing GHS 200,000, with a life-span of five years and a terminal value of GHS 5,000. Profits before depreciation from the project will be GHS 15,000 p.a. However, there will be cash flows which will differ from profits by the built-up of working capital during the first year of operations and its run-down during the fifth year, amounting to GHS 8,000.

Tax-allowance on the equipment is estimated at 20% p.a. on a reducing balance basis. At the end of the project's life a balancing charge or allowance will arise equal to the difference between the scrap proceeds and the tax written down value.

Tax is payable one year after the end of the accounting year on which it is based, at a rate of 30%. The start of the project is definitely, the start of the accounting year. Cost of Capital is 12%. You are required to examine the viability of this project.

7.18 Chapter References and Bibliography

[1] Becker, W., Rowson, J., Oakley, J. E., Yoxall, A., Manson, G., & Worden, K. (2011). Bayesian sensitivity 612 analysis of a model of the aortic valve. Journal of Biomechanics, 44(8), 1499–1506. 613 https://doi.org/10.1016/j.jbiomech.2011.03.008.

[2] Koks, E. E., Rozenberg, J., Zorn, C., Tariverdi, M., Vousdoukas, M., Fraser, S. A., ... & Hallegatte, S. (2019). A global multi-hazard risk analysis of road and railway infrastructure assets. *Nature communications*, *10*(1), 2677.

[3] Lindsay, R. & Sametz, W.A. (1963). *Financial Management: An Analytical Approach* (Home- wood, Ill.: Richard D. Irwin, Inc.

[4] Malenko, A. (2019). Optimal dynamic capital budgeting. *The Review of Economic Studies*, *86*(4), 1747-1778.

[5] Ribeiro, A., Silva, C. S. J. E., Ferraz Filho, A. C., & Scolforo, J. R. S. (2018). Financial and risk analysis of African mahogany plantations in Brazil. *Ciência e Agrotecnologia*, *42*(2), 148-158.

[6] Robichek, A. A., & Myers, S. C. (1966). Conceptual problems in the use of risk-adjusted discount rates. *The Journal of Finance*, *21*(4), 727-730.

[7] Saltelli, A., Aleksankina, K., Becker, W., Fennell, P., Ferretti, F., Holst, N., ... & Wu, Q. (2019). Why so many published sensitivity analyzes are false:

A systematic review of sensitivity analysis practices. *Environmental modelling & software*, *114*, 29-39. 10.1016/j.envsoft.2019.01.012.

[8] Waters D (2011) *Quantitative Methods for Business*, 5th ed. Pearson Education Limited, London.

[9] Weitzman, M. L. (2010). Risk-adjusted gamma discounting. *Journal of Environmental Economics and Management*, *60*(1), 1-13.

7.19 Recommended Reading List

[1] Albrecht, G. R. (2011). A review of the three arguments used to justify including a risk-premium in the discount factor. *Journal of. Legal Economics.*, *18*, 1.

[2] Schwab, B. (1978). Conceptual problems in the use of risk-adjusted discount rates with disaggregated cash flows. *Journal of Business Finance & Accounting*, *5*(4).

[3] Tibiletti, L. (2022). One-size risk-adjusted discount rate does not fit all risky projects. *The Journal of Risk Finance*, *23*(3), 289-302.

[4] Galigekere, V. P., Onar, O., Pries, J., Zou, S., Wang, Z., & Chinthavali, M. (2018, June). Sensitivity analysis of primary-side LCC and secondary-side series compensated wireless charging system. In *2018 IEEE Transportation Electrification Conference and Expo (ITEC)* (pp. 885-891). IEEE.

CHAPTER 8

VALUATION OF BUSINESSES

8.1 Overview

Valuation of business is an important exercise since it can help identify mispriced companies or securities or determine what projects a company should invest in. However, intrinsic value is a concept that refers to a security's perceived value on the basis of future earnings or other attributes that are not related to a firm's market value. Therefore, the work of analysts when doing valuation is to know if an investment or a company is undervalued or overvalued by the market.

Objectives of the Chapter

This topic seeks to achieve the following objectives:

- To explain what is meant by business valuation;
- To explain the concept of standard of value and premise of value in business valuation;
- To examine the main factors that trigger business valuation; and
- To explain the various the main methods of business valuation with worked examples.

> **Key Words Used in the Chapter**
> - Assets-based approach
> - Capitalizing earrings
> - Fair market value
> - Going concern approach
> - Liquidation value
> - Premise of value
> - Standard of value
> - Super-profit approach

8.2 Definition of Valuation of Business

Valuation of business refers to the process and set of procedures used to measure or estimate the economic worth (value) of an owner's interest in a business. Valuation is a concept used by financial market participants to estimate the price that they (buyers) are willing to pay or receive (sellers) to affect the sale of a business.

As the name suggests, a business valuation determines the value of a business or company. During the process, all areas of a business are carefully analyzed, including its financial performance, assets and liabilities, market position, and future growth potential. Ultimately, the goal is to arrive at a fair and objective estimate, which can be useful in making business decisions and negotiations.

Knowing how much a business is worth can be useful in a variety of scenarios. For example, the Ghana Revenue Authority may use business valuation methods to determine taxes on a company. Small business owners can also use business valuation methods to figure out how much they can sell their business for. The most common place to find business valuations is the finance industry, though. Certain careers in finance rely on business valuation to inform investing decisions. Investment bankers, for example, use a variety of business valuation methods to figure out how much a company is worth for a merger or acquisition. Business valuation can also help determine if a company is worth investing in. The valuation of entities is a complex task due to the fact that they operate as branded businesses, wherein a substantial portion of the alienable value is represented by the brand asset. Empirical evaluation of enterprises that possess substantial intangible assets presents a challenge for conventional financial valuation methods (Lie & Lie 2002).

8.3 Standard of Value

This refers to the hypothetical conditions that will be used to calculate the company's valuation. It is concerned with determining the type of value used in a certain transaction. Depending on the circumstances, each of these four company valuation factors will yield a different figure indicating the value of the firm. This version attempts to convey value as a function of context or to a specific owner or purchaser, as well as worth in relation to the multiple contexts to which the standard is applied. Just as liquidation value would be an inappropriate metric to use to determine the value of a going concern in an M&A transaction, fair market value may be insufficient to reflect value in shareholder disputes where discounts for lack of control and marketability would devalue the interests of an oppressed minority.

The four criteria used to determine a company's worth are as follows:

8.3.1 Fair Market Value

Businesses are appraised using the fair market value (FMV) criterion from the perspective of a neutral third party, or rational investor. The fair market value criterion seeks to ascertain how the market perceives the worth of the firm in question. The FMV criteria assesses value through the eyes of a reasonable third-party investor, such as a stock buyer. Therefore, when the term "fair market value" is applied universally, it refers to the amount that a commodity would be exchanged for in a transaction involving two parties who are willing to do business together, have adequate knowledge of each other, and are not coerced in any way. In publicly traded markets, Anderson (2009) suggests that the definition of "fair market value" is frequently straightforward to implement. The estimation of equity value in publicly traded companies is possible in such markets based on the quantity of outstanding shares and actual market transactions involving equity shares. "The price, expressed in cash equivalents, at which property would change hands in an open and unrestricted market between a hypothetical willing and able buyer and a hypothetical willing and able seller acting at arm's length, when neither is under compulsion to buy or sell and both have reasonable knowledge of the relevant facts." FMV business valuations are used to estimate value for transactions, investment decisions, and legal procedures, and they serve as the foundation for the vast majority of property tax assessments.

8.3.2 Investment Value

This measure of value refers to a company's worth to a certain party or investor and is sometimes referred to as strategic value. Due to the anticipation of business synergy, the value of a firm to a rival, supplier, or customer is often greater than it would be to a reasonable third-party investor. Investment value fluctuates based on the worth of the business to the particular buyer; for instance, the firm may be more valuable to one rival than to another. In merger and acquisition (M&A) transactions, investment value is nearly invariably the metric used to calculate value. It is essentially a value estimate based on a stake that the merged firm will be more valuable and create more profits. Goodwill is the premium paid for a firm beyond the fair market value of its physical and intangible assets.

8.3.3 Fair Value

This is a value metric that is commonly used in accounting or regulatory reporting; while it generally correlates to fair market value, the two are not identical. Fair value as a legal metric may be used in shareholder disputes or divorce processes, depending on the nation. To ensure that dissident parties are not penalized for the lack of control that led to the dispute, the fair value would eliminate discounts for lack of marketability and lack of control. Furthermore, unless a party's commercial interest is sold to a third party, loss of control often has little impact on value. In M&A transactions, the acquiring company allocates purchase prices based on fair value. All other valuation rules are based on the assumption that the business will continue to operate, either independently or as part of a larger corporation. Clearly, a problematic company is less valuable than a wanted, growing business. As a result, liquidation value will take into account value in the context of a company's dissolution. The liquidation value is calculated using fundamentally different assumptions than the continuing company valuation. In general, the firm will not have enough cash flows to cover its operational expenses or debt commitments, forcing it to file for bankruptcy or dissolve. Insolvent businesses, on the other hand, may have significant intellectual property (IP). Customers, patents, trademarks, and copyrights all have the potential to increase the value of intellectual property.

8.3.4 Liquidation Value

All other valuation rules are predicated on the assumption that the business will continue to operate, either independently or as part of an acquiring company. Clearly, a troubled firm is less valuable than a desired, thriving enterprise. Consequently, liquidation value will be considered in the context of a company's dissolution. The liquidation value computation is based on fundamentally different assumptions than the valuation of a continuing company. Generally, the firm will not have sufficient cash flows to cover its operational expenditures or debt commitments and will be forced to file for bankruptcy or dissolve. However, insolvent firms may own significant intellectual property (IP). Customers, patents, trademarks, and copyrights may add to the value of intellectual property. The value of the assets will be determined based on a rapid and piecemeal sale.

8.4 Premise of Value

This refers to the value that is related to the assumptions, such as the going concern. It is based on the most likely scenario involving a collection of transactional events that may be important to the subject property's worth. The facts and circumstances related to the asset to be valued, as well as the motivation for completing the valuation, should be expressed in the valuation assumption. Many components of the valuation will be affected by the premise, including the valuation base, procedures, and methodology, among others. Before it may be included in the engagement letter, the client and the valuer must agree on the concept of value. Furthermore, the value premise must be documented. Examples include:

Going-Concern Value
The worth of a firm is calculated on the assumption that it will continue to function in the future.

Liquidation
The net sum that would be obtained if the business was ended and all assets were auctioned off in pieces.

Orderly Liquidation Value
Assets are liquidated in a timely manner

Forced Liquidation
Assets are liquidated as rapidly as possible, for example, through auction sales.

8.5 Reasons for Performing a Valuation
The fundamental premise of relative valuation methods is that, on average, the market accurately determines asset prices. Because these methods depend on the market values of similar companies, they can be wrong over time if a whole sector consistently undervalues or overvalues during a certain period (Mizik & Jacobson, 2009).

Some of the main reasons for performing a valuation are listed below:

- **Buying or selling a Business**
  Buyers and sellers will typically have a difference in the value of a business. Both parties would benefit from a valuation when making their final decision on whether to buy or sell and at what price.

- **Strategic planning**
  A company should only invest in projects that increase its net present value. Therefore, any investment decision is essentially a mini-valuation based on the likelihood of future profitability and value creation.

- o **Capital financing**

    An objective valuation may be useful when negotiating with banks or any other potential investors for funding. Documentation of a company's worth and its ability to generate cash flow enhances credibility with lenders and equity investors.

- o **Securities investing**

    Investing in a security, such as a stock or a bond, is essentially a bet that the security's current market price is not reflective of its intrinsic value. A valuation is required to determine the intrinsic value.

8.5.1 Factors that Influence Valuation of Businesses

Company/ Firm Size

Company size is a commonly used factor when valuing a company. Typically, the larger the business, the higher the valuation will be. Smaller companies often lack market power and suffer more from the loss of key leaders. In addition, larger businesses likely have a well-developed product or service and, as a result, more accessible capital.

Profitability of the Firm

Is your company earning a profit? If so, this is a good sign, as businesses with higher profit margins will be valued higher than those with low margins or profit losses. The primary strategy for valuing your business based on profitability is to understand your sales and revenue data.

Sales and Revenue Targets

Valuing a business based on sales and revenue uses your totals before subtracting operating expenses and multiplying that number by an industry multiple. Your industry multiple is an average of what businesses typically sell for in your industry, so if your multiple is two, companies usually sell for two times (2x) their annual sales and revenue.

Market Traction and Growth Rate

Your business is evaluated in comparison to your competitors when evaluating a company based on market traction and growth rate. Investors are interested in the size of your industry's market share, the extent to which you control it, and the speed at which you can capture a percentage of the market. The valuation of your business will increase as you accelerate your market entry.

Sustainable Competitive Advantage

What sets your product, service, or solution apart from competitors? With this method, the way you provide value to customers' needs will differentiate you from the competition. If this competitive advantage is too difficult to maintain over time, this could negatively impact your business's valuation. A sustainable competitive advantage helps your business build and maintain an edge over competitors or copycats in the future, pricing you higher than your competitors because you have something unique to offer.

Future Growth Potential

Is it anticipated that your market or industry will expand? Alternatively, is there potential for the business to broaden its product line in the future? The valuation of your company will increase if investors are aware that your business is expected to expand in the future. The financial sector is founded on the pursuit of precise definitions of future valuation and current growth potential.

All of the aforementioned characteristics must be taken into account; however, the key to comprehending future value is to ascertain which factors are more significant than others. Various metrics are employed to evaluate public and private enterprises, contingent upon the nature of the business.

8.5.2 Asset-Based Approach to Business Valuation

Basically, this valuation method sums up all the investments in the business. And this can be done using:
    a) Going-concern or
    b) Liquidation basis

8.5.3 Going-Concern Approach

This method enumerates the net balance sheet value of the assets of the business and subtracts the value of its liabilities.

The value of a company that is determined based on the assumption that it will continue to operate for an extended period is known as the "going concern value." In contrast, the liquidation value is based on the assumption that the company will shortly cease operations. The discrepancy between the value of the continuing concern and the company's value if it were liquidated is comprised of intangible assets and goodwill.

For example, a reputable textile company that continues to operate is able to maintain its ability to sell its brand-name products at a premium in order to generate earnings. Subsequently, the "going concern value" would be employed to determine its value.

However, in the event that the company ceases operations, it will be necessary for it to liquidate its assets, including fabric and stitching machines, in order to satisfy its account payables and prevent bankruptcy. In this scenario, the firm's value would be determined by the amount it would be worth if it were to cease operations and be liquidated.

The buyer typically pays a price that exceeds the value of the assets being acquired by the target company when one company acquires another. The company's reputation in the marketplace or the value of its continuing operation as a going concern are the reasons for the increased cost.

8.5.4 Liquidation Asset-based Approach

This method ascertains the net cash that would be received if all assets were liquidated and liabilities were settled. The liquidation value is an asset-based approach that is determined by the value that the company would receive if it were to promptly sell the asset on the open market. When we state that an asset can be sold immediately, we mean as soon as possible, typically within six to twelve months. This approach evaluates the asset's age, degree of deterioration, and recent technological advancements in pertinent fields.

The book value and the liquidation value are significantly different. This is due to the fact that assets that lack book value may still have a liquidation value.

This is a common occurrence for assets that are rapidly depreciated or written off. Moreover, the company's assets may appreciate in value over time, regardless of whether this development is recorded in the company's accounts.

The liquidation plan is predicated on the premise that the company has failed and must promptly dispose of its assets. The assets may be sold as part of a systematic procedure, such as the liquidation of an insolvent corporation. The book value adjustment methodology does not account for the urgency of the sale or the prospective market price of the asset in the event of the company's insolvency.

8.5.4.1 Limitations of Liquidation Assets-Based Approach
1. Failure to account for the entity's value as a going concern.
2. Inability to calculate the value of intangible assets in an acceptable manner. This is especially significant for a wide variety of businesses just beginning operations. These assets are notoriously difficult to value due to the fact that they frequently only have worthwhile the business is operating, such as:
   - ✓ Brand recognition;
   - ✓ Intellectual property;
   - ✓ Industry repute;
   - ✓ Human capital (knowledge or expertise);
   - ✓ Property rights (trademarks, trade secrets, patents, copyrights. etc.,

8.5.5 Income Approach to Business Valuation
This income approach is used to ascertain the fair market value by dividing the benefit stream generated by the subject or target firm by a discount or capitalization rate. Essentially, the income approach is a business valuation technique that employs an income approach to determine the value of a firm by considering the predicted future value of the company, the annual rate of return, and the present cash flow.

A discount or capitalization rate is used to convert the stream of benefits into present value. The discount rate is frequently employed in DCF (discounted cash flow) valuations to estimate the cost of capital for the business and calculate the NPV of a series of projected cash flows.

8.6 Present Value of Future Receipts (PVFR)

The present value of a company's anticipated future profits or financial flows is considered when determining the value of a business using the income method. The company's earnings are initially estimated, and the projected cash flows or future profits are subsequently adjusted to reflect changes in growth rates, tax structures, and other factors, among others.

This valuation procedure indicates that the procuring entity (purchaser) is purchasing a stream of future returns (cash flows). The purchaser acquires the disparity between its own cash flows prior to the acquisition and the combined companies' cash flows subsequent to the acquisition, as stated by Samuels et al. (1999). In order to calculate the NPV, it is necessary to estimate, discount, and sum this discrepancy.

The receipts from the purchase can be expressed mathematically as:

$$PVr = \frac{C}{V}\left[1 - \frac{1}{(1+r)^n}\right] \quad \text{Equation-------8.1}$$

Where:
PVr = Present Value of returns
C = increase in the annual cash flow of the purchasing as a result of the acquisition
r = Discount factor
n = Number of years

Illustration 8.1

Adom Company Ltd. has purchased XYZ Ltd., and as a result of the acquisition, the annual cash flow of Adom Company has increased by GHS 35,500.00, the appropriate discount factor (rate) is 10%, and the number of years over which the returns will be taken into account is 50 years. The value of the acquisition can be calculated as follows:

$$PVr = \frac{35,500}{0.10}\left[1 - \frac{1}{(1.10)^{50}}\right]$$

$$= 355{,}000\ (1-0.0085)$$

$$= 355{,}000\ (0.9915)$$

$$= \underline{\mathbf{GH}¢\ \mathbf{351{,}982.50}}$$

Illustration 8.2

Assume that detailed forecasts of the cash flows are made for the first five years with the following cash flow estimates: 20,000, 32,000, 45,000, 29,000, and 26,000, with an appropriate discount rate of 10%. Also assume that these cash flows are expected to grow at an annual rate of 4% (p.a.). The horizon is taken as 50 years, and cash flows beyond this point are ignored; hence, the value of the company to be purchased is estimated as follows:

$$\frac{20{,}000}{(1.10)^1} + \frac{32{,}000}{(1.10)^2} + \frac{45{,}000}{(1.10)^3} + \frac{29{,}000}{(1.10)^4} + \frac{26{,}000}{(1.10)^5} + \frac{26{,}000(1.04)}{(1.10)^6} + \frac{2{,}600(1.04)^{45}}{(1.10)^{50}}$$

$$= \frac{20{,}000}{1.1} + \frac{32{,}000}{1.21} + \frac{45{,}000}{1.331} + \frac{29{,}000}{1.4641} + \frac{26{,}000}{1.61051} + \frac{27{,}040}{1.772} + \frac{151{,}870.57}{117.30}$$

$= 18{,}181.82 + 26{,}446.28 + 33{,}809.17 + 19{,}807.39 + 16{,}143.95 + 15.26 + 1{,}294.92$

$$= \underline{115{,}698.79}$$

8.6.1 Problems of PVFR:
1. Difficulty of forecasting future annual cash flows
2. The choice of appropriate discount rate based on risk element
3. The Estimated numbers of years' cash flows on which the calculation will be based.

8.7 Valuation by Capitalizing Earnings

The capitalization of earnings is a method that can be employed to determine the value of a company. This method is employed to ascertain the net present value (NPV) of an organization's anticipated future cash flows or profits. NPV is an acronym for "net present value." To determine this evaluation, the anticipated future profits of the organization are initially divided by the capitalization rate, and the resulting sum is then multiplied by the same rate. This procedure is repeated in order to determine the final number in accordance with the formula:

$$\text{Business value} = \frac{\text{Annual Future Earnings}}{\text{Required Rate of Return}} = \frac{AFE}{r} \quad \text{Equation --------- 8.3}$$

AFE= Annual future earnings (cash flow)
r = Required rate of return

This is one of the most straightforward methods of evaluating the value of a company. Here, a predetermined conception of the rate of return that an investor (purchaser) would anticipate in this specific investment case is established by determining the earnings of the company to be purchased. This is followed by the calculation of a capital sum that would generate such a return.

Key steps:
- Select the past period for the investigation;
- Estimate the maintainable profits (earnings) after making adjustment for directors' remuneration, depreciation or bad debt;
- Estimate the acceptable normal rate of return on capital invested in a similar type of company, considering the industry effect; the size of company and the level of capital earring; and
- Capitalize the maintainable the maintainable rate of return.

Illustration 8.3
Assume that XYZ Company Ltd. is engaged in the management of automobile assembly. In the year 2019, the Board of Directors of the company was presented with a takeover offer, which they subsequently discussed. They spoke about the offer, and in the end, they decided that what they really wanted was for the Chief Financial Officer of the company to give them a presentation. The required rate of return for the company was established at 15.5 percent, and the company's future profit projections came in at GHS 60 million. Ascertain the value of the firm.

$$\text{Business value} = \frac{\text{Annual future earnings}}{\text{Required rate of return}}$$

$$= \frac{AFE}{r}$$

$$= \frac{GHS\ 60{,}000{,}000}{0.155}$$

= **GHS 387,096,774.19**

Hence, the value of the Company is **GHS 387,096,774.19**

Illustration 8.4

Assume that the maintainable earnings after corporate tax of a company is GHS 1,000,000, and the normal rate of return for such companies is 20%. The purchase price is computed as:

$$\frac{1{,}000{,}000}{0.20}$$

= **GHS 5,000,000.00**

8.8 Super-Profit Approach (SPA)

This is the most frequently implemented valuation methodology. The objective of this approach is to establish a standard rate of return for assets of a specific nature. However, it may be feasible to generate profits that exceed this standard level over a specified period of time. Therefore, the investor will acquire a number of years of supernormal profits in addition to the normalized value of the assets.

Steps Required in SPA

a. Value the net asset of the business on a going-concern basis.

b. Establish an acceptable rate of return on assets of this type.
   c. Find the annual profits that would be assumed to result from the use of the assets so as to earn the rate established in (b)
   d. Estimate the profits that can be expected to be earned by the business over the next few years.
   e. Deduct the acceptable profit amount in (c) From the estimated profit in(d)
   f. If the estimate is higher the difference is regarded as super-profit.
   g. Multiply the super-profits by a factor to be agreed: say 5 or 10 to represent the number of year's super-profits being purchased.
   h. The value of the business is **(a)** plus **(g)** (that is the value of the net assets plus, say 10years purchase of super-profits.

Illustration 8.5

Assume that the net assets of the business are valued at GHS 800,000 and the normal rate of return on such an investment is 10%.

From steps (b) these steps can be followed:

c) A 10% return on 800,000 results in profits of GHS 80,000.

d) Assume profits are estimated as being GHS150,000 for the next few years.

e) The difference between the estimated and the acceptable level is
   GHS (150,000 – 80,000) = GHS 70,000

f) there is a super profit of GHS 5,000 per annum

g) It is agreed to purchase 10years super-profits = 70,000 x 10years

h) The value of the company would compute as follows:

Net assets valued at GHS 800,000 + 10 years super-projects
GHS 800,000 + 700,000

= GHS 1,500,000.00

Illustration 8.6

ABI Company Ltd. is a medium-scale company noted for the production of high-quality local aluminum products. In recent years, the company has experienced turbulence in its business operations as a result of unending cash flow problems due to an expected fall in local demand. An investor, Mr. AFUMI, has expressed an interest in acquiring ABI Company Ltd. for the strategic reason of turning it around. The valuation of the company (ABI) is based on a super-profit approach, as agreed by the negotiating parties. The net assets of the company are valued at GHS 5 million, and the normal rate of return on such investments is estimated to be 10% p.a. over the life-span of the company. Information available indicates that ABI Company Ltd. is expected to make a profit of GHS 850,000.00 p.a. over the next few years as compared to its previous annual profit of GHS 500,000.00. As part of the negotiations, the investor has agreed to the purchase of eight years' supper profits. You have been engaged as the financial consultant to value ABI Company Ltd. based on the super-profit approach. Compute the economic value of ABI Company Ltd.

Solution

Steps:

i. Value of the net assets of **ABI Company Ltd.** = **GHS 5,000,000.00**

ii. Normal profit level based on the normal rate of return of 10% on the net asset value:

$$= \frac{10 \times 5,000,000.00}{100}$$

= **GHS 500,000.00**

iii. Expected future profit = **GHS 850,000.00**

iv. Super-profit Computation
Super profit = Expected future profit minus Normal annual profit

$$= 850,000.00 - 500,000.00$$

= GHS **350,000.00** per year

Super profit for 8years = GHS 350,000 x 8

= **GHS 2,800,000.00**

Valuation of **ABI** Company Ltd.
Total purchase value = net asset value + 15-years super profits

$$=5,000,000.00 + 2,800,000.00$$

$$= \underline{\textbf{GHS 7,800,000.00}}$$

8.9 Discounted Cash Flow (DCF) method

Many businesses value themselves using the discounted cash flow (DCF) method, which is an example of an income strategy. This approach is based on the idea that a company's total worth may be calculated by adding the present value of its predicted future profits to the present value of its terminal value. The procedure begins with a forecast of the company's cash flow over a specified future time period.

In accordance with Mizik & Jacobson (2009), conducting a DCF valuation necessitates the estimation of future cash flows and a discount rate that is contingent upon the firm's level of risk.

Then, the probability of getting each individual cash flow at the projected period is included in the discount rate used to determine its present value. Items including capital expenditures, operational expenses, income, and working capital are projected as accurately as possible.

The DCF method is utilized by professional analysts and investors at investment banks. It is used for determining the amount of money that should be paid for a business.

Here is the equation for finding the DCF:

$$DCF = CF_1/(1+r)^1 + CF_2/(1+r)^2 + \ldots + CF_n/(1+r)^n$$

This is essentially what the DCF equation accomplishes. It converts the expected future cash flows from an investment into their present value today. Obviously, this is predicated on the compounded rate of return you may reasonably expect to obtain with your money today. Analyzing the predicted discounted cash flows can help you decide which investments are viable and which are not, whether you are preparing to acquire an entire firm or have someone invest in your business.

With that established, let us apply the DCF method to determine the worth of a firm. Assume you are an investor who has been given a proposal to buy a 10% interest in a company that has been on the market for a long time. And in this instance, you are also extremely familiar with the owner.

This company has been passed down through four generations and is currently going strong. It expands at a pace of roughly 5% every year. It currently generates around GHS 2,000,000 in free cash flow per year. So, if you agree to invest 10% in the firm, you will receive GHS 200,000 every year in cash. And it would continue to increase at a rate of 5% every year.

The corporation will provide GHS 200,000 this year. Certainly, you will receive GHS 210,000 the next year, GHS 220,500 the next, etc. (this is obviously assuming that the growth estimates are accurate). Your firm's ownership is worth the sum of all future cash flows. Given that this is a private firm deal with limited liquidity, imagine you want a 15% annual return. If you know you can achieve this rate of return on the investment, you would only buy this business stake if it was cheap enough. All future cash flows are discounted at 15% compounded.

That is with each of those cash flows being discounted to their present value per the subsequent table:

Table 8.1 Discounted Cash Flows

Years	Actual CF @5% Growth GHS	DF @15%	PV Future CF GHS
1	200,000.00	0.870	174,000
2	210,000.00	0.756	158,760
3	220,500.00	0.657	144,868.5
4	231,525.00	0.572	132,432.3
5	243,101.25	0.497	120,821.32
6	255,256.31	0.432	110,270.73
7	268,019.13	0.376	100,775.19
8	281,420.08	0.327	92,024.37
9	295,491.09	0.284	83,919.47
10	310,265.64	0.247	76,635.61
NPV			1,194,507.49

8.10 Market Value Approach

This valuation method attempts to establish the value of a business by comparing it to similar businesses that have been sold recently. The market comparison approach, or market-based approach, refers to a business valuation technique in which, irrespective of the asset under valuation, prices of comparable assets are made and proper adjustments for other similar variables such as quantities, qualities, or sizes are made. For instance, when you want to determine the value of equity shares, you should look at the recent selling price of similar equity shares. Since the share ownership of a company is usually identical, the recent selling price of the shares will provide a good estimation of their fair value.

8.11 Approaches to Market Comparison Methods

Under the market approach, a valuation analyst can select from a variety of different approaches to determining an asset's worth using a variety of different methodologies. The names of the procedures are chosen in accordance with the origin of the known values that serve as recommendations. Under the market approach, the two primary approaches to value that are utilized are as follows:

- **Public Company Comparisons**

The use of valuation indicators from firms that have been traded publicly is required in order to conduct the public company comparison. These companies are thought to be appropriately comparable to the entity under consideration. Direct comparison is difficult to achieve in most circumstances due to the fact that the majority of publicly traded firms are not only larger but also more different from the topic at hand. In spite of this, the direct comparison criterion needs to have a little bit of wiggle room in it so that public firms that have comparable business characteristics are not prevented from providing direction on the value of the subject company.

In most cases, guideline firms are companies that have been traded publicly in an industry that is either comparable to or identical to that of the subject company.

- **Precedent Transactions**

This requires generating value through the use of price multiples that are founded on the observed transactions of other businesses operating in the same industry as the subject firm. It is predicated on the notion that access to detailed information on a company's financial standing is difficult to come by, whereas transaction value is readily available. In addition, there exist databases of valuations that may be investigated for proof of previous actuals and valuations.

8.11.1 Key Comparison Indicators

The valuer needs to take into account a number of elements in order to determine whether or not one firm is comparable enough to the other to be employed in the process of calculating the value of the other company. Some of these considerations are as follows:
- Whether or whether the businesses in question are active participants in the same market;
- To what extent do they contend with one another for the same business?
- Regardless of whether they provide the same items or services;

- The geographical locations of the businesses; and
- Whether or whether they make earnings that are comparable to us.

Advantages
1. It is not complicated and only requires some easy calculations.
2. It utilizes data that is both actual and available to the public.
3. It is not contingent on speculative projections in any way.

Disadvantages
1. Both the quantity of data that can be accessed and the quality of the data both become problematic as a result of utilizing this technique.
2. There is a possibility that it will be difficult to find transactions or firms that are identical to one another. The majority of the time, there is not a sufficient number of organizations or transactions that are analogous to the one that is being considered.
3. When compared to other options, this one provides a significantly lower level of adaptability.

8.12 Chapter Review Questions

1. Define the term 'Valuation of business'
2. Distinguish between standard of value and premise of value.
3. Explain the main criteria used to determine the standard of value.
4. Explain the main reasons why business valuation takes place.
5. Examine the following methods of business valuation:
    i. Asset-based approach to business valuation.
    ii. Income-based approach to business valuation.
    iii. Market value approach to business valuation.

6. ABC Co. Ltd. has purchased ABA Co. Ltd. and as a result of the acquisition, the annual cash flow of ABC has increased by GH₵2,500.00 and the appropriate discount factor (rate) is 12% and the number of years over which the returns will be taken place into account is 30yrs. Compute the value of the acquisition.

7. Assume that the detailed forecasts of the cash flows are made for the first five years with the ff. cash flow estimates: 10,000, 15,000, 25,000, 20,000 and 25,000 with appropriate discount rate of 12%. Also assume that these cash flows are expected to grow at an annual rate of 5% (p.a.). The horizon is taken as 45years, and that cash flows beyond this point are ignored. Compute the value of the company to be purchased.

8. ABAMA Company Ltd. is a medium-scale company noted for the production of high-quality local aluminum products. In recent years the company is experiencing turbulence in its business operations as a result of unending cash flow problems due to an expected fall in local demand. An investor, Mr. AFUMI has expressed an interest in acquiring ABAMA Company Ltd. for the strategic reason of turning it around. The valuation of the company (ABC) is based on a super-profit approach as agreed by the negotiating parties. The net assets of the company are valued at GHS 3.6 million and the normal rate of return on such investment is estimated to be 4.5% p.a. over the life-span of the company. Information available indicates that ABAMA Company Ltd. is expected to make a profit of GHS 300,000.00 p.a. over the next few years as compared to its previous annual profit of GHS 600,000.00. As part of the negotiations, the investor has agreed the purchase of 18 years' supper-profits. You have been engaged as the Financial Consultant to value ABAMA Company Ltd. based on the Super-profit approach. Compute the economic value of ABAMA Company Ltd.

9. Assume that XYZ Company Ltd., is engaged in the management of automobile assembling. In the year 2022, the Board of Directors of the company were presented with a takeover offer, which they subsequently discussed. They spoke about the offer, and in the end, they decided that what they really wanted was for the Chief Financial Officer of the company to give them a presentation. The required rate of return for the company was established at 15.5 percent, and the company's future profits projections came in at GHS 40 million. Ascertain the value of the firm. Assume that the maintainable earnings after corporate tax of a company is GHS 100,000 and the normal rate of return in such companies is 15%.

8.13 Chapter References and Bibliography

[1] Anderson, P. L. (2009). The value of private businesses in the United States. *Business Economics*, *44*(2), 87-108.

[2] Lie, E.& Heidi J. L. (2002). Multiples used to estimate corporate value, *Journal of Financial Analysts*, 58 (2), 44–54.

[3] Mizik, N., & Jacobson, R. (2009). Valuing branded businesses. *Journal of Marketing*, *73*(6), 137-153.

[4] Trugman, G. R. (2016). *Understanding business valuation: A practical guide to valuing small to medium sized businesses*. John Wiley & Sons.

8.14 Recommended Reading List

[1] Damodaran, A. (2009). *The dark side of valuation: Valuing young, distressed, and complex businesses*. Ft Press.

[2] Lerm, M., Rollberg, R., & Kurz, P. (2012). Financial valuation of start-up businesses with and without venture capital. *International Journal of Entrepreneurial Venturing*, *4*(3), 257-275.

[3] Palepu, K. G., Healy, P. M., Wright, S., Bradbury, M., & Coulton, J. (2020). *Business analysis and valuation: Using financial statements*. Cengage AU.

[4] Pratt, S. P. (2006). *The market approach to valuing businesses*. John Wiley & Sons.

CHAPTER 9

BUSINESS ETHICS

9.1 Overview

According to the viewpoint of an individual, the primary purpose of an organization is to generate income. However, from a human perspective, the primary reason for the existence of an organization is to supply human beings with a variety of goods and services. An organization may have the expectation that the individual goals or objectives it pursues will not be in direct opposition to those of society. However, since human beings are in charge of running a business organization, and since every individual human being has his or her own distinctive outlook on life, it is not required that the decisions and actions of a business organization conform to the expectations of society. For instance, a company may have great success in terms of profits and market standing but fail to live up to its social responsibilities despite its commercial achievements. This question inspired the development of the concept of ethics, which seeks to answer it by drawing a connection between what is morally right and wrong and what is for the collective and individual good.

Objectives of the Chapter

The objectives of the chapter are:

- To explain what business ethics are;
- To outline and explain the key essentials of business ethics;
- To examine the key values of business ethics;
- To identify and explain the key business ethics;
- To explain the advantages of sound business ethics;
- To examine the drawback to business ethics; and
- To examine Svensson and Wood's model of business ethics.

> **Key Words Used in the Chapter the Chapter**
>
> ✓ Accountability
> ✓ Business ethics
> ✓ Code of ethics
> ✓ Technology ethics
> ✓ Values of business ethics

9.2 Definition of Business Ethics

The ancient Greek term "ethos" refers to a community's or group's prevalent ideals, norms, and character. The word "ethos" derives from this ancient Greek term. Therefore, ethics may be regarded as the study of moral behavior and the establishment of right and wrong in an individual's acts based on the declared and established norms of moral conduct by society in a specific field of endeavor. This notion of ethics applies to several disciplines, including business, medicine, law, and politics. Ethical behavior may be defined as a collection of norms or a system of regulations that a society imposes on its members in order to achieve human goals.

The word "business ethics" refers to the values, practices, and rules that influence decision-making and the handling of company-related conflicts or concerns. Therefore, when we speak of "business ethics," we mean the set of rules and principles for behaving morally in the context of the corporate world. One of the most essential considerations is how an organization's practices and processes correspond to its broader goals. It is essential to establish an honest connection, not just with consumers but also with the wider public, when operating a business. Ethical business practices include, but are not limited to, treating employees with respect, charging consumers reasonable pricing, offering high-quality goods and services, earning a fair profit, utilizing honest and precise weights and measures, and other practices. Drucker (1981) posits that the fulfillment of role obligations by its constituents is a critical factor in the well-being of any organization.

Donaldson & Dunfee (1994) contend that ethical dilemmas in business can be addressed through the lens of social contract theory. The concept is that, in theory at least, human beings tacitly concur with the formation of societies and at least tacitly agree to laws and regulations governing their behavior in order to live in harmony and achieve their own objectives in relation to others.

A number of philosophers have contended that ethical relativism, the notion that there are no universal moral principles, does not follow from cultural differences and, as a result, cannot be resolved. Nevertheless, Bowie (1996) contends that cultural distinctions should not be conflicted with moral disputes that are unresolvable.

White (2001) contends that modern corporate society creates more intricate ethical concerns. In the past few years, the scope of these concerns has increased. Initially, they were nearly entirely focused on fraudulent behavior or personnel issues in the workplace. These concerns used to receive practically no attention until recently, and even then, they were largely aimed at unethical activity in the workplace or by individuals.

Ethics in business not only helps firms make moral and ethically sound judgments but also helps them develop trust so that they may conduct themselves in a manner that stakeholders view as fair and honest. The owners (investors), paid managers, and staff are all governed by these principles while making ethically pleasing judgments and establishing consumer trust.

This framework outlines the behavior that employees are expected to display in their dealings with one another and with those outside the organization. In addition, it specifies the moral standards upheld by the organization as well as the role it plays within the greater community. Modern businesses formulate their codes of conduct in the form of policies in order to achieve two objectives simultaneously: to reconcile their roles as public citizens with the requirements of their businesses, which are to produce high-quality goods and services while maximizing profits. Businesses in the modern period develop their rules and standards of behavior in order to accomplish these two objectives.

9.3 Principles of Business Ethics

- **Solicit commitment from top management**
  Leadership in an organization is critical to developing an integrity-based culture. They act as a moral compass for the entire organization. To increase performance and establish ethical behavior among business personnel, the CEO and other top-level managers must show a strong personal commitment to ethical conduct. Their adherence to the code of ethics will serve as an example to the rest of the workforce, who will be more inclined to follow suit. They are in charge of motivating employees to progress the organization and preserve its key values.

- **Formulate a policy document on 'code of ethics'**
  Companies with effective ethics programs define organizational-wide norms of behavior in writing. We refer to this collection of spelled-out principles for correct behavior as "code." The code of conduct addresses a variety of issues, including product quality and safety, basic honesty, legal compliance, financial transparency, marketing tactics, employment practices, workplace health and safety, and so forth. An organization cannot function unless certain rules and regulations are strictly followed.

- **Establish compliance mechanisms**
  It is not enough to just publish the code of conduct without also putting mechanisms in place to ensure that workers follow it and that the company's behavior is compatible with the ideas it promotes. During the recruiting process, for example, it is critical to ask candidates about their personal beliefs and ethics, and it is also critical to develop a method for workers to report any instances of unethical behavior anonymously through suggestion boxes fitted at vantage points within the organization.

- **Measure results**
  It is not enough to just publish the code of conduct without also putting mechanisms in place to ensure that workers follow it and that the company's behavior is compatible with the ideas it promotes. During the recruiting process, for example, it is critical to ask candidates about their

personal beliefs and ethics, and it's also critical to develop a method for workers to report any instances of unethical behavior anonymously.

- **Apply punitive measures or sanctions to unethical behaviors**
  Any unethical behavior should be treated with a fair and equitable penalty or punitive action to dissuade others from indulging in the same behavior. The punishments should be imposed without fear or favor on anybody, and they should be applied fairly to everyone. Under no circumstances should any type of compromise be contemplated.

- **Involve employees at all levels**
  Contributions from workers at every level of an organization are necessary in order to make it possible for ethical business practices to be implemented. As a result, it is essential for companies to include their employees in the ethical initiatives they undertake. For example, a company might get together a small number of its employees to discuss the most significant ethical policies it has and to get a feel for how workers feel about those policies.

9.4 Values of Business Ethics

The seven widely acknowledged corporate ethics principles that guide a company's code of conduct Accountability, care and respect, honesty, healthy competition, loyalty, openness, and respect for the rule of law are among the business ethics principles.

- **Accountability**
  Accountability means businesses taking full responsibility for their actions or practices. This includes any bad decisions taken or unethical business practices followed during the course of the firm's dealings.

- **Care and Respect**
  Mutual respect must be maintained among the stakeholders, such as business owners (investors), employees, lenders, account payables (suppliers), and customers (consumers). Businesses need to ensure a safe

working space for employees and encourage a respectful relationship between all stakeholders.

- **Honesty and Integrity**
  Transparent communication between business owners and employees is much desired. This characteristic helps build trust and establish a relationship between employees and the business. Transparency is also applicable to business relationships with its customers.

- **Healthy Competition**
  Businesses should encourage healthy competition among their workforce and reduce conflicts of interest. This will minimize organization conflict, reduce striving and tension among employees, and encourage teamwork and harmonious relationships.

- **Loyalty and Fair Conflict Resolution Mechanisms**
  All disagreements between businesses and their employees should be resolved internally, away from the eyes of the public. More out-of-court settlement, mainly through alternative dispute resolution currently being promoted by the Judicial Service of Ghana, should be encouraged. Employees are to stay faithful to upholding the business vision and promoting business brands. Businesses are also to stay faithful to agreements with employees. Unreasonably interpreting agreements or not respecting commitments is considered unethical business practice.

- **Full Information Disclosure**
  Important information disseminated among a business's customers, employees, or partners is to be provided comprehensively. This includes both positive and negative information, terms and conditions, or any other crucial information, as it is against business ethics to withhold or hide relevant facts.

- **Respect for Rules and Laws (Rule of law)**

Businesses have a duty to uphold and respect corporate laws, rules, and regulations such as the Companies Code Act 179 of 1963, the Incorporated Private Partnership Act of 1962 (Act 152) and the Labour Act of 2003 (Act 651), etc. These laws and rules should serve as guiding business principles and practices that ought to be respected and observed by businesses and their employees alike, as any act that flouts such laws is considered unethical.

9.5 Types of Business Ethics

There are various types of business ethics adopted by businesses, depending on the nature or location of the business. Here are some standard ethical practices adopted by different businesses:

- **Personal Responsibility**
  A level of personal responsibility is expected from business employees. This responsibility may include completing an assigned task, reporting to work at the expected time, or being honest in the workplace. Employees are also expected to own up to their mistakes and work towards correcting them.

- **Corporate Responsibility**
  Businesses should honor their responsibilities to their employees, partners, and customers. They need to respect the interests of all parties involved with the business. These interests may take the form of written contracts, verbal agreements, or legal obligations.

- **Social Responsibility**
  Businesses have a responsibility to the environment where their operations are located. Therefore, businesses are to work towards ensuring environmental protection and giving back to the community through empowerment or investments that improve societal values. One key way businesses have been able to achieve this is through a practice called corporate social responsibility (CRS), which has geared corporations towards environmental protection, community development, and improving the working environment by focusing on people. Figure 1 below outlines the four pillars of CSR. Corporate social responsibility refers to a concept that considers the business as part of society and helps the society address some of its social challenges. Hence, businesses factor economic, social, and environmental concerns into their business activities while simultaneously looking to achieve their aims and objectives.

- **Technology Ethics**

  With businesses now moving their operations to the digital space through the adoption of online market place (e-commerce) practices and the emergence of artificial intelligence (AI), technology-related business ethics are necessary. These ethics include customer data protection, customer privacy, customer personal information protection, fair intellectual properties practices, etc.

- **Trust and Transparency**

  Trust and transparency need to be maintained with stakeholders, including customers, investors, and employees. Businesses must maintain transparency in financial reports to partners and not conceal relevant information from customers.

- **Fairness**

  Biases and personal beliefs are to be avoided in business decision-making processes. The business must ensure a fair and equitable chance for everyone and boost their growth and empowerment.

9.6 Advantages of Ethics in Business

The benefits of business ethics include:

1. **It attracts customer loyalty**

   Customers and investors would rather work with companies that are transparent, so businesses that practice ethics in their dealings with customers and investors can gain a competitive advantage.

2. **It improves corporate image**

   The image of a company is improved when it complies with the standards of business ethics. This makes the company more appealing to potential employees, customers, and investors.

3. It serves as a source of motivation
When business ethics are upheld in business, it helps to create a motivating work environment that employees love to be a part of because it aligns their morals with the morals of the company.

4. It helps to avoid law breaking and prevent payment of fines
Businesses can avoid future legal action, such as large legal fines or the failure of the business as a result of non-compliance with rules and regulations, if they comply with the rules and regulations as soon as possible.

9.7 Drawbacks of Ethics in Business
The drawbacks of business ethics include:

- **It involves a lot of time wasting**
  It takes time for a company to develop, implement, adjust, and maintain its ethics in business, which is especially true when the company is just beginning to recover from a reputation scandal that was caused by poor ethics. Because of the consistently shifting legal requirements and ethical standards that apply to businesses, ethics training needs to be ongoing.

- **Possibility of conflict**
  The possible conflict or trade-off between ethics and the maximization of profitability Business ethics can impact a company's ability to maximize profit opportunities. For example, an ethical company with a manufacturing plant in a developing country would not try to reduce labour costs through unethical means. Such methods could include increasing profits by paying low wages or forcing employees to work unpaid overtime. Instead, an ethical business would ensure that a nurturing work environment is created, even if it means lower profits.

9.8 Svensson and Wood's Model of Business Ethics
Business is established and allowed to exist because, in capitalist societies, it is deemed to have a central and pivotal role in the betterment of society (Joyner & Payne, 2002). When members of a society view this role as not being fulfilled,

individuals, in the extreme, disrupt business forums to protest against the ideologies being touted, such as in the case of globalization.

Society is predicated upon behaviors that it expects will advance itself, and it is not interested in behaviors that will force society to regress. The rights of freedom of speech and of assembly must be lauded because they are an integral part of a group of rights that define who we are. Such rights allow us, as a society, to be self-critical and to re-examine the precepts upon which we claim to be civilized. Also, society does have expectations of business and of its business leaders.

Business can be pure hell because it is relentless in the pursuit of its goals—goals that need to be aligned with those of the society to whom it is responsible, to whom it should have allegiance, and to whom it should ultimately seek to be subservient. These expectations of ethical behavior in business lead to a set of antecedents that frame the business environment in which corporations seek to exist. Each one of these antecedents is important, for they shape the ways in which a society comes to view its corporations and their subsequent performances. These antecedents all conspire independently and collectively to foster behaviors that are seen as acceptable by society.

Corporate scandals involving Enron and notable others have led to the Sarbanes-Oxley Act (Thomas et al., 2004). The US Sentencing Guidelines of 1991 mitigate penalties dependent upon the ethical processes and procedures that corporations have in place to attempt to ensure that the company maintains ethical business practices (McKendall et al., 2002). Governments have also set up watchdogs to monitor the practices of business.

According to Svensson & Wood (2008), the business ethics model is comprised of three principal components:
- Expectations;
- Perceptions; and
- Evaluations.

That is, expectations, perceptions, and evaluations that are interconnected by five sub-components (i.e., society expects; organizational values, norms, and beliefs; outcomes; society evaluates; and reconnection). The introduced model makes a contribution to the creation of a conceptual framework for business ethics. These, according to them, are interconnected by five sub-components (i.e., society expects, organizational values, norms and beliefs, outcomes, society evaluates, and reconnection).

Table: 9.1 Svensson and Wood's Model of Business Ethics

Expectations (Societal)	Perceptions (Values, Norms & Beliefs)	Evaluations (Societal)
o Government Legislation o Lobby Groups o Institutional Responsibilities o Increased Education o Power of Media o Socially Responsible Managers o Professional Associations o Competition o International Business with Integrity	o Leadership Relationships o Staff Relationships o Shareholder Relationships o External Stakeholder Relationships o Supplier Relationships o Customer Relationships o Competitor Relationships	o Economic Outcomes o Lawful Behavior o Better Corporate Citizens o Pay Appropriate Taxes o Environmentally Friendly o Employees Retained o Services Retained o Products Acceptable

9.9 Chapter Review Questions

1. What are business ethics?
2. Examine the key principles of business ethics
3. Explain the main values underlying the concept of business ethics
4. Identify the types of business ethics
5. What are the main advantages and disadvantages of business ethics?
6. Examine Svensson and Wood's model of business ethics

9.10 Chapter References and Bibliography

[1] Bowie, N. (1996). *Relativism, cultural and moral. Ethical issues in business,* ed. T. Donaldson and P. R. Werhane. Upper Saddle River, NJ: Prentice Hall.

[2] Donaldson, T. & Dunfee, T. (1994). Toward a unified conception of business ethics: Integrative social contracts theory. *Academy of Management Review*, 18 (2), 22–284.

[3] Drucker, P. F. (1981). What is business ethics. *The public interest, 63*(2), 18-36.

[4] Joyner, B. E. & D. Payne: 2002, Evolution and Implementation: A study of values, business ethics and corporate social responsibility, *Journal of Business Ethics* 41, 297–311.

[5] McKendall, M., B. DeMarr and C. Jones-Rikkers: 2002, Ethical Compliance Programs and Corporate Illegality: Testing Assumptions of the Corporate Sentencing Guidelines, *Journal of Business Ethics* 37, 367–383.

[6] Svensson, G., & Wood, G. (2008). A model of business ethics. *Journal of Business Ethics, 77*, 303-322.

[7] Thomas, T., Schermerhorn, J.R. & Dienhart, J.W. (2004). Strategic leadership of ethical behavior in business, *Academy of Management Executive* 18(2), 56– 66.

[8] White, G. W. (2001). Business ethics. *Journal of Business & Finance Librarianship, 6(4), 49–49.* doi:10.1300/J109v06n04_05

9.11 Recommended Reading List

[1] Crane, A., Matten, D., Glozer, S., & Spence, L. J. (2019). *Business ethics: Managing corporate citizenship and sustainability in the age of globalization.* Oxford University Press, USA.

[2] De George, R. T. (2005). A history of business ethics. In *Paper delivered at the third biennial global business ethics conference. Santa Clara, CA: Markkula Center for Applied Ethics*, 337-359.

[3] Dewey, J., & Tufts, J. H. (2022). *Ethics.* DigiCat.

[4] Micewski, E. R., & Troy, C. (2007). Business ethics–deontologically revisited. *Journal of Business Ethics*, 72, 17-25.

[5] Murphy, P. E. (1988). Implementing business ethics. *Journal of Business Ethics*, 907-915.

[6] Trevino, L. K., & Nelson, K. A. (2021). *Managing business ethics: Straight talk about how to do it right.* John Wiley & Sons.

[7] Velasquez, M. G. (2018). *Business ethics: Concepts and cases.* Pearson.

CHAPTER 10

LEASE OR BUY DECISION

10.1 Overview

This chapter introduces readers to one of the most common decision-making processes in finance. When a firm or even an individual desires to obtain a non-current asset (i.e., a machine or piece of equipment), the entity may have to decide whether to buy the said item outright or to lease it from a supplier or an owner. Making this decision requires some fundamental analysis. This is the subject of this chapter.

Objectives of the Chapter

This chapter seeks to achieve the following key objectives:

- To explain the nature of lease and buy decision;
- To examine the nature and implications of financing decision;
- To evaluate the nature and implications acquisition decision; and
- to examine the fundamental analysis of choosing lease or buy.

Key Words Used in the Chapter

- ✓ Leasing
- ✓ Lessor
- ✓ Lessee
- ✓ Operating lease
- ✓ Finance lease
- ✓ Sale-and-lease-back

10.2 Meaning and Nature of Lease or Buy

A lease or buy decision is the process of deciding and choosing between an outright purchase or acquisition of an asset, usually a non-current asset, and renting or leasing the asset from a supplier or external party. This requires a comparative analysis of these two options (buy or lease). The analyzes involve evaluating the costs and benefits of the buying decision and the leasing option.

10.3 Lease or Buy Decision Process

A business may encounter a dilemma regarding the acquisition of a new non-current asset, and if the decision is made to acquire the asset, the company must decide between financing it with a bank loan or opting for a lease agreement. This is commonly known as a 'lease versus buy' decision, which should be carefully evaluated in two distinct stages.

- **The acquisition decision (or investment decision).**
  The initial stage involves determining whether or not to acquire the asset. This determination is made under the assumption that the asset will be bought.

- **Identifying the acquisition option**
  When the acquisition is decided, an entity will further identify and evaluate the acquisition options. Basically, acquisition options include outright acquisition or rent/lease.

- **The financing decision.**
  The next step involves making a financing determination. This phase of the decision-making process entails choosing the optimal financing method for the acquisition. Essentially, it involves deciding whether to purchase the asset outright (i.e., with cash, funded by a bank loan, credit, or a combination of these) or opt for a lease agreement.

10.4 Financing Decision and Options in Assets Acquisition

Once the determination has been made to acquire the assets, the subsequent step involves making the financing decision, which entails selecting the most suitable method of financing for the asset. The financing decision becomes relevant only after the investment decision has been finalized, and that decision is to move forward with the project. In order for this to occur, the net present value (NPV) of the project must be positive, taking into consideration the cash cost of the asset. Subsequently, the finance decision seeks out a more cost-effective alternative for financing the asset. The preferred method of financing is the one that offers the lowest present value (PV) of cost. Should a firm choose to invest in an asset, it has the option to finance the asset through one of the methods below:

- The investment can be financed by utilizing the company's regular capital structure, thereby employing the WACC, or by purchasing the asset;
- Obtain financing for the asset through a designated loan from either the bank or the vendor (i.e. purchase the asset); and
- Enter into a lease agreement for the asset where the bank or the vendor maintains ownership of the asset, while the company is able to utilize the asset and make lease payments (i.e. lease the asset).

10.5 Understanding Buying Decision

A buy decision is the act of deciding on the outright purchase or acquisition of an asset, usually a non-current asset, rather than renting or leasing the asset from a supplier or external party. If the firm buys an asset instead of leasing, the following will apply:

- The company is accountable for maintenance and insurance;
- The company has the ability to claim wear and tear deductions on the asset for tax reasons; and
- When the asset reaches the end of its useful life, its residual value will provide a financial benefit to the company.

10.5.1 Implications of Acquisition Decision (Buying)

i. The firm becomes the owner in right, control and risk.
ii. The firm or the user is eligible to receive tax-deductible depreciation on the asset
iii. The firm can obtain tax credit or benefit for the interest paid on the loan used to finance the asset.

10.6 Understanding Leasing Decision

A leasing decision is the process of deciding and choosing to acquire an asset, usually a non-current asset, through renting or leasing instead of a direct or outright purchase from a supplier or external party. If a firm leases the asset, the following will apply:
- The entity assumes the risks and rewards of ownership without legal ownership of the asset (i.e. a Finance lease);
- The entity is eligible to expense the lease payments; and
- The entity is not entitled to claim wear and tear allowances due to not being the legal owner of the asset.

10.6.1 Type of Leasing Arrangement

There are two types of leasing arrangements, namely finance and operating leases. These classes have been popularized in financial accounting as finance leases (right-to-use assets) and small-item or value leases. However, this section does focus on the traditional accounting insight into leasing.

1. Finance Lease

A lease is considered a finance lease when it conveys most of the risks and rewards associated with ownership. In a finance lease, the lessor retains ownership of the asset while the lessee has possession and enjoys the benefits. The lessee is responsible for paying the finance charge. There are two distinct lease periods within the finance lease, namely the primary lease period and the secondary lease period. The primary lease period encompasses the anticipated economic lifespan of the leased asset. During this period, the lessor assumes responsibility for both the capital and the projected return on the asset. On the other hand, the secondary lease period pertains to the duration for which the lessee has the option to rent the asset for a nominal fee.

2. Operating Lease

In an operating lease agreement, the lessee is granted the use of an asset and is obligated to pay rent. However, the duration of the lease is significantly shorter than the anticipated economic lifespan of the asset. An operating lease is categorized as such when it does not involve the transfer of a significant portion of the risks and benefits associated with ownership.

10.6.2 Features of a Finance Lease

The lessee is granted the opportunity to acquire the asset from the lessor at a later date, with the predetermined purchase price significantly lower than the anticipated fair value of the asset when the purchase option becomes exercisable.

The lease duration covers a substantial portion of the anticipated economic lifespan of the asset. Upon commencement of the lease, the current value of all forthcoming lease payments equals or exceeds a significant portion of the fair value of the leased asset.

The leased asset is so specialized that it can only be utilized by the lessee without requiring significant modifications. The underlying asset is uniquely tailored for the lessee, with no foreseeable alternative use for the lessor upon the conclusion of the lease period.

10.6.3 Advantages of Leasing

1. The firm can prevent incurring the expenses of obsolescence if the lessor fails to accurately predict the obsolescence of assets and sets the lease payment at an insufficient level.
2. By opting for a lease agreement, a lessee can evade numerous restrictive covenants that are typically imposed on long-term loans.
3. Leasing, particularly operating leases, can offer the firm the necessary financial flexibility.
4. Through sale-leaseback arrangements, the firm has the opportunity to enhance its liquidity by converting an existing asset into cash, which can subsequently be utilized as working capital.

10.6.4 Disadvantages of Leasing

1. A lease does not incur any specified interest expenses.
2. The lessor obtains the salvage value of an asset, if applicable, upon the expiration of the lease agreement.
3. The lessee is typically restricted from making enhancements to the leased property or asset without obtaining consent from the lessor.

4. Even if an asset leased by a lessee becomes obsolete, they are still obligated to make lease payments for the remaining duration of the lease.

10.6.5 Implications of Lease Financing Decision
1. The user does not have ownership of the asset in the eyes of the tax authorities.
2. The finance company, being the asset owner, receives the tax-deductible depreciation.
3. Although the user does not receive any tax-deductible depreciation, they can fully offset the rental payment against their tax liability.

10.7 Fundamental Analyzes for Choosing Lease or Buy
Choosing to lease or buy is not a matter of guesswork. It requires fundamental analysis, comparative evaluation, and a cost-benefit profile. These analyzes are basically classified into two categories:
- Quantitative analysis; and
- Qualitative analysis.

10.7.1 Quantitative Analysis
Quantitative analysis is the foremost analysis required to make an informed decision on leasing or buying. The results of the analysis are the 'necessary conditions' while the qualitative results are the 'sufficient conditions'. The quantitative analysis uses cost and benefit data to determine the appropriate decision.

10.7.2 Qualitative Analysis
Other than quantitative analysis, qualitative analysis is based on recognizing relevant and irrelevant cost-benefit analyzes to make an informed decision on leasing or buying. Relevant cost-benefit analysis aids in improving the frequency of making decisions about leasing or buying. There are some important factors that a firm would consider before making a decision to either lease or buy the asset or item. The results of the qualitative analysis may be sufficient to make a determination based on the approach (lease or buy) that is

more cost-effective. At times, the qualitative analysis addresses any concerns a firm cannot measure specifically.

10.7.3 Qualitative Factors to Consider in Lease vs. Buy Analysis

In order to conduct a lease versus buy analysis, it is imperative for an organization to possess a comprehensive comprehension of its current operational status. Numerous inquiries need to be raised, with the following four being the primary areas of concentration:

1. **Length of expected use:**

How long will you need the item?

The number of years or periods the asset or item will be needed and used could determine whether to lease or buy. All other things being equal, when an asset is an integral part of a business operation and could be used for a relatively long time or throughout the time of the business's existence, buying may be more appropriate. However, if the asset is required for a fixed period or shorter duration, then a lease may be more suitable, holding other factors constant.

2. **Nature and frequency of change:**

The nature and how frequently the asset changes or becomes obsolete also influence the lease or buy decision. When an asset needs to be regularly updated to keep up with technological advancements, firms normally opt for a lease so that they can always have access to the latest equipment. On the other hand, when the asset is unlikely to change, firms may consider buying it while holding other factors constant.

3. **Cost and Budget Constraint**

What is feasible for your budget?

The cost of the asset or the item may influence a firm's decision to either lease or buy. When the firm does not have the required capital or funds to acquire the asset, it may consider a lease decision. When a lease agreement for an asset or an item may seem like a more cost-effective option, it is crucial to understand the terms of the lease. On the other hand, all other things being equal, when the leasing analysis does not ensure cost-effectiveness, then the firm would also make a decision to buy the asset or the item.

4. **Ownership of the asset or the item**

Does the asset need to be customized?

When it is necessary to emboss or customize the asset or item, then leasing may not be the most suitable option. A firm gains control over assets immediately after it purchases the asset and becomes the rightful owner of the item. It is more convenient to buy the asset and have it embossed or customized rather than negotiate the modifications with the lessor.

5. **Financial strength to maintain the asset**

Have the firm examined the business's financials?

The financial performance of a firm is a significant factor in a lease or buy decision. Acquiring a lease can alleviate concerns about capital constraints, particularly for newer businesses. It is necessary to assess whether the firm can sustain the financial obligations associated with the lease before accepting the lease terms. On the other hand, when a decision is made to buy the asset or item, it is also necessary to examine the additional cost to be incurred to maintain the asset in the day-to-day running of the business, thus holding all other factors constant.

6. **Expected revenue**

When making a decision to lease or buy effectively, the expected revenue generated with respect to the production volume of the asset or the item in the production process could influence the decision-making process. An analysis of both the lease and buy decisions is necessary to determine which of the decisions will ensure that revenue and profitability can be maximized. It is advisable to opt for the financing decision that will increase profitability, holding all other factors constant.

Illustration 10.1

BRIC Limited has decided to lease a machine to make a product that requires two sequential operations (Operation 1 and Operation 2) on the same machine. The machine is fully utilized. BRIC Limited would have to incur a material cost of GHS 24 per unit. Instead of carrying out Operation 1, BRIC Limited could buy components for GHS 30 per unit. This would allow production to be increased because the machine has to deal with only Operation 2.

Operation 1 takes 0.13 hours of machine time, and Operation 2 takes 0.25 hours of machine time. Labour and variable overheads are incurred at a rate of GHS 32 per machine hour, and the finished products sell for GHS 55 per unit. Assuming the output is 1,000 units.

Required

Should BRIC Limited lease the machine to make the entire product internally or buy in the components and complete them in Operation 2?

Solution:

It is necessary for BRIC Limited to take into consideration all the incremental cash flows or costs caused by any decision that would be made. The machine running costs are already fully utilized on Operations 1 and 2 and will remain fully utilized, but only on Operation 2. Therefore, the machine running costs will not change, and this running cost is irrelevant to BRIC Limited when making an informed decision on leasing or buying.

With respect to the materials, if the buy-in option is accepted, the material cost increases from GHS 24 to GHS 30 per unit.

The production volume can increase by 52% because currently each item takes 0.25 hours in Operation 2, but 0.13 hours per unit will be released by Operation 1, which will now not be needed.

The following would occur (ignoring labor and variable overheads, which we know to be constant):

DETAILS	GHS
Increase in revenue (50% extra could be produced) = (1,000 x 50% x 55)	27,500
Increase in costs (material/buy-in costs only) = (1,500 x 30) – (1,000 x 24)	21,000

Therefore, it is worth buying in as incremental revenue exceeds incremental costs.

10.8 Relevant Cash Flow Analysis of Lease or Buy

In practice, the lease or buy decision is premised on the outcome of the analysis of relevant cash flow. Firms or decision-makers often conduct comparative analyzes of the relevant cash flow emerging from buying and leasing to make an informed decision.

10.8.1 Cash Flow Analysis for Buying Decision

The relevant cash flows from buying decisions include:
  i. The purchase cost of the asset (usually at time 0 of the cash flow);
  ii. Any residual value at the end of the asset's life;
  iii. Any associated tax implications due to tax allowable depreciation;
  iv. The tax cash flows which consist of the tax effect on tax of higher or lower annual cash profits;
  v. The expected benefits and costs from the project, such as extra cash revenues and cash expenses each year;
  vi. Working capital requirements;
  vii. Do not include the interest payments or the tax relief arising on them in the NPV calculation;
  viii. The acquisition decision should be reached using the normal NPV method of investment appraisal; and
  ix. The cost of capital should be the company's normal (after-tax) cost of capital.

10.8.2 Cash Flow Analysis of Lease Financing Decision
The relevant cash flows would be:
   i. The lease payments; and
   ii. Tax relief on the lease payments.

10.9 Relevant Cash Flows for Lease or Buy Decision
Relevant cash flows are any cash flows that hold significance to a given financing decision of choosing either lease or buy, vary in response to the financing option, and cannot be disregarded so long as a particular financing decision holds true. Thus, cash flows that relate solely or purposefully to a particular financing option This means that all relevant cash flows for lease financing are irrelevant or do not exist for the buying decision. Similarly, relevant cash flows for buying decisions are also irrelevant or do not exist under lease financing. The only cash flows that hold relevance are those that will be altered due to the chosen financing method. To summarize, the pertinent cash flows can be outlined as follows:

1. **Purchase price of the asset**
   - If the acquisition of the asset is financed through a bank loan, it is necessary to discount the cash flows for the bank loan to a present value at the after-tax cost of borrowing. Conversely, the present value of the cash flows associated with a loan (comprising interest payments and the tax relief on interest payments) discounted at the after-tax cost of capital equals the loan amount.

   - This implies that the borrowed amount can be utilized in lieu of discounting future interest and tax relief on that interest. The present value (PV) of the opportunity to acquire the asset through a loan decreases due to the decrease in tax payments resulting from claiming capital allowances on the asset. Consequently, the net PV of the cost is the loan amount minus the PV of the tax advantages from capital allowances.

2. **Tax Savings on Capital Allowances**
Rules in regards to capital allowances are as follows:

- A business purchasing an asset for its operations is eligible to claim capital allowances;
- Similarly, a business entering into a finance lease for an asset can also claim capital allowances; and
- However, a business leasing an asset under an operating lease cannot claim capital allowances.

These are claimed by the lessor. When deciding between borrowing to purchase an asset or leasing it under an operating lease, this tax implication should be considered. The tax effect of capital allowances does not apply to the decision between borrowing to purchase an asset or leasing it under a finance lease.

3. Rentals
The lessee's rental payments add to the cost of borrowing or purchasing the asset in the case of both finance leases and operating leases.

4. Tax Relief on the Rentals
You can fully deduct operating lease rental payments, which provides tax relief. This means that the tax benefits associated with these rentals are additional to the decision of whether to borrow and purchase an asset or lease it under an operating lease. On the other hand, only the interest portion of a finance lease rental is eligible for tax deduction. Consequently, the tax relief on rentals is only incremental to the financing decision when considering borrowing, purchasing an asset, and leasing it under a finance lease.

5. Disposal Proceeds
The lessee lacks ownership of the asset; thus, they are unable to reap any advantages from the asset's sale upon reaching the end of its useful life. This aspect is an additional consideration in the financing decision.

6. Cost of Capital
It is crucial to utilize the post-tax cost of borrowing as our discount rate since the interest payments receive tax relief. This rate is applied to both leasing and buying, as all financing cash flows are deemed risk-free. The post-tax cost of borrowing can be calculated by multiplying the cost of borrowing by (1 minus

the tax rate). However, in cases where the company is not liable to pay taxes, the pre-tax rate would be utilized instead.

10.10 Computation of Lease or Buy Decision

The lease-versus-purchase decision involves the application of capital budgeting methods.
1. First, we determine the relevant cash flows and then apply present value techniques.
2. The following steps are involved in the analysis:

   - **Step 1**: Find the after-tax cash outflows for each year under the lease alternative.

   - **Step 2**: Find the after-tax cash outflows for each year under the purchase alternative.

   - **Step 3**: Calculate the present value of the cash outflows from Step 1 and Step 2 using the after-tax cost of debt as the discount rate.

   - **Step 4:** Choose the alternative with the lower present value of cash outflows.

Illustration 10.2

Sammy & Co. Ltd. has made the decision to purchase a new machine at a cost of GHS 12,800. We expect the machine to have a lifespan of five years. The company can claim a tax-allowable depreciation of 25% annually on a reducing balance basis for this investment. A taxation rate of 30% is applicable to operating cash flows, with payments made one year after they occur. Sammy & Co. Ltd. intends to finance the new plant by means of a five-year fixed-interest loan at a pre-tax cost of 11.4% per annum. The principal is repayable in five years' time. A leasing company has also suggested a finance lease spanning five years with an annual payment of GHS 2,840 to be made in advance. The residual value of the machine for both financing options will be zero.

Required:

Evaluate the two options for acquiring the machine and advise Sammy & Co Ltd. on the best alternative.

Solution

Table 10.1: Tax Relief Computation

Year	Details	WDV	Tax Saved (30%)	Timing
0	Cost	12,800		
1	Capital allowance	3,200	960	2
		9,600		
2	Capital allowance	2,400	720	3
		7,200		
3	Capital allowance	1,800	540	4
		5,400		
4	Capital allowance	1,350	405	5
		4,050		
5	Disposal proceeds	0		
	Balance allowance	4,050	1215	6

After-tax Cost of Capital

After-tax cost of capital = 11.4% x (1 – 30%)
After-tax cost of capital = 8%

Table 10.2: Cost of Buying

Year	0	1	2	3	4	5	6
Plant	(12,800)						
Tax savings			960	720	540	405	1,215
Net Cash flow	(12,800)		960	720	540	405	1,215
DCF @ 8%	1.000	0.926	0.857	0.794	0.735	0.681	0.630
Present Value	(12,800)	0	823	572	397	276	766
NPV	(9,967)						

Table 10.3: Cost of Leasing

Year	Details	Cashflows	DCF @ 8%	Present Value
0-4	Lease payment	(2,840)	1 + 3.312	(12,246)
2-6	Tax savings (30% x 2,840)	852	3.697 (W1)	3150
				(9,096)

Table 10.4: Working 1

6-year cumulative present value factor 8%	4.623
1 Year present value factor 8%	(0.926)
	3.697

Decision Rule
Therefore, the cost of leasing is lower than the cost of buying, so the plant should be acquired under a finance lease.

Illustration 10.3
BRIQ Company Limited is in the process of considering the acquisition of a new machine tool with a price tag of GHS 24,000. Options are available for either leasing or buying the equipment. The company is currently subject to a tax rate of 40%. The specifics of the situation are as follows:

o **Lease:**
The company is set to acquire a 5-year lease with yearly end-of-year payments amounting to GHS 7,000. The lessor will cover all maintenance expenses, and the lessee will have the opportunity to buy the machine for GHS 5,000 once the lease ends.

o **Purchase:**
The machine's purchase would be financed by the firm through a 5-year loan with an interest rate of 9%. The loan would necessitate end-of-year installment payments amounting to GHS 6,170. Additionally, the firm would allocate GHS 2,500 per year for a service contract that encompasses all maintenance expenses. However, the firm would be responsible for covering insurance and

other associated costs. Furthermore, the firm intends to retain the machine and utilize it even after the completion of its 5-year recovery period.

- Cost of capital is at 6%
- The company will use MACRS 5-year recovery period for the depreciation of the machine in which the values are as follows:

Year	Rate
1	20% of the asset's value
2	32% of the asset's value
3	19 % of the value of the asset
4	12% of the value of the asset
5	12% of the value of the asset

Solution

Lease Option

The after-tax cash outflow from the lease payments can be found as follows:
After Tax Outflow from Lease = GHS 7,000 x (1 - t)
= GHS 7,000 x (1 - 0.40)
= GHS 4,200

In the last year, the total cost of the purchase option, which amounts to GHS5,000, will be combined with the lease outflow of GHS 4,200, resulting in a year 5 outflow of GHS 9,200 (4,200 + 5,000).

Table 10. 5: Cost of Leasing

Year	1	2	3	4	5
After tax cashflows	4,200.00	4,200.00	4,200.00	4,200.00	9,200.00
DCF @ 6%	0.943	0.890	0.840	0.792	0.747
Present Value	3,960.60	3,738.00	3,528.00	3,326.40	6,872.40
Total Present Value	21,425				

Buying Option

Initially, it is necessary to calculate the annual interest component of each loan payment, as only the interest portion is eligible for tax deductions, as illustrated in Table 10.6.

Table 10.6: Calculation of Annual Interest

Year	Bal at start	Interest (3)	Liability for the period	Installment Payment	Balance at Close
		9% @ 1			
1	24,000	2,160	26,160	6,170	19,990
2	19,990	1,799	21,789	6,170	15,619
3	15,619	1,406	17,025	6,170	10,855
4	10,855	977	11,832	6,170	5,662
5	5,662**	510	6,172**	6,170	0

Table 10.7: Annual Interest Component of Each Loan Payment

At year-end	Bal at beginning (1)	Loan payment (2)	Interest (3)	Principal (4)	Bal at close (5)
		3 + 4	9% @ 1	2 – 3	1 – 4
1	24,000	6,170	2,160	4,010	19,990
2	19,990	6,170	1,799	4,371	15,619
3	15,619	6,170	1,406	4,764	10,855
4	10,855	6,170	977	5,193	5,662
5	5,662**	6,170	510	5,660**	0

Table 10.8: Buying Cost

Year	1	2	3	4	5
Loan payments	6,170.00	6,170.00	6,170.00	6,170.00	6,170.00
Maintenance costs	2,500.00	2,500.00	2,500.00	2,500.00	2,500.00
Depreciation	4,800.00	7,680.00	4,560.00	2,880.00	2,880.00
Interest	2,160.00	1,799.00	1,406.00	977.00	510.00
Total Deductions	9,460.00	11,979.00	8,466.00	6,357.00	5,890.00
Tax shield (40% * Total Deductions)	3,784.00	4,791.60	3,386.40	2,542.80	2,356.00
After tax cashflows (LP + MC - TS)	4,886.00	3,878.40	5,283.60	6,127.20	6,314.00
DCF @ 6%	0.943	0.890	0.840	0.792	0.747
Present Value	4,607.50	3,451.78	4,438.22	4,852.74	4,716.56
Total Present Value	**22,067**				

Decision Rule
The asset should be purchased because it has the highest cashflows of the present value of GHS 22,067 than the cashflows of the present value of the leasing.

Illustration 10.4
Kalala Ltd. has opted to invest in a new milling machine. The machine is priced at GHS10,000 and is projected to have a useful life of five years, with a trade-in value of GHS2,000 at the end of the fifth year. The company must now decide on the financing approach for this project.
   a. Kalala Ltd. could purchase the machine for cash, using bank loan facilities on which the current rate of interest is 13% before tax.
   b. Kalala Ltd. has the option to enter into a leasing agreement for the machine, which would involve making a payment of GHS 2,400 annually for the next five years.

The tax rate stands at 30%. In the event of purchasing the machine, the company will have the opportunity to avail a full tax depreciation allowance in the initial year. The payment of tax is deferred by a year.

Required:
Evaluate the two options for acquiring the machine and advise Kalala Ltd., on the best alternative.

Solution

After-tax cost of capital
After-tax cost of capital = 13% x (1 – 30%)
After-tax cost of capital = 9%

Table 10.9: Tax Relief Computation

Year	Details	WDV	Tax Saved (30%)	Timing
0	Cost	10,000		
1	Capital allowance	2,000	600	2
		8,000		
2	Capital allowance	2,000	600	3
		6,000		
3	Capital allowance	2,000	600	4
		4,000		
4	Capital allowance	2,000	600	5
		2,000		
5	Disposal proceeds	(2,000)	600	6
	Balance allowance	0		

Table 10.10: Cost of Buying

Year	0	1	2	3	4	5	6
Equipment	(10,000)						
Tax savings			3,000				
Trade-in-value						2,000	
Balancing charge (30% x 2,000)							(600)
Net Cash flow	(10,000)		3,000			2,000	(600)
DCF @ 8%	1.000	0.917	0.842	0.772	0.708	0.650	0.596
Present Value	(10,000)	0	2,526	0	0	1,300	(358)
NPV	(6,532)						

Table 10.11: Cost of Leasing

Year	Details	Cashflows	DCF @ 8%	Present Value
1-5	Lease payment	(2,400)	3.890	(9,336)
2-6	Tax savings (30% x 2,400)	720	3.569 (W1)	2,570
				(6,766)

Table 10.12: Working 1

6-year cumulative present value factor 8%	4.486
1 Year present value factor 8%	(0.917)
	3.569

Decision Rule

The cost of leasing is higher than the cost of buying, so the machine should be purchase since it has the cheapest option.

10.11 Chapter Review Questions

1. Ben & Sam Ltd. is evaluating the possibility of purchasing a personal computer valued at GHS 100,000. The computer is projected to have a useful life of five years. The company is considering two options for acquiring the computer: borrowing GHS 100,000 from the bankers at an annual interest rate of 15% or leasing it.

In order to make an informed decision, the company needs to determine the annual lease rentals that would be equivalent to the loan option. The following additional information has been provided for your consideration:

   a. The principal amount of the loan will be paid in five annual equal installments.
   b. Payments for interest, lease rental, and principal repayment are scheduled for the final day of each calendar year.
   c. The total expense of the computer will be depreciated evenly over the computer's useful life, and this depreciation will be tax-deductible.
   d. With an effective tax rate of 35% and an after-tax cost of capital of 9%, the company's financial situation is stable.
   e. At the conclusion of the 5th year, the computer will be sold for GHS 3,400. A 9% commission on the sale price will be paid out.

You are required to **c**ompute the annual lease rentals payable by Ben & Sam Ltd. which will result in indifference to the loan option.

2. A company is interested in acquiring an asset that costs GHS 50,000. The company has received an offer from a bank to borrow the required amount at an interest rate of 18%. The loan is repayable over a period of 5 years in installments. Alternatively, a leasing company has presented a proposal to the company, offering to lease the asset for a yearly rental fee of GHS 140 per GHS 500 of the asset's value.

This lease agreement would also be for a duration of 5 years, with payment due at the end of each year. For tax purposes, the asset's depreciation rate is set at 20% on the Written Down Value (W.D.V.), without any additional shift allowance. The estimated salvage value of the asset at the end of the 5-year period is GHS 500.

You are required to evaluate whether the company should accept the proposal of Bank or leasing company, if the effective tax rate of the company is 50%.

3. The following are the details regarding the machine to be given on lease by Heavy Com Ltd.

1. The machine's cost to the lessor is GHS 200,000, with 80% financed through debt and the remaining balance through equity. The cost of debt before tax is 20%, while the cost of equity is 16%.
2. The lessor falls into the 35% tax bracket. The machinery's depreciation rate is 20% using the diminishing balance method.
3. At the end of the 5th year, the machines have a scrap value of GHS 25,000.
4. The estimated annual cost for maintenance and general administration related to the machine is GHS 3,000.
5. The lessee agrees to make the following payments:
    - Annual rent of GHS 72,000 for 5 years. The payment is to be made at the end of each year;
    - The security deposit of GHS 6,000 which is refundable at the end of the lease period without interest; and
    - Management fees (non-refundable) payable at the inception of the lease period is GHS 5,000.

You are required to decide whether the lessor should lease the machine using the internal rate of return method.

4. ATUAS Co. Ltd. is currently evaluating the potential acquisition of a machine with a price tag of GHS 640,000. In the event of purchasing the machine, the company would need to allocate GHS 50,000 annually for maintenance costs. After a period of three years, the machine would be sold for GHS 100,000. On the other hand, ATUAS Co. Ltd. has the option to obtain the machine through a lease, which would require an annual lease rental of GHS 240,000. ATUAS Co. Ltd. is eligible to claim capital allowances on a 25% reducing balancing basis.

The company is subject to an annual tax rate of 30% on its profits, and all tax obligations are settled retrospectively. The accounting year for ATUAS Co. Ltd. concludes on 31 December. If the decision is made to purchase the machine, the payment will be made in January of the first year of operation. Conversely, if the machine is leased, the annual lease rentals will be paid in January of each operational year. (assuming an after-tax borrowing rate of 7%).

Required: Evaluate whether ATUAS Co. Ltd. should purchase or lease the new machine.

5. Level Wise Limited management has made the decision to acquire a machine that has a cost of GHS 31,500 and a lifespan of 4 years. The expected scrap value of the machine is estimated to be GHS 2,500. Tax payment is due one year after it is incurred, and the tax rate is set at 30%. The company can claim tax allowable depreciation at a rate of 25% per year on a reducing balance basis. Alternatively, the company has the option to lease the asset under a finance lease arrangement, with an annual rental fee of GHS 10,000 for 4 years in arrears. If the company chooses to purchase the machine, it can borrow funds at an interest rate of 10% to finance the acquisition.

Required: Should the company buy or lease the asset.

10.12 Chapter References and Bibliography

[1] Athanassakos, G., & Klatt, M. (1993). Lease or Buy: How Recent Tax Changes Have Affected the Decision. *Can. Tax J.*, *41*, 444.

[2] Berlin, J. W., & Lexa, F. J. (2006). An analysis of the buy-vs-lease decision. *Journal of the American College of Radiology*, *3*(2), 102-107.

[3] Gansler, J. S., Lucyshyn, W., & Rigilano, J. (2014). *Rethinking the Lease vs. Buy Decision*. Acquisition Research Program.

[4] Goela, N., & Bisman, J. E. (2013). A Model and Research Agenda for Lease Decision Making. *Indonesian Management and Accounting Research*, *12*(1), 64694.

[5] Hackert, A., & Byers, S. (2024). *Lease or buy?* Society for Case Research

[6] Harwood, G. B., & Hermanson, R. H. (1977). The lease-or-buy decision reconsidered. *Journal of Accountancy*, *143*(000006), 81.

[7] Herst, A. C. (2012). *Lease or purchase: Theory and practice*, (4). Springer Science & Business.

CHAPTER 11

FUNDAMENTALS OF MERGERS AND TAKEOVERS

11.1 Overview

Takeovers and mergers are important in the world of corporate finance. When there are no chances for organic growth, they can be a valuable external growth source for many businesses, but they can also be a continual threat to some businesses' ability to survive. Probably the most crucial issue facing all organizational managers today is managing change.

Objectives of the Chapter

This chapter seeks to achieve the following key objectives:

- To explain the concept of Mergers and Takeovers;
- To ascertain why companies, Merge or Takeover;
- To examine the motives of Mergers and Takeovers;
- To measuring the success of Mergers and Acquisitions;
- To examine some scenarios for failure of Mergers and Acquisition; and
- To explain the concept of Reverse Takeovers.

Key Words used in the Chapter

- ✓ Merger
- ✓ Acquisition
- ✓ Takeover
- ✓ Reverse takeover

11.2 The Concept of Mergers and Takeovers

Mergers and acquisitions represent a form of non-organic growth. Mergers involve the consolidation of two entities into one, while takeovers or acquisitions occur when one entity purchases another and integrates it into its own operations. This can take the form of a business purchasing another company or a management team buying out the business from its owners. Mergers and takeovers are often pursued by companies looking to expand their market share, diversify their product offerings, or enter new markets. By combining resources, expertise, and customer bases, companies can achieve economies of scale, increase efficiency, and drive growth. Mergers and takeovers can also be a strategic way for companies to gain access to new technologies, intellectual property, or talent. By acquiring a company with valuable assets or capabilities, a business can strengthen its competitive position and drive innovation. However, mergers and takeovers can also be complex and risky endeavors. Integration challenges, cultural differences, and regulatory hurdles can all pose obstacles to a successful merger or takeover. It is crucial for companies to carefully plan and execute these transactions to ensure they deliver the intended benefits and create long-term value for shareholders.

11.3 Distinction Between Mergers and Takeovers

The concepts of merger and acquisition primarily pertain to the amalgamation of two or more corporate entities with the aim of attaining enhanced synergies. The reasons for engaging in either agreement encompass the expansion of operations, attaining a larger market share, cost reduction, or profit augmentation. Nevertheless, there exist notable distinctions between the two, which are succinctly outlined in the subsequent Table 11.1.

Table 11.1: Distinction Between Merger and Takeover

Distinctiveness	Merger	Takeover/Acquisition
1. Procedure	The procedure involves two or more companies or firms joining to form a new business entity.	The procedure involves one company or firm completely taking over the operations of another through a majority or 100% shareholding.
2. Nature of Consent	Under a merger, mutual consent is required between or among parties.	Under acquisition or takeover, the decision is usually not based on mutual consent. This sometimes leads to what is termed a hostile takeover.
3. Nature of New Identity	Under the merger, the merged entities operate under a new identity or name.	The target or acquired firm mostly operates under the name of the associated parent company. In another stream, the acquiree retains its original name or identity if the parent company allows it.
4. Degree of Benefit	Under a merger, the entities or parties involved can reap the advantages of coming together, as they are able to sustain their operations and leverage their combined resources to enhance the overall efficiency of the newly formed entity.	Under a takeover or an acquisition, the buyer or acquirer can reap numerous advantages, including but not limited to acquiring fresh shares, bolstering their capital, and venturing into untapped markets. Consequently, the acquiring entity tends to derive greater benefits compared to the purchased company, which typically either dissolves or continues its operations under the acquiring company's identity.

Table 11.1 Cont'd.: Distinction Between Merger and Takeover

Distinctiveness	Merger	Takeover/Acquisition
5. Comparative Size	Normally, the parties involved in a merger have similar size and scale of operations.	Under takeover or acquisition, the acquirer is larger and financially stronger than the target company.
6. Nature of power	Merger leads to the dilution of power between the parties involved.	Under takeover or acquisition, the acquirer exerts absolute or higher power over the acquiree.
7. Nature of shares	Under a merger, the firms involved issue new shares.	New shares are not normally issued. It only happens when the acquisition is based on share exchanges.

11.4 Types of Mergers

Mergers are often categorized as horizontal, vertical or conglomerate mergers.

- **Horizontal Merger**

A horizontal merger is the result of two competitors merging, or two businesses with comparable output levels and operating in the same industry. A recent example of a horizontal merger is the combination of Hewlett-Packard and Compaq. A horizontal merger may face opposition on antitrust grounds if the combined company experiences an increase in market dominance that will have anti-competitive repercussions. Nonetheless, governments everywhere have been lax in recent years, permitting numerous horizontal mergers to occur without opposition.

- **Vertical Merger**

Combinations of businesses with a buyer-seller connection are known as vertical mergers. This can involve moving forward or backward in the production process to secure an outlet for a company's product or supply of raw materials. It involves two companies operating at separate stages of production within the same industry. An example of a vertical merger is when Merck, the Royalgest pharmaceutical business in the world, bought Medco, the

Royal gest US retailer of inexpensive prescription drugs. Merck became the largest pharmaceutical firm and the largest integrated producer and distributor of pharmaceuticals as a result of this acquisition. Antitrust authorities did not object to this transaction either, despite the fact that the merger obviously created a stronger company.

- **Conglomerate Merger**

When there is no buyer-seller relationship and the companies are not competitors, a conglomerate merger takes place. This also entails the purchase of a business that operates in an entirely unrelated industry to the acquirer. For example, the tobacco corporation Phillip Morris purchased General Foods, despite the fact that these two businesses were in very different industries.

11.5 Types of Takeovers

- **Friendly Takeovers**

Friendly takeover refers to a situation in which two companies mutually agree for one to assume control and management of the other. Ideally, the management of the company recommends and accepts the offer when it believes that doing so will benefit the shareholder more.

- **Hostile Takeovers**

A hostile takeover occurs when the target company opposes the takeover and gains control of the business through an unwilling purchase. The acquiring company can acquire the target company through two methods: either by silently buying enough stock of the company in the open market (a process known as a creeping tender offer) to force a management change or by participating in a proxy fight in which it tries to convince a sufficient number of shareholders to replace the current management with the new one.

- **Reverse Takeovers**

A reverse takeover occurs when a smaller company buys a larger corporation or when a private company buys a public company.

- **Backflip Takeovers**

A reverse takeover occurs when the acquiring company becomes a subsidiary of the business that it has just purchased. Takeovers of this kind are uncommon.

11.6 Why Companies Merge and Takeover

A company's decision to buy or combine with another is influenced by various factors, such as strategic objectives, overcapacity, or the goal of controlling capacity in the industry. Research indicates various justifications and motivators for mergers, highlighting the importance of strategic planning. Firms merge and takeover based on underlying rationales and drivers:

11.6.1 Some Underlying Rationales

Several primary rationales determine the nature of a proposed merger or acquisition. These rationales are:

Strategic Rationale

The strategic rationale involves using mergers or acquisitions to achieve strategic objectives, such as controlling capacity in a specific sector. However, these are not always central to achieving strategic objectives. Alternatives include acquiring a successful company or developing a research and development division to catch up with established players. Successful entry into new markets requires prior product production or expertise.

- **Speculative Rationale**

The speculative rationale involves acquiring a company as a commodity, potentially in a developing field, to share its potential profitability without major strategic realignment. This approach is high-risk, even with carefully selected targets.

- **Management Failure Rationale**

Mergers or acquisitions can be imposed due to management failures, strategy alignment errors, or market changes. This can result in misaligned strategies, as customers' demands and competitors' actions may change the company's direction.

- **Financial Necessity Rationale**

Financial need may necessitate mergers and acquisitions at times. A business may find that it is losing value due to a lack of confidence from shareholders if its strategy is out of alignment. Sometimes the only way to solve this issue is to either purchase smaller, more successful enterprises or merge with larger, more successful ones.

- **Political Rationale**

Political influences are increasingly impacting mergers and acquisitions, with government policies encouraging large public-sector organizations like health trusts and banks in Australia to aggressively pursue overseas acquisitions due to local legislation.

11.6.2 Merger and Takeover Drivers

Some typical merger drivers are considered below:

1. A Requirement for Specialist Skills and/ or Resources

Sometimes a business would look to merge with or buy another business because it wanted to obtain a certain resource or set of skills that the other business owned. This kind of merger or acquisition usually happens when a smaller business has spent years developing highly valuable specialized skills, and it would take a lot of time and resources for the acquiring corporation to acquire these same skills.

2. National and International Stock Markets

Changes in the price of shares can be strong motivators for mergers and acquisitions. During a boom in the stock market, it becomes more convenient to utilize the acquirer's shares rather than cash for the transaction, which tends to make acquisition activity more appealing. On the other hand, a declining stock market may result in potential targets having a reduced market value, making them more appealing for a cash purchase.

3. Diversification Drivers

A business may wish to diversify into other markets or industries in order to balance the portfolio's risk profile. Diversification has clearly become less popular as a risk-management tactic in recent years. Diversification and unrelated acquisitions, according to a number of academics and industry experts, do not actually lower an organization's risk profile. The claim that an organization has less developed the specialized tools and approaches required to address unique difficulties relating to any one of its ranges of business activities the more diverse it is serves as evidence for this notion.

4. **Capacity Reduction**

A sector's overall production may surpass or be close to demand, resulting in a low product value. In certain situations, a corporation may find it advantageous to purchase or merge with a rival to gain more influence over the overall production of the industry.

5. **Vertical Integration**

To lower the risk profile attached to a supplier and guarantee supply continuity, a business can try vertical integration, for instance, with a supplier of a critical supply.

6. **A Drive for Increased Management Effectiveness and Efficiency**

A certain business may lack managerial experience in one or more crucial areas. These areas might be considered "important" if they are crucial to a new growth area the business is trying to build or if they have to do with achieving recently defined new strategic goals.

7. **A drive to Buy into a Growth Sector or Market**

Businesses may utilize mergers or acquisitions to break into a desired new industry or market, especially if they anticipate future growth in that industry or market.

8. **National and International Consolidation**

When suitable businesses are accessible for acquisition or merger within the same broad geographic area, this kind of driver arises.

11.7 Motives or Purpose of Mergers and Takeovers

1. Procurement of Supplies
Acquisitions may be made in order to protect the source of intermediate or raw material supplies, to achieve purchasing efficiencies through discounts, lower overhead, reduced shipping costs, etc., and, ultimately, to standardize the materials.

2. Revamping Production Facilities
Acquisitions aim to achieve economies of scale by combining production facilities, standardizing product specifications, and improving quality, while also acquiring improved production technology and know-how to reduce costs.

3. Market Expansion and Strategy
M&A aims to eliminate competition, protect markets, acquire new outlets for product development, reduce advertising costs, improve public image, and control patents and copy rights.

4. Financial Strength
Enhancing liquidity and cash flow is one of M&A's main goals. Their ability to take advantage of tax savings and automatically increase capacity stems from the sale of excess and out-of-date assets.

5. General Gains
The goal of M&A is to enhance one's reputation and draw in top-tier management expertise to oversee operations. Better client satisfaction and services for product users are among the general benefits of M&A.

6. Development Plans
The development ambitions of the offeror company support the acquisition's goal. The strategy could involve growing the business, adding more funding, eradicating rivals, fortifying its position in the market, etc. Therefore, when choosing a good partner for a merger or acquisition in business combinations, the goals and specifications of the offeror company are quite important.

11.8 Concept of Merger and Takeover Waves: Similarities and Differences

A merger and takeover or acquisition wave (M&A wave) refers to a period of heightened merger activity or surge in mergers and acquisitions within a specific sector or industry, which can vary in duration depending on market performance and the involvement of companies. Throughout merger and acquisition waves, publicly traded companies tend to be more active as buyers compared to private firms, primarily due to their enhanced access to financing and more easily tradable stocks.

M&A Waves turn to have:
M&A waves commonly occur during periods of sustained high rates of economic growth, low or falling interest rates, and a rising stock market.

Differences
Historically, each merger wave has differed in terms of a specific development, such as the emergence of a new technology; industry focus, such as rail, oil, or financial services; degree of regulation; and type of transaction, such as horizontal, vertical, conglomerate, strategic, or financial.

11.8.1 Key Determinants of Merger and Takeover Waves
There are several factors that influence M&A waves. The primary causes are shocks, high liquidity, low financing costs, and overvaluation. Besides these primary determinants, there are several other key contributors. The factors are explained as follows:

1. ***Shocks:*** M&A waves occur when companies respond to industry shocks, such as deregulation, the emergence of new technologies, changes in distribution channels, the introduction of substitute products, or a sustained increase in commodity prices. These events often lead companies to acquire either entire companies or certain parts of other companies.

2. ***High Liquidity and Low Financing***: In the absence of sufficient liquidity to finance deals, shocks alone will not trigger a wave of merger activity.

However, if there is ample liquidity and low-cost capital readily available, it can lead to a surge in M&A activity even without industry shocks.

3. **Overvaluation**: Managers utilize overvalued stocks to acquire the assets of undervalued companies. For mergers and acquisitions to occur in waves, the valuations of multiple companies must increase simultaneously. Managers whose stocks are considered to be overvalued tend to acquire companies whose stock prices are undervalued.

4. **Market Conditions**: M&A waves often coincide with periods of economic growth and stability, as companies are more willing to take on the risks associated with mergers and acquisitions when the economy is performing well. Low interest rates and high stock market valuations can also encourage companies to pursue M&A opportunities.

5. **Industry Trends**: Certain industries may experience M&A surges or waves due to specific trends or challenges within the sector. For example, technological advancements or regulatory changes can prompt companies to seek mergers or acquisitions in order to stay competitive or expand their market share.

6. **Company Strategies**: Individual companies may also drive M&A waves or surges through their own strategic initiatives. For example, a company may pursue acquisitions as part of a growth strategy, seeking to enter new markets or diversify their product offerings. Additionally, companies may engage in mergers and acquisitions to achieve cost savings through economies of scale or to gain access to new technologies or intellectual property.

11.8.2 Measuring the Success of Mergers and Acquisitions

Merger success can be categorized by factors such as immediate liquidation, short-term financial gains, and the creation of long-term synergies. High success rates occur when mergers force the firm into liquidation, while low success rates occur when focusing on short-term financial gains.

Thus, it makes sense to think about merger success in terms of both short- and long-term metrics.

11.8.3 Short-term Measures of Success

There are several well-documented short-term effects of a merger announcement.
1. Upon announcement, the target company shares' value typically increases, while the acquiring company's shares' value remains static or declines.
2. Pre-announcement rumors often lead to an increase in the price of target company's shares before the announcement.
3. The acquisition's short-term financial success is significantly influenced by the target share price rise, often leading to the acquirer paying an inflated price for the target.
4. The inflationary premium, which is the difference between pre-rumor value and merger bid value, often leads to the overvaluation of acquired companies, especially when multiple bidders exist.
5. Shareholders may have different views on success in acquisitions, with target shareholders who sell shares at a premium rate making more money than they would have otherwise.
6. Shareholders who remain with the target and continue to hold shares in the merged company may have a different long-term perspective.

11.8.4 Long-term Measures of Success
1. The long-term view of a merger's success is complex and influenced by various variables, with two main areas of focus in financial terms;
   - payment method;
   - implementation.
2. The merger deal is typically financed through cash, shares, or a combination of both.
3. Cash deals involve selling existing shares for cash, while share deals involve receiving new shares for existing ones. In a buoyant economy, more deals involve shares.

4. Cash-paying companies often have higher debt and undervalued stock, and long-term shareholder performance may be lower for shares-paid mergers due to economic depression.
5. In a robust economy, companies that have invested in shares can expect better long-term performance.
6. The literature highlights the long-term issue of ineffective implementation, as numerous mergers prolong the process beyond its initial purpose.
7. Implementation plans often change during integration due to inadequate planning or unaddressed integration problems.

11.9 Some Scenarios for Failure of Mergers and Acquisition

The success of a merger or acquisition can be challenging to determine in the short or long-term, with primary reasons for a relatively unsuccessful outcome.

1. An Inability to Agree on the Terms

Senior managers at the two organizations may not be able to agree on terms for the proposed merger, which might mean that it never gets enacted. Due to the expenses and lost time in these situations, the merger must be deemed a failure.

2. Overestimation of the True Value of the Target

Acquirers often overpay for targets due to short-term share price rises and long-term inaccurate valuations due to poor due diligence or potential sector changes, resulting in overpayment.

3. A Failure to Realize all Identified Potential Synergies

The potential to create and take advantage of synergies frequently influences the fundamental reasoning for mergers and acquisitions. When planning, these possible synergies could seem possible, but in practice, they might be much harder to realize and take advantage of than first thought.

4. An Inability to Implement Change

A significant quantity of change is produced by a large-scale merger or acquisition. Every department within each organization may experience changes of differing degrees in the event of an equal merger. When it comes to creating and executing change, some businesses excel more than others. There may occasionally be a fundamental inability to successfully plan and handle change. In other situations, there could be a strong cultural resistance to change.

5. A Failure to Achieve a Technological Fit

Failure to attain technological fit is a common source of issues in mergers and acquisitions. Businesses typically take several years to establish their unique technological methods for manufacturing and technologies, and each system is typically very individualistic. Combining two very distinct technological systems might be very challenging. The expenses of doing so in full can be unaffordable in certain circumstances.

11.10 Reverse Takeovers

Acquisitions when the purchase price is paid in newly issued shares by the acquiring company occasionally result in reverse takeovers. Reverse takeovers occur when one company buys another and the acquired company's shareholders end up controlling the combined company.

Illustration 11.1

Existing Condition Before Takeover:
- Payne Ltd. has 20,000 ordinary shares in issue.
- Kaa Ltd. also has 20,000 ordinary shares in issue.

Transaction/Takeover Action:
- Payne Ltd. buys the entire share capital of Kaa Ltd. and
- pays for them by issuing 60,000 new ordinary shares to the owners of Kaa Ltd.

Condition after the Transaction:
- Payne Ltd. owns 100% of Kaa Ltd.
- The original owners of Kaa Ltd. own 75% (60,000 shares out of 80,000 shares) of the combined entity.

Implication:
Payne Ltd. is the legal acquirer but in effect, Kaa Ltd. has taken over Payne Ltd. (because its original owners now control it). This is a typical case of reverse takeover.

11.10.1 Uses of Reverse Takeovers
A private firm can employ a reverse takeover to become public without having to make an initial public offering.

11.10.2 Benefits Reverse Takeovers
Reverse acquirers benefit from being traded without the costs and delays of an IPO process.
1. Due to their increased liquidity, the shares that the legal subsidiary's original owners currently own may appreciate.
2. The company's access to financial markets has increased.
3. The company can effectively utilize share option schemes to motivate its directors and other employees.
4. One possible use for the shares is acquiring other businesses.

11.11 Due Diligence: Mergers and Takeovers
Due diligence is not only fundamental but also critical in merger and takeover transactions. Whenever an individual makes a purchase, there is always a potential risk that the item they are acquiring may not align with their initial perception. Difficulties may arise in situations where the seller possesses undisclosed information that is not accessible to the buyer.

For example, a buyer may purchase a used car without knowing that it has a history of mechanical issues or has been involved in a previous accident. Without this crucial information, the buyer may end up spending more money on repairs than they initially anticipated. In other cases, sellers may use deceptive marketing tactics or withhold important details about a product in order to make a sale. This can result in buyers feeling cheated or taken advantage of, leading to a breakdown in trust between the two parties.

Taking over or merging with another entity bears certain similarities, yet undoubtedly, there are significantly greater financial implications involved. To mitigate these risks, there is a need for due diligence.

Due diligence in mergers and takeovers is the process or set of tools used to fully understand the target company's financial, legal, operational, and market aspects. This is done by thoroughly investigating and analyzing the target entity's business processes, key personnel, financial records, legal documents, operational procedures, and overall business performance in order to lower the risk that comes with a merger or takeover. A sound due diligence process helps the buyer assess the potential risks and benefits associated with the transaction.

11.11.1 Types of Due Diligence
There are different types of due diligence. The types of due diligence of interest are dependent on the aspects of transactions prone to severe risk. Nevertheless, there are basically four different types of due diligence in mergers and takeovers:

Financial Due Diligence
This involves scrutinizing the target entity's management account, projections, and financial statements, including the statement of financial position, profit or loss and other comprehensive income, and the statement of cash flow. This analysis helps the buyer understand the entity's financial health, profitability, and potential for future growth. It also helps identify any potential financial risks, such as undisclosed liabilities or overstated assets. In financial due diligence, the examiner will examine, among others:
- Financial statements, including statements of financial position, profit or loss, and other comprehensive income, and statements of cash flow;
- Management account; and
- Prospective financial information includes projections and associated assumptions.

Legal Due Diligence
This involves reviewing contracts, agreements, licenses, permits, and any legal disputes or litigation involving the target entity. This examination ensures that the buyer is aware of any legal obligations, potential liabilities, or regulatory compliance issues that may impact the transaction or the future operations of the acquired entity. Under legal due diligence, the examiner will examine, among others:
- Hidden warranties;
- Asset security;
- Legal disputes; and
- Potential break clauses in supply contracts that could lead to customer loss.

Operational Due Diligence
This focuses on evaluating the target entity's operational processes, supply chain management, production capabilities, and overall efficiency. This assessment helps the buyer understand the operational strengths and weaknesses of the target entity and identify any potential operational risks or areas for improvement. The examiner or consultant will examine, among others:
- Operational process;
- Supply chain management;
- Production capabilities; and
- Operational efficiency.

Market Due Diligence
This is due diligence that involves conducting market research and analysis to assess the target entity's competitive position, industry trends, and market potential. This information helps the buyer evaluate the target entity's market value and growth prospects. The examiner or the consultant will conduct and examine, among others:
- Market research;
- Target entity's competitive position;
- Industry trend of the target entity; and
- Market potential.

11.11.2 Objectives of Due Diligence

The primary objective of due diligence is to mitigate transactional risks. Additionally, there are several secondary objectives, including:

 i. Verifying the accuracy of information and assumptions that form the basis of a bid;
 ii. Offering an independent evaluation and examination of the target business;
 iii. Identifying and quantifying potential areas of commercial and financial risk;
 iv. Providing reassurance to financial providers;
 v. Assessing the legal and regulatory compliance of the target business;
 vi. Evaluating the target business's operational efficiency and effectiveness;
 vii. Identifying any potential conflicts of interest or ethical concerns;
 viii. Evaluating the target business's customer base and market position;
 ix. Assessing the target business's management team and their capabilities;
 x. Identifying any potential environmental or sustainability risks; and
 xi. Identifying any potential cultural or organizational integration challenges in case of a merger or acquisition.

11.12 Mergers and Acquisitions in Ghana- The Motivation Behind

According to research, mergers and acquisitions in Ghana are primarily driven by developments at the economic, legal, and technological levels (Ghana's Mergers and Acquisitions Report 2017). In essence, the absence of laborious and disorganized bureaucratic regulatory structures and requirements that used to disrupt and obstruct mergers and acquisitions processes have all been revised in recent years with the introduction of new legislation and guidelines that have created a procedure that is both expedient and comprehensive for mergers and acquisitions.

According to the Monetary Policy Report published by the Bank of Ghana in July 2021, regulatory reliefs and policy measures have continued to support the performance of the banking sector, which has resulted in an increase in business transactions in Ghana, including mergers and acquisitions (M&A) transactions or other business transactions. Within the context of the success story of companies and the economy of Ghana as a whole, mergers and

acquisitions have firmly proven to be a force to be reckoned with. This is because a huge number of enterprises have taken this adventurous route.
(Source:https://www.bog.gov.gh/banking_sect_report/banking-sector-developments-report-july-2021)

13.13 Laws that Support M&A's in Ghana

Typically, M&A transactions among public companies in Ghana is regulated by the following:
- Legislation such as the Securities and Exchange Commission Code on Takeovers and Mergers 2008 (SEC Rules);
- The Companies Act (Act 992);
- Securities Industry Act, 2016 (Act 929);
- Corporate Governance Code for Listed Companies 2020; and
- Constitution of the Company.

11.14 Examples of Mergers and Acquisitions (M&A's) in Ghana

1. Vodafone Ghana

In August 2008, Vodafone Ghana purchased a 70% ownership stake in Ghana Telecom from the government of Ghana for US$900 million. This was another transaction that occurred. Ghana Telecom was the third-largest telecommunications firm and a prominent fixed-line provider at the time. Vodafone Ghana anticipated that the advantages would encompass exposure to the expanding Ghanaian telecoms sector. Vodafone Ghana experienced a rise in the number of mobile phone subscribers subsequent to the purchase. The company's market share was 21.92 percent as of April 2016. This resulted in Vodafone Ghana being the second-largest operator in the country.

2. Ecobank and The Trust bank

The parent firm of the Ecobank Group, Ecobank Transnational Incorporated (Ecobank), purchased a sizeable ownership share in The Trust Bank, Ghana Limited, in 2011. This transaction took place in 2011. (TTB). At the time, the transaction was initiated with the intention of satisfying the requirement imposed by the Bank of Ghana (BoG) that local banks must recapitalize to the tune of sixty million Ghana cedis by the end of 2010.

3. First Atlantic Merchant Bank Limited and Energy Commercial Bank

Energy Bank and First Atlantic Bank completed a merger in order to satisfy the minimum capital requirement of GHS 400 million. Energy Bank was unable to raise the necessary funds to comply with the new BoG GHS 400 million capital requirement at the time. The two banks executed a Memorandum of Understanding to consolidate their operations in order to conform to the new MCR established by the BoG.

4. Express Life

After receiving clearance from the National Insurance Commission, Prudential Life PLC made the announcement that they would be acquiring Express Life in December of 2013. (NLC).

5. Fidelity and ProCredit

In 2014, Fidelity Bank purchased 100% ownership of ProCredit Savings and Loans Company Ltd. ("ProCredit Ghana") from its two shareholders, ProCredit Holdings and the DEON Foundation of the Netherlands. This occurred subsequent to the acquisition's approval by the Bank of Ghana. The acquisition was designed to facilitate the transfer of ProCredit Ghana's qualified workforce and robust SME processes to Fidelity Bank, hence improving the bank's offerings to Ghanaian firms. Fidelity Bank was the third-largest bank in terms of branch network at the time of the purchase, with 80 branches, 300 agencies, and more than 100 ATMs.

6. Provident Life

An acquisition of a controlling share in Provident Life Assurance was made by Old Mutual in 2013. In 2013, the South African insurance business finished the process of purchasing the interest from the indigenous company, and it was formally launched the following year in 2014.

7. Airtel and Tigo

Tigo, which was formerly owned by Millicom, became the second-largest mobile operator in Ghana in 2017 following the merger between Bharti Airtel and Tigo. AirtelTigo was established as a consequence of the combined telecommunications corporations' decision to merge the identities of both companies, despite the fact that many Ghanaians had anticipated a name change. The objective of the merger, which was the first of its type in the telecoms sector, was to increase market share in Ghana, a country with one of the highest rates of mobile phone usage in Africa.

8. Omni Bank and Bank Sahel Sahara

The merger procedure between OmniBank Ghana Limited and Sahel Sahara Bank Ghana Limited (BSIC) was finalized in 2019. The merger's theme is "Together, we provide you with more." Effective March 4, 2019, the two entities were merged into a single organization. OmniBSIC Bank Ghana Limited is the current operational name. After the merger, a statement was released stating that it "needed to boost capital in order to comply with the new Bank of Ghana Minimum Capital Requirement of GHS400 million." This merger is a combination of the strengths of two big banks in a variety of financial services, which will allow the combined firm to provide additional options, expand access, and appeal to the banking public.

(Source: *https://www.pulse.com.gh/bi/strategy/7-merger-and-acquisitions-of-the-decade-in-ghana/gnmyxjb*).

11.15 Chapter Review Questions:

1: In your own view, what are the key distinctive features of mergers and takeovers or acquisitions

2. Explain the main types of:
    a) Mergers
    b) Takeovers/acquisition

3. Explain five (5) factors that typically drive entities to pursue mergers.

4. Why is due diligence important in the mergers and takeovers process?

5. Explain financial due diligence and outline three (3) source documents for financial due diligence. With the aid of a hypothetical scenario explain a reverse takeover.

11.16 Chapter References and Bibliography

[1] Clark, F. (2019). *The Fundamentals of Statutory Mergers* (Master's thesis, University of Pretoria (South Africa).

[2] Distler, J., & Distler, J. (2018). Fundamentals of mergers & acquisitions. *Acquisitions by Emerging Multinational Corporations: Motivation and Performance of Transactions in Western Europe and North America*, 9-63.

[3] Dreher, M., & Ernst, D. (2016). *Mergers & acquisitions*. UVK Lucius.

[4] Flom, J. H. (1999). Mergers & (and) Acquisitions: The Decade in Review. *U. Miami L. Rev.*, *54*, 753.

[5] https://www.bog.gov.gh/banking_sect_report/banking-sector-developments-report-july-2021)

[6] https://www.pulse.com.gh/bi/strategy/7-merger-and-acquisitions-of-the-decade-in-ghana/gnmyxjb).

[7] Ghana's Mergers and Acquisitions Report 2017).

[8] Golubov, A., Petmezas, D., & Travlos, N. G. (2013). Empirical mergers and acquisitions research: A review of methods, evidence and managerial implications. *Handbook of research methods and applications in empirical finance*, 287-313.

[9] Malik, M. F., Anuar, M. A., Khan, S., & Khan, F. (2014). Mergers and acquisitions: A conceptual review. *International Journal of Accounting and Financial Reporting*, *4*(2), 520.

[10] Monetary Policy Report published by the Bank of Ghana in (July 2021).

CHAPTER 12

VALUATION FOR MERGERS AND ACQUISITIONS

12.1 Overview

Mergers and acquisitions (M&A) valuations serve various purposes such as due diligence, negotiation, and establishing a business's price. Identifying the intended use of the valuation is crucial in selecting the appropriate valuation method. Additionally, it is important to assess the data accessible for conducting the valuation.

Objectives of the Chapter:

- To examine the nature of valuation;
- To estimate whether valuation is an art or science;
- To examine the Valuation methods; and
- To examine the concept of Synergy in Mergers & Acquisitions.

Key Words used in the Chapter

- ✓ Predatory
- ✓ Target
- ✓ Valuation
- ✓ Synergy

12.2 Overview and Nature of Valuation

The ability of the predatory company to assign value to the business it is attempting to acquire is a crucial factor in any takeover. A predatory firm might then compare the value it has determined for its target with the anticipated cost of the purchase. If the target company's share price exceeds the market price, a bidder's success is unlikely, as shareholders are unlikely to accept the offer. The purchasing business must therefore estimate the target company's value when bidding for both public and private enterprises in order to determine what price it could be willing to offer. It is not necessary to value the target company as a whole; rather, only the equity shares must be valued. Sadly, valuing a company may be a highly complex process. This is because numerous approaches to valuation can be employed. In this way, a lot of people view business valuation as more of an art than a science.

12.3 Valuation as an Art or Science

It is critical to keep in mind that company valuation for merger or acquisition purposes is not an exact science. While methods of valuation exist, they are all predicated on approximations and conjecture. Thus, valuation methods can be used to determine an offer price or to justify an offer price. Nevertheless, the final price is typically determined through negotiation, and the management of the bidding company must exercise their judgment in determining the highest price they are willing to pay. The only "correct" valuation is the price proposed by the bidder and accepted by the shareholders of the target company. This implies that the bidder's price, which the target company's shareholders accept, is the only reasonable value.

When drafting a takeover offer, a corporation should analyze the various valuations that are generated by different methodologies of valuation. The price at which shares of the target firm should be offered should then be determined by judgment rather than an objective value, making it more of an art and less of a science.

12.4 Determinants of Pricing of a Merger or Takeover Bid

When contemplating an acquisition of another business, there are several crucial aspects to consider before determining the potential offer price.

These include:

1. Synergy

Synergy arises when two organizations' assets and/or activities complement each other in such a way that the total of their outputs before the merger is less than their combined output after the merger, as in the case of the 1 + 1 = 3 effect.

2. Real Options

Legal possibilities to grow operations or redeploy may arise from a purchase at some point in the future. A real option is a decision to make a move at a later date, usually contingent on how the firm performs. A purchase has some worth if it produces actual options, such as the ability to eventually expand into a new geographic market.

3. Risk Exposure

Acquisitions and mergers have the potential to change the larger company's asset beta and exposure to market risk. Before concealing a takeover offer or determining an appropriate offer price, the acquiring business ought to contemplate the potential alterations to its risk exposures and their potential magnitude.

4. Financing

A large amount of funding is frequently needed for an acquisition, thus, the company making the acquisition must think about its options for raising the funds. When the purchasing firm is similarly highly geared, it could be challenging to get additional debt financing in order to buy the highly geared target company. The dividend policy may be affected by the use of retained earnings to fund acquisitions.

5. Valuation Assumptions

During a takeover procedure, the target business's directors and the company making the takeover proposal each make their own valuations of the target company. Assumptions underpin valuations, yet many of these assumptions are based on opinions rather than concrete data. Certain forecasts, such as those about the target company's free cash flows or the growth rate of its future profits, may not be accurate. The directors of the company putting up the takeover offer should think about an initial offer price and a price they might be ready to go up to in order to allow for pricing talks.

12.5 Valuation Methods

Although the valuations produced by each approach will differ, they can all offer helpful information and aid in determining the appropriate offer price. Be ready to apply each of the many methods of valuation, and then have a discussion about the estimations and presumptions that underpin the valuation. There are two major methods for appraising businesses. The valuation of a business can be determined using:
1. The value of the assets of the company itself; and
2. The future earnings or cash flows expected from the ownership and utilization of its assets can be analyzed.

Going concern valuation involves various techniques to create various valuations of a company, each with its own advantages and disadvantages. The appropriateness depends on the acquirer's intentions, such as breaking up the acquisition or integrating assets. Now, each of the several approaches to company valuation is examined in turn and demonstrated using a numerical example.

Illustration 12.1

NYQ PLC has a weighted average cost of capital of 14%, a P/E ratio of 37.4, and dispersed earnings of GHS 145.4 million. It is in the process of acquiring Ndori Kaa PLC, which has the following financial information:

Table 12.1: Financial Data on NYQ PLC

	GHS' millions
Profit before interest and tax	132
Interest paid	14.4
Corporate tax	35.28
Distribution earnings	82.32
Current dividend	30p
Last 4 years dividends	20p, 24p, 24p, 28p
Earnings per share	33.4p
P/E ratio	25.74
Market price of ordinary shares	4.3
Equity beta	2.34

Table 12.1: Statement of Financial Position

	GHS million	GHS million
Fixed asset		530
Current assets	120	
Current liabilities	86	34
		564
10% debentures		144
		420
Financed by:		
Ordinary shares (50p)		246
Reserves		174
		420

Ndori Kaa PLC anticipates that the projected synergies from the takeover will allow it to sustain an annual growth in distributable earnings of 5%. Additionally, the business will be able to sell redundant assets, freeing about GHS 120 million in one year. The overall market return is 15%, whereas the risk-free return is 9%.

12.5.1 Stock Market Valuation

1. Any investor who wishes to outperform the market needs to become an expert in stock valuation. In its most basic form, stock valuation is a technique for ascertaining a stock's theoretical or intrinsic worth.

2. The calculation of this valuation approach is simple: it involves multiplying the number of ordinary shares in a firm by their current market value. The stock market's efficiency will, of course, determine whether this is a fair price.

3. Since only a tiny percentage of a business's shares are traded at any given time, it must also be acknowledged that the quoted share price of a firm does not reflect the worth of all of its shares.

4. Furthermore, if the target firm has issued ordinary shares but they are not regularly traded, or if the target company has not been floated at all on a recognized stock exchange, this form of valuation is unlikely to be available.
   - From Ndori Kaa, the number of ordinary shares is 246 / 0.50 = 492m
   - Stock market valuation = 492m * 4.3 = GHS 2,116m
   - Stock market valuation serves as a starting point for takeover purposes, representing the minimum acceptable price for target shareholders.
   - The floor value will be boosted with a substantial purchase premium to encourage shareholders to relinquish their shares.
   - The market value of the target company is not fully reflected due to the lack of consideration for the predatory company's post-acquisition intentions.

12.5.2 Asset Valuation
There are several different ways in which a company's assets can be valued.

12.5.2.1 Book Value
1. One of many valuation techniques, or a way to place a lower bound on a company's value, is the net assets valuation method. It is unlikely to yield the most realistic value on its own.
2. By dividing the total number of shares by the net tangible assets, the value of an equity share is calculated using this method of valuation.
3. The value of the tangible non-current assets (net of depreciation) plus the current assets less all liabilities is what is referred to as net tangible assets in the statement of financial position.
4. Unless they have a commercial value (such as patents and copyrights, which might be sold), intangible assets (such as goodwill and research costs) should be eliminated.
    - Mathematically, the book or asset valuation can be defined as:
    - Net Asset Value (NAV) = fixed assets + net current assets minus long-term debt.
    - From Ndori Kaa, NAV = GHS 530m + GHS 34m – GHS 144m
    = GHS 420m.

12.5.2.2 Realizable or Break-up Value
- It is feasible for assets to be appraised using their net realizable value as opposed to their stock book prices.
- The amount that could be obtained if the target company's assets were sold on the open market is the basis for this valuation. Formally speaking, it is the remaining value that remains after creditors are paid off, assets are realized, and liquidation expenses are subtracted.
- Theoretically, a company's market value ought to exceed its break-up value or remain unchanged. A company's market value is lower than its break-up value, suggesting undervaluation due to stock market inefficiencies, potentially allowing a predatory company to profit without risk.

- o The net realizable value of a company's assets is challenging due to historical cost, property underestimation, stock overestimation, unique assets, and provisions for unforeseen liabilities.
- o Book values may overestimate realizable value, and financial position figures may underestimate property value. Unique assets may not be easily sold, and provisions for unforeseen liabilities may be necessary.
- o In the case of most takeovers, the break-up values are not the most appropriate method of valuation anyway, as very few takeovers involve a total break-up of the victim company.

12.5.2.3 Replacement Value
- o This approach looks at how much it would cost to buy a target company's assets on the open market.
- o The replacement cost estimates of asset values are more relevant than historical cost estimates, which gives it an edge over a book valuation. Regretfully, goodwill is not taken into consideration.
- o It also calls for identifying the distinct assets of the business and figuring out how much each one would cost to replace.
- o It will be challenging to locate secondhand assets in comparable conditions, given most corporate assets are only partially utilized.
- o Due to a lack of information, we have not calculated the realizable and replacement values of Ndori Kaa's assets.

12.5.2.4 Factors to Consider when Selecting Assets Valuation Bases
The following list should give you some idea of the factors that must be considered.
1. Do the assets need a professional valuation? If so, how much will this cost?
2. The question is whether liabilities, such as deferred taxation, are accurately quantified, if any contingent liabilities exist, and if balancing tax charges will arise upon disposal.
3. The current assets' valuation, collectability, realizability, and physical location of all assets, especially those abroad, may be crucial for determining their saleable condition.

4. The question is whether it is possible to accurately assess hidden liabilities, including redundancy payments and closure costs.
5. The statement of financial position values should accurately reflect the break-up values of assets in an available market.
6. Are there any prior charges on the assets?
7. The business's revaluation and replacement policy, as well as the valuation's bases, are crucial factors in estimating future cash flows from the asset.
8. The question suggests that there may be factors that suggest the overall business valuation is significantly higher than the individual asset valuation.
9. What shareholdings are being sold? If a non-controlling interest is being disposed of, the realizable value is of limited relevance as the assets will not be sold.

12.5.3 Going-Concern Valuation

If the predatory firm intends for the target company to remain in operation without major modifications for the foreseeable future, rather than dismantling or selling off its assets after the acquisition, then the target company should be valued as a going concern. The value of a firm as a going concern can be determined in a variety of ways. Now, these are taken into account and quantitatively demonstrated concerning Ndori Kaa PLC.

12.5.3.1 Capitalized Earnings Valuation

The valuation method involves capitalizing a company's annual maintainable expected earnings by a required earnings yield, considering historical earnings and potential future earnings increases due to synergy or economies of scale, and adjusting the discount rate accordingly. The valuation using this method is as follows:

$$\text{Capitalized earnings value} = \frac{\textit{Annual maintainable expected earnings}}{\textit{Required earnings yield}}$$

- In this example, the approximated capitalization rate is as follows:
- Required earnings yield = EPS/share price = (33.4/4.3) x 100 = 7.8%

- Current distributable earnings can be capitalized if they are equivalent to annual maintainable expected earnings and are used to calculate the current financial statement.
- Capitalized earnings value = GHS 82.32m / 0.078 = GHS 1,055m
- This method offers a forward-looking measure of expected earnings, enabling forecasting of future performance, but also introduces uncertainty due to accounting policies and the treatment of exceptional items.

12.5.3.2 Price/Earnings Ratio Valuation

This valuation method involves multiplying the target company's distributable earnings by an appropriate P/E ratio, where:

$$\text{P/E ratio} = \frac{\text{Market value of company}}{\text{Distributable earnings}}$$

- The P/E ratio selected, including the predator's and victim's P/E ratios, significantly influences the valuation of Ndori Kaa PLC. The following results were obtained from Ndori Kaa PLC:

Company value = 25.74 x GHS 82.32 = **GHS 2,119m**

- The P/E ratio of a company is the reciprocal of its earnings yield, and if a predatory company believes it can improve its victim's performance, it can use its own P/E ratio.

Company value = 37.4m x GHS 82.32m = **GHS 3,079m**

- To predict future predatory/victim performance, a weighted average of Ndori Kaa and NYQ's P/E ratio, based on their current distributable earnings, is more appropriate.

= [25.74 x (82.32/227.72)] + [37.4 x (145.4/227.72)] = 33.18

Company value = 33.18 x GHS 82.32m = **GHS 2,731m**

o The method of calculating post-merger P/E ratios is straightforward, but its valuation varies widely, posing challenges due to the use of different bases and the difficulty in estimating appropriate post-merger P/E ratios.

12.5.3.3 Significance of high P/E ratio
A high P/E Ratio may indicate:

1. Expectations that the EPS will Grow Rapidly
Many small, fast-growing companies are valued on high P/E ratios, with some reaching high valuations before making any profits based on expected future earnings.

2. Security of earnings
A similar company with more uncertain earnings would be valued at a lower P/E ratio than a well-established, low-risk corporation.

3. Status
A quoted company bids for an unquoted company, expecting a higher P/E ratio on its shares due to lower risk and the advantage of easily sold shares in a stock market.

12.5.3.4 Problems with Using P/E Ratios
Using quoted companies' P/E ratios to value unquoted companies can be challenging, as a P/E ratio must be guessed using similar quoted companies as a guide.
1. Finding a quoted company with a similar range of activities can be challenging due to their often-diversified nature.
2. If a company's earnings are erratic or the reported share price is unusual—perhaps as a result of a takeover bid—a single year's P/E ratio would not be appropriate for assessing its financial standing.
3. The use of a P/E ratio trend involves utilizing historical data to predict the future performance of an unquoted company.
4. The capital structure of the quoted company and the unquoted company could differ.

12.5.4 Guidelines for a P/E Ratio-Based Valuation

The ultimate offer price for an acquisition of an unquoted firm will be negotiated; however, the following is a summary of some of the criteria that influence the valuer's selection of the P/E ratio.

1. General economic and financial conditions.
2. An unnecessarily low valuation can be obtained by using current P/E ratios if the industry as a whole is experiencing a loss of trust.
3. The nature of the industry and its prospects.
4. The project's magnitude and standing within the sector. A greater P/E ratio should be applied when evaluating the shares of an unquoted firm because it may pursue a listing on its own if its earnings are increasing annually.
5. Marketability in shares without stock market quotations is restricted, requiring higher yields due to the diversity of shareholdings and principal shareholder financial status.
6. Profit estimates and past profit records can provide a more reliable valuation, especially when compared to industry levels over time.
7. Asset backing and liquidity.
8. A high gearing ratio typically indicates higher financial risk for ordinary shareholders and necessitates a higher rate of return on equity.

12.5.4.1 Use of a Bidder's P/E Ratio

Sometimes a bidder's business will assess a target company's worth based on its greater P/E ratio. This may be a risky assumption to make because it presumes that the bidder can enhance the target's operations. Using an adjusted industry P/E ratio or another technique would be preferable.

12.5.4.2 Use of Forecast Earnings

When considering a company's acquisition, it is crucial to assess the target company's forecast earnings, ensuring they are future, maintainable earnings. Forecasts of earnings growth should only be used if:

1. There are good reasons to believe that earnings growth will be achieved;
2. A reasonable estimate of growth can be made; and
3. The target company's directors provide accurate forecasts in good faith, using reasonable assumptions and fair accounting policies.

12.5.5 Dividend Valuation Model (Gordon Growth Model)

The Gordon growth model can be used to assess a company's value by calculating the present value of future dividends that will be paid on its shares. Below is the estimation:

$$P_0 = \frac{D_0(1+g)}{(r-g)}$$

Where:
D_o = Current total dividend payment
g = Expected annual growth rate of dividends
r = Required rate of return of the company's shareholders

- To apply this model to Ndori Kaa PLC, we need to calculate its annual growth using its historical dividend values.

$$= 20 \times (1+g)^4$$
$$= \underline{30}$$

Hence:

$$g = \sqrt[4]{\frac{30}{20}} - 1$$

$$= \underline{10.7\%}$$

- To calculate the total amount of recent dividends (Do), multiply the dividend per share by the number of Ndori Kaa's shares.
= 0.30 x 492m shares = **GHS 147.6m**

- The required return of Ndori's shareholders is now required, using the target company's rate of return instead of the predatory companies, as former shareholders are being asked to sell their shares. We can calculate the required number of Ndori's shareholders by using the CAPM and the data supplied earlier:

r = 9% + 2.34 x (15% - 9%) = 23%

- If we put our calculated data into the Gordon model we obtain:
  - Company value = $\dfrac{GHS\ 147.6m \times (1+0.107)}{(0.23-0.107)}$

$$= \underline{\textbf{GHS 1,328m}}$$

12.5.5.1 Assumptions in the Dividend Valuation Model
The dividend valuation model is underpinned by some assumptions that you should keep in mind.
1. The model fails to consider shareholders' diverse expectations and motivations, as investors act rationally and homogeneously, focusing on dividends over future capital appreciation.
2. The current year's dividend (D_o figure) does not significantly differ from dividend trends, but an adjusted trend figure based on past dividends may be more suitable.
3. The method uses reasonable estimates for future dividends, prices, and cost of capital, but may not accurately predict future costs due to historical trends or uncertain earnings forecasts.
4. Discounted cash flow arithmetic can be used to model investors' attitudes toward different cash flows at different times.
5. Directors use dividends to indicate a company's position strength, but companies that pay zero dividends do not have zero share values.
6. Dividends either show no growth or constant growth. If the growth rate is estimated using Gordon's growth approximation (g = br), then the model assumes that the percentage of profits retained in the business and the return on those retained profits, b and r, are constant values.
7. Other influences on share prices are ignored.
8. The company's earnings will increase sufficiently to maintain dividend growth levels.

12.5.5.2 Discounted Cash Flow Valuation
The difference between the current amounts of Ndori Kaa's pre- and post-acquisition cash flows is the maximum price that NYQ should be willing to spend for the company:

$$PV_{X+Y} - PV_Y$$

Discounted cash flow valuations are preferred but face numerous problems before useful information can be obtained from them for determining a target company's value.

1. The challenge lies in accurately estimating future cash flow predictions, considering expected synergy benefits, and determining the expected growth rate of these cash flows.
2. The company must select a suitable timeframe for estimating future cash flows and determining its terminal value at the end of the period.
3. The predatory company's cost of capital is the most suitable discount rate, but it's challenging to calculate. In cases where the victim company's risk characteristics differ, the CAPM can be used to determine a more appropriate discount rate.
4. The difference between Ndori Kaa PLC's pre- and post-acquisition cash flows is insufficiently determined, but using distributable earnings as an approximate substitute can provide insight.

	GHS
Current distributable earnings	145.4m
Ndori Kaa's distributable earnings	82.32m
Total Post-acquisition earnings	**227.7m**

5. NYQ anticipates being able to raise profits by 5% annually. Additionally, NYQ anticipates being able to sell extra assets in a year for GHS 120 million. If a superior option isn't available, we can reduce using NYQ's WACC:

	GHS
Present value of post-acquisition earnings	
[(227.7 x 1.05) / (0.28 − 0.05) + (120 / 1.28)]	1,133m
Present value of pre-acquisition earnings (145.4 / 0.28)	519m
Maximum price that NYQ should prepare to pay	**614m**

This valuation is based on the assumption that growth in distributable earnings will occur only if the acquisition goes ahead and uses the Gordon model.

12.6 Concept of Synergy and Determination

Acquiring companies typically pay a significant premium on the stock market value of the companies they purchase. The primary reason behind this is the *concept of synergy, where the merger benefits shareholders by increasing the post-merger share price through the potential value of synergy*. Rational owners would be unlikely to sell if they could benefit more from not selling, which means buyers must pay a premium to acquire the company, regardless of the pre-merger valuation. This premium represents the future prospects of the seller's company and a portion of the post-merger synergy that the buyers anticipate achieving.

Another name for synergy is the "1 + 1 = 3" effect. It is the idea that, following a merger or purchase, the combined value of two independent organizations will be greater than their combined value as separate entities. Opportunities to increase earnings may present themselves when two distinct entities merge to become a single business.

12.6.1 Categories of Synergy
Three categories could be used to classify synergies:

1. Revenue Synergies
Revenue synergies are gains in overall sales revenue that occur from a combination of greater combined market shares after a merger or acquisition. It is unusual for revenue synergies to occur, but they might occur in the following circumstances:
- The acquisition or merger of a company expands its reach, enhances brand promotion, and boosts market share due to the new brand image attracted by customers; and
- The acquisition or merger creates a larger company capable of bidding for large contracts, such as government supply, which was previously impossible for smaller companies.

2. Cost Synergies

Cost synergies occur when a merger or takeover leads to cost reductions due to improved efficiency, such as combining administrative functions or warehouse facilities, and may also result in staff redundancies.

3. Financial Synergies.

A larger company or group can raise finance cheaper due to access to financial markets and lower credit risk, allowing it to borrow from banks at lower interest rates.

12.6.2 Synergic Equation of Mergers and Takeovers

To determine whether a deal is sensible, the following equation provides a useful approach to considering synergy and calculating the minimum required synergy. In essence, the success of a merger is determined by whether the buyer's value is enhanced through the transaction.

The equation for calculating the minimum required synergy is as follows:

Minimum Required Synergy (MRS) = (Offer Price - Pre-Merger Market Value) / Pre-Merger Market Value

This equation helps buyers determine the minimum amount of synergy needed to justify paying a premium for the acquisition. If the calculated synergy is achievable and exceeds the minimum required synergy, the merger is likely to be successful in enhancing shareholder value.

Illustration 12.2:

The Board of Ebie Tra Ebie Ltd. has decided to acquire Suro Krosona Ltd. The current data for these companies is as follows:

Table 12.3: Financial Data

	Ebie Tra Ebie Ltd.	Suro Krosona Ltd.
Earnings After Tax (EAT) GHCm	500	100
Number of shares outstanding	50	25
Earnings per share (EPS)	5	2
Price/Earnings (P/E) in times	5	2.5
Market Price Per Share (MPS)	50	10

Ebie Tra Ebie Ltd. has engaged you as a consultant to advise on this merger and takeover transaction. Your advice should answer the following questions:
  a) Determine the swap ratio based on current market prices?
  b) What is the post-merging EPS of Ebie Tra Ebie Ltd.?
  c) Determine the expected MPS of Ebie Tra Ebie Ltd. in the post-merging period, assuming the P/E ratio of Firm A remains unchanged.
  d) Determine the market value of the merged firm.
  e) Calculate the gain/loss for shareholders of the two independent companies, after the merger.
  f) Determine the upper and lower limits for the swap ratio beyond which the two firms would not go for the acquisition or merger

Solution:
  a) For illustrative purposes, we ignore the formal report format as consultants. The swap ratio is also called the exchange ratio. The swap or exchange ratio is the ratio of the number of shares of one company to be issued for each share of the other company received. Normally, it is pegged as a ratio of the MPS of the target firm to the MPS of the

acquirer or the predatory firm. This requires that for every share in the target firm, how many shares in the acquirer will be issued?

This is given as the ratio of the MPS of the target (MPSt) to the MPS of the acquirer (MPSa).

$$\frac{MPSt}{MPSa} = \frac{10}{50}$$

$$0.2 : 1$$

b) Post merging EPS of Ebie Tra Ebie Ltd.

Post-merger EPS = $\frac{NY_a + NY_t \pm Adj}{SO_a + NS} = \frac{500 + 100}{[50 + (0.2*25)]}$

$$\frac{600}{55}$$

GHS10.91

Where:

NYa and NYt are the net income of acquirer and target, respectively, and Adj is the incremental adjustment from the merger. This can be plus or minus. SO is the number of acquirer's shares outstanding; NS is the number of new shares issued by the acquirer.

c) The expected MPS of Ebie Tra Ebie Ltd. in the post-merging period

Post-merger MPS = $P/E_{Ebie} * EPS_{pm} = 5 * 10.91$

GHS54.55

Where:

P/E$_{ebie}$ is the P/E ratio of Ebie Tra Ebie Ltd.
EPS$_{pm}$ is the EPS of Ebie Tra Ebie Ltd. in the post-merger

d) The market value (MV) of the merged firm

MV after merger = $MPS * Total\ Shares\ outstanding\ in\ the\ merged\ firm$

= 54.55 * 55

= **GHS3,000.25**

e) **Gain or Loss**

Table 12.4: Gain or Loss for Shareholders of the Two Independent Companies, After the Merger.

Estimation of Combined Gains/Loss	GHS	GHS
Post-Merger Market value [54.55*55]		3,000.25
MV of Ebie Tra Ebie before merger [50*50]	2,500.00	
MV of Suro Krosona Ltd. before merger [10*25]	250.00	(2,750.00)
Gains from Merger		**250.25**
Estimation of Gains/Loss (Ebie Tra Ebie)		
Post-Merger Market value [54.55*50]		2,727.50
MV of Ebie Tra Ebie before merger [50*50]		(2,500.00)
Gains from Merger		**227.50**
Estimation of Gains/Loss (Suro Krosona Ltd.)		
Post-Merger Market value [54.55*5]		272.75
MV of Ebie Tra Ebie before merger [10*25]		(250.00)
Gains from Merger		**22.75**

f.) The upper and lower limits for the swap ratio are beyond which the two firms would not go for the acquisition or merger.

   i. *The lower-limit exchange ratio is determined from the perspective of the target entity. This is the lowest or minimum exchange ratio acceptable to the shareholders of the target entity (in this case, Suro Krosona Ltd.) to the extent that the existing wealth is not reduced.*

   ii. *The Upper limit exchange ratio is determined from the perspective of the acquirer. This is the highest or maximum exchange ratio*

acceptable to the shareholders of the acquiring entity (in this case Ebie Tra Ebie Ltd.) to the extent that the existing wealth is not diluted.

Table 12.5: Lower Limit Gains -EbieTra Ebie

Lower Limit (based on gains accruing to Ebie Tra Ebie):	GHS	GHS
Post-Merger Market value [54.55*55]		3,000.25
Pre-merger (or minimum post-merger) value acceptable to shareholders of Suro Krosona Ltd. [10*25]		(250.00)
Maximum acceptable MV of Ebie Tra Ebie in post-merger		**2,750.25**
Desired post-merger MPS of Ebie Tra Ebie (Divided by the number of equity shares outstanding [2,750.25/50]	55.00	

Number of equity shares required to be issued in Ebie Tra Ebie to have the desired MPS of GHS55 and to have a post-merger value of GHS250 of Suro Krosona Ltd. is given as:
    = Post-Merge Value of Suro Krosona Ltd. divided by the desired MPS
    = GHS250/GHS55
    = 4.55 shares
 The Existing number of Equity shares outstanding in Suro Krosona Ltd. is 25
       Share exchange ratio (4.55/25) = 0.18:1 or 1: 5.6
 Therefore, for every 5.5 shares of Suro Krosona Ltd., 1 share in Ebie Tra Ebie will be issued. This is the lowest or minimum exchange ratio acceptable to Suro Krosona Ltd. Any ratio lower than this will decrease their existing wealth of GHS250.		

Upper Limit (based on Gains accruing to Suro Krosona Ltd.)	GHS	GHS

Post-Merger Market value [54.55*55]		3,000.25
Pre-merger (or minimum post-merger) value acceptable to shareholders of Ebie Tra Ebie Ltd. [50*50]		(2500.00)
Maximum acceptable MV of Suro Krosona Ltd. in post-merger		**500.25**

Since the post-merger market value of Ebie Tra Ebie remains unchanged at GHS2,500 and so the number of its outstanding shares (50) and MPS of GHS50, the number of equity shares required to be issued in Ebie Tra Ebie to have an MPS of GHS50 and to have a post-merger value of GHS500.25 of Suro Krosona Ltd. is given as:

= Post-Merge Value of Suro Krosona Ltd. divided by the desired MPS
= GHS500.25/GHS50   = 10 shares

The existing number of Equity shares outstanding in Suro Krosona Ltd. is 25

Share exchange ratio (10/25) = 0.40:1 or 1: 2.5

Therefore, for every 2.5 shares of Suro Krosona Ltd., 1 share in Ebie Tra Ebie Ltd. will be issued. This is the highest exchange ratio acceptable to shareholders of Ebie Tra Ebi, as any ratio higher than this will dilute their existing wealth of GHS2,500.00.

Illustration 12.3

The following information is available about Eiiii Hmmmm Company Limited.

Table 12.6: Financial Data on Eiiii Hmmmm

Eiiii Hmmmm	GHS (000)
Tangible non-current assets	500
Intangible non-current asset	150
Current assets	<u>120</u>
	770

Ordinary shares of Ghc.1	100
Revaluation reserves	160
Retained profits	290
	550
Bank loans	180
Current liabilities	40
	770

Required:

Provide an asset-based valuation of the share to **Eiiii Hmmmm**

Solution

1. The book value of the net assets is GHS 550,000 or GHS 5.50 per share (550/100). However, this valuation is based on the assumption that the tangible non-current assets are suitably valued and that GHS 150,000 represents a realistic value for the intangible non-current asset.
2. It is therefore, unlikely that the target company shareholders will accept an offer below GHS 5.50 per share, and the offer will almost certainly need to be higher than GHS 5.50 if the takeover is to succeed.
3. Valuations based on other valuation methods should be compared with assets-based valuations. There should be some concern (for the bidding company) if a valuation based on expected earnings, dividends, or cash flow is lower than the asset-based valuation.

Illustration 12.4

The share price of ABC Company is currently GHS 850. The cost of equity capital is 15%. The annual dividends have just been paid. It is expected that the annual dividend next year will be GHS 35 per share and that the annual dividends will then grow at a constant annual rate into the foreseeable future.

Required

1. Calculate the expected annual growth rate in dividends from next year onwards.

2. Suppose that the stock market now receives new and unexpected information about the company that makes investors re-assess the future annual dividends. Investors now expect that the annual dividend next year will be 10% lower than previously and that the annual growth in dividends in subsequent years will be only 5%.

Solution:

a. Let the annual growth rate in dividends be g.

$$850 = \frac{35}{(0.15 - g)} = g$$

$$\underline{= 11\%}$$

b. The annual dividend next year is now expected to be GHS 31.50
[35 − (35 * 0.10)]

$$MV\ (Ex\text{-}div) = \frac{31.5}{(0.15 - 0.05)}$$

$$\underline{= GHS\ 315}$$

Illustration 12.5

You are given the following information regarding Kobiri & Sons Company Limited, an unquoted company:

Issued Ordinary Capital is 200,000 shares at GHS1. Extracts from Profit and Loss for the year ended December 31, 2023 are given in Table 12.7:

Table 12.7: Extracts from Profit and Loss Account

	GHS	GHS
Profit before tax		130,000
Less tax		60,000
Profit for the year		70,000
Dividend: Preference	10,000	
Ordinary	18,000	28,000
Retained profit		42,000

You have found that the PE ratio of a similar quoted company obtained from the stock exchange is 12.

Required:
Your uncle wants to acquire 50% of Kobiri & Sons Company Limited; advise him the value to pay.

Illustration 12.6

Price = EPS x PE ratio

$$EPS = \frac{Earnings - Preference\ share\ div}{Number\ of\ shares}$$

$$EPS = \frac{70,000 - 10,000}{200,000}$$

EPS = **GHS 0.3**

Kobiri & Sons Company Limited is not quoted, but the PE ratio of a similar company is 12. The 12 will be marked down by 25% to cater for the non-marketability of Kobiri & Sons Company Limited shares.

Hence:
Applicable PE ration = 75% x 12
= 9
Price = 0.3 x 9

= **2.7 per share**
No. of shares to acquire = 50% x 200,000
= 100,000

Therefore, the value = 200,000 x 2.7
= **540,000**

Illustration 12.7
The abridged Statement of Financial Position of Bukyeewonye Ltd. as at 31/12/2022 is given Table 12.8.

Table 12.8: Statement of Financial Position of Bukyeewonye Ltd.

	GHS
Fixed assets (Net)	225,000
Net current assets	50,000
	275,000
Represented by:	
Ordinary shares	100,000
Reserves	175,000
6% Debentures (115 per 100)	**275,000**

You ascertain the following relevant information:
a) The debenture is now trading at GHS 115 per every GHS 100.
b) The market value of goodwill not recorded in the books is GHS 25,000.
c) The current market value of freehold property exceeds the book value by GHS 15,000.
d) All other assets are estimated to be realizable at their book values.

Required:
You are required to value 85% holding of ordinary shares on a net asset's basis.

Solution

Table 12.9: Valuation of 85% Holdings in Bukyeewonye Ltd.

	Book Values GHS	Realizable Values GHS
Fixed Assets	225,000	240,000
Goodwill		25,000
Adjusted Fixed Assets	225,000	265,000
Net Current Assets	50,000	50,000
	275,000	315,000
Debentures	(100,000)	(115,000)
Net Assets	175,000	200,000
Value of 85% holding	**148,750**	**170,000**

12.7 Chapter Review Questions

1. In mergers and takeovers, there is a need for valuation of shares of some sort. Experts have described valuation as more of an art than science. Explain.
2. Explain five (5) factors to be considered in pricing a takeover bid.
3. In mergers and takeovers, one (1) + one (1) is not always equal to 2: Discuss
4. Explain the statement 'Valuation is both an art and science'
5. Micky Ltd. is an Accra-based Clothing Company owned and managed by its two founders. The company has been selling to only domestic consumers in Ghana since inception. The founders think it is time to extend the operations of the company to foreign markets, particularly those in neighboring West African countries. Moving into foreign markets requires additional financing and capabilities, which the company does not have. The owners have agreed on ceding 40% stake in their company to a strategic investor who would provide the additional financing and capabilities needed to compete successfully in the international business environment.

However, they are not sure of what range of prices to accept for the shares they would give up.

Below is a summary of financial data for Micky Ltd. for the recent financial year.

Issues Shares	1 million
	GHS'000
After-tax profit	4,800
Total dividends	960
Property	25,250
Current assets	12,650
Long-term borrowings	4,550
Current liabilities	5,550

The following information are relevant to the position and value of Micky Ltd.:
   a. The assets of Micky Ltd. were calculated just after the recent financial statements were published. Inventories and trade receivables, which are

included in current assets, were written down by GHS 40,000 and GHS 47,500 respectively. Property, plant and equipment were valued at GHS 26,200,000.

b. Micky Ltd. falls into the fabrics and clothing industry. The average P/E ratio for listed equity stock in the industry is 10. The average required return on listed equity stocks in the industry is 16%.

c. Marketability of shares in Micky Ltd. is limited as its equity stock is not listed on the stock exchange. Consequently, investors demand a marketability risk premium of 7% above the industry average required return on equity in order to invest in the equity stock of Micky Ltd.

d. Earnings and dividends of Micky Ltd. are expected to grow by 5% every year to perpetuity.

Required:

i. Estimate an appropriate required rate of return on the equity stock of the Micky Ltd.

ii. Estimate a range of suitable considerations for 40% stake in Micky Ltd. using the net assets method, P/E ratio method, and dividend valuation method.

6. Royal Limited is considering a takeover bid for Ben & Co. Limited, another company in the same industry. Little is expected to have earnings next year of GHS 43,000. If Royal acquires Ben & Co. Limited, the expected results from Ben & Co. Limited will be as follows:

	Year after the Acquisition		
	Year 1 GHS	Year 2 GHS	Year3 GHS
Sales	100,000	140,000	160,000
Cash costs/expenses	60,000	80,000	90,000
Capital allowances	10,000	15,000	20,000
Interest charges	5,000	5,000	5,000
Cash flows to replace assets and finance growth	12,500	15,000	17,500

i. From year 4 onwards, it is expected that the annual cash flows from Ben & Co. Limited will increase by 4% each year in perpetuity.
ii. Tax is payable at the rate of 30%, and the tax is paid in the same year as the profits to which the tax relates.
iii. If Royal acquires Ben & Co. Limited, it estimates that its gearing after the acquisition will be 35% (measured as the value of the debt capital as a proportion of its total equity plus debt). Its cost of debt is 7.4% before tax. Royal has an equity beta of 1.60.
iv. The risk-free rate of return is 6%, and the return on the market portfolio is 11%.

Required:
a. Suggest what the offer price for Ben & Co. Limited should be if Royal chooses to value Ben & Co. Limited on a forward P/E multiple of 8.0 times
b. Calculate a cost of capital for Royal
c. Suggest what the after price for Ben & Co. Limited might be using a DCF-based.

12.8 Chapter References and Bibliography

[1] Aluko, B. T., & Amidu, A. R. (2005). Corporate business valuation for mergers and acquisitions. *International Journal of Strategic Property Management*, 9(3), 173-189.

[2] Aydin, N. (2017). Mergers and acquisitions: a review of valuation methods. *International Journal of Business and Social Science*, 8(5), 147.

[3] Ferris, K., Petitt, B., & Ferris, K. R. (2013). *Valuation for mergers and acquisitions*. Pearson.

[4] Fiorentino, R., & Garzella, S. (2013). The synergy valuation models: towards the real value of mergers and acquisitions. *International Research Journal of Finance and Economics*, (124).

[5] Petitt, B. S., & Ferris, K. R. (2013). *Valuation for mergers and acquisitions*. FT Press.

[6] Ray, K. G. (2022). *Mergers and acquisitions: Strategy, valuation and integration*. PHI Learning Pvt. Ltd.

CHAPTER 13

FINANCING OPTIONS FOR ACQUISITIONS

13.1 Overview

Acquisitions have significant financial implications for the companies involved, with different financing methods having different financial implications. The predatory company must consider satisfying the needs of shareholders in both the acquired firm and the acquiring firm (predator).

Objectives of the Chapter

This chapter addresses the following key objectives:

- To examine the Financing methods of M&A;
- To identify the strategic and tactical issues relating to M&A;
- To examine Merger regulation and control;
- To evaluate the bidding processes and bid defenses;
- To examine the economic gains and cost of mergers; and
- To analyze All-share transaction.

Key Terms Used in the Chapter

- ✓ Bid
- ✓ Control
- ✓ Economic gains
- ✓ All-share transaction
- ✓ Cash offers
- ✓ Vendor placing

13.2 Financing Methods

Currently, in mergers and acquisitions (M&A) transactions, there are several financing methods for an investor or the acquirer to purchase shares or capital contributions in the target company. The following are the financing methods the acquirer can adopt:

13.2.1 Cash Offers

Here, cash is used to buy shares of the target firm. The target company's shareholders are drawn to a cash offer because they know exactly how much money they would get in exchange for giving up their shares. After receiving their monetary compensation, stockholders of the target business can then make adjustments to their portfolios. Cash issues often arise from external sources, such as debt finance, borrowed money from banks, or debt securities. This is often used in leveraged takeovers, where large amounts of cash are borrowed for payment. Companies with high gearing may struggle to find sufficient banks or financial intermediaries to provide the required debt financing.

Advantages of Cash Offers to The Bidding Company and its Shareholders
1. There are also significant advantages to cash offers for the bidding company and its shareholders.
2. It allows them to see exactly how much is being offered to the victim company.
3. Cash offers will not impact the predatory company's equities shares issue number, preventing dilution of earnings per share.

13.2.2 Share-for-Share Offers

- In this case, the shareholders of the victim firm receive an offer to exchange their shares in their own company for a predetermined number of shares in the predatory company.
- One benefit of a share-for-share offer for the victims' shareholders is that, despite the company being a part of a larger enterprise, they still retain an equity interest in the business they originally invested in.

- Furthermore, they are not liable for any capital gains taxes resulting from the sale of their shares, nor are they charged brokerage fees for reinvesting any funds received.
- Equity payments are more expensive than cash offers for acquiring companies and shareholders. The predatory company may increase shares, leading to a possible decrease in share price, dilution of control, and a decrease in gearing, potentially increasing the predatory company's capital cost.

13.2.3 Vendor Placings and Vendor Rights
- These funding strategies are riffs on the cash offer concept, taking advantage of a gap in the accounting standards definition of a merger to permit corporations to apply merger accounting rules to the post-merger company instead of takeover accounting rules.
- A takeover occurs when a corporation makes cash offers to target company shareholders; merger accounting is not applicable in this situation.
- In a vendor placement, the target firm's shareholders are offered shares by the purchasing business, with the option to retain their shareholding.
- On the other hand, the purchasing business concurrently makes arrangements for the payment of cash to the shareholders of the target company and the placement of the new shares with institutional investors.
- The only way a vendor rights issue differs from this is in the ultimate destination of the shares being offered. The shares are made available to the shareholders of the acquiring firm rather than being placed with institutional investors.

13.2.4 Security Packages
These days, it is uncommon for predatory companies to pay target firm stockholders with instruments other than their ordinary shares. Financing takeovers have not involved much use of security packages, which can comprise bonds, convertibles, and preference shares.

13.2.4.1 Problems of Associated with Security Packages

The problems of using these securities as a method of payment are as follows:

1. **Straight debentures and Loan Stock**

The acceptability of ordinary debt securities from the perspective of the target company's shareholders is a significant issue with employing them as a payment method. It may not sit well with investors to swap their shares in the victim firm for debt securities with low risk and low return, if they had previously purchased shares to fulfill their preferences for high risk and high return.

2. **Convertible Bonds**

Offering convertible bonds to victim company shareholders can partially resolve problems with straight bonds. Convertibles offer shareholders future corporate growth and delay EPS dilution. Banks may not lend money to predatory companies due to post-acquisition gearing levels, but target shareholders may accept convertibles as payment, expecting reduced gearing levels.

3. **Preference Shares**

Preference shares are even less frequently used as a form of payment than bonds. Because preference dividends are less flexible than regular share distributions, preference shares are less appealing to predatory companies than ordinary stock. Preference dividends cannot be deducted from taxable profit since they are payouts of after-tax profit.

4. **Mixed Bids**

Mixed bids, where a share-for-share offer is supported by a cash alternative, are gaining popularity due to their perceived acceptance by target shareholders and the requirement for companies to acquire 30% or more shares to make a cash offer at the highest price.

13.3 Strategic and Tactical Issues

When a business engages in acquisitional behavior, it needs to carefully examine the approach and methods it will take. It must be satisfied that acquisition is a more cost-effective option than organic expansion or the independent acquisition of necessary assets before engaging in takeover activities. A predator may pay over the odds or, in the worst instance, not be able to capture its victim at all if the proper tactics and strategic process are not used. After a business is pleased with these aspects, it should proceed with the strategic strategy to acquire a target business.

13.3.1 Strategic Strategy Procedures
1. Identify suitable target companies.
2. Obtain as much information about the target companies as possible.
3. The process involves valuing each potential target company based on the obtained information and determining the maximum purchase price for each option.
4. Decide which of the potential target companies is most appropriate.
5. Decide upon the best way to finance the acquisition.

13.4 Shareholding and its Implication
A summary of levels of shareholding and their associated implication is given in Table 13.1.

Table 13.1 Level of Share Holdings and Associated Implications

Voting Right	Implications
90% and above	Once 90% of shares are held the company has a right to purchase compulsorily the remaining shares.
75% and above	The acquiring company can change the articles of association of the company taken over and put it into liquidation.
50% and above	The company can influence dividend policy and appoint management.
30% and above	It imposes effective control on public companies and hence requires the launch of a formal takeover bid.
25% and above	Minority influence on dividend policy and management.
10% and above	Can prevent a complete takeover.

13.5 Merger Regulation and Control

Two types of regulation govern merger and takeover activity, which are characterized as legal controls and self-regulatory controls.

13.5.1 Legal Controls

A variety of statutory restrictions apply to takeover activity, the most significant of which is the Fair-Trading Act of 1973. According to this Act, any merger and acquisition involving the creation of a business that holds a larger than 25% market share or the acquisition of assets costing more than a specific sum of money must be reviewed by the Director General of Fair Trading. After gathering data on mergers and acquisitions that fit these requirements, the Director General contacts the Secretary of State to inquire about whether he believes a particular merger or acquisition ought to be looked into by the Monopolies and Mergers Commission (MMC). The criteria that are considered in deciding whether a merger should be referred are meant to indicate whether a merger will maintain or promote the public interests as regards:

- Effective competition within the industry;
- The interests of consumers, purchasers, and users of the goods and services in the industry are influenced by quality, price, and variety; and.
- The reduction of costs and the introduction of new products and techniques.

13.5.2 Self-Regulatory Controls

When social interests are involved in economic activity, laws are applied with the intention of regulating the activity to protect the interests of the general public. Any type of takeover or merger involving the individual and collective interests of various parties—shareholders, creditors, employees, and customers—is referred to as a business combination. Every nation has developed legal regulations governing the establishment and structure of businesses in order to protect the general welfare and the interests of its customers. The Stock Exchange has a rule book for member companies to follow, addressed to the Securities and Investment Board. It also requires member companies to keep shareholders informed.

13.6 The Bidding Processes

When a business makes a bid, it frequently consults with financial advisors, such as merchant banks; therefore, it is critical that the business thoroughly considers the strategies it will use. The acquiring business will try to pay as little as possible below the maximum amount it has decided it is willing to pay. Throughout the bidding process, adherence to the City Code is required. The goal of this is to safeguard the interests of the various participating shareholder groups. The following processes are included in the code:

1. The acquiring company must inform potential victims five days after acquiring a five percent stake to prevent dawn raids, allowing victims to prepare for potential attacks;
2. After 30% of the victim company's shares are held, the predatory must offer a cash offer to all remaining shareholders at the highest price paid in the previous 12-month period;
3. The acquiring company must inform the target company's board of its offer's nature and terms, which are then shared with the victim company's board by shareholders;
4. After receiving the offer, the victim company's board will evaluate its acceptability, and the acquiring company may need shareholder approval for the proposed bid;
5. An unconditional offer occurs when the acquiring company acquires over 50% of the victim company's shares, giving existing shareholders 14 days to sell or become minority shareholders; and
6. Partial bids, where the acquiring company bids for a specific percentage of the victim company's share capital, are only permitted under specific circumstances and require approval from the takeover panel.

13.7 Takeover Bid Defenses

A company's management must determine whether to accept a bid for its shares or to reject it. If they want to reject the offer, they ought to do so on the basis that it is not optimal for their shareholders, not only because they do not want to risk losing their jobs. It may be challenging for management to persuade shareholders to reject the proposal if it seems to be in their best financial interests to accept it. Management must inform shareholders of their decision to oppose the bid. Bid defenses can be conveniently grouped into two, and they are:

13.7.1 Pre-Bid Defenses

Pre-bid defenses are implemented in advance of a formal takeover bid in order to make a company difficult and costly to acquire, hence discouraging bids from being made in the first place. This defense is strengthened if management can identify the potential of a takeover offer well in advance of its official launch by keeping an eye on the composition of its share ownership. The following are some of the methods by which management can accomplish these goals, all of which are in line with the goal of optimizing shareholder wealth:
- Improving operational efficiency;
- Examining asset portfolios and making necessary divestments;
- Restructuring of equity;
- Ensuring good investor relations; and
- Managing retrenchment devices.

13.7.2 Post-bid Defenses

Target corporations utilize post-bid defenses to block a bid once it has been submitted. Frequently employed post-bid defenses consist of the following:
- A pre-emptive circulation of shareholders;
- Formulation of a defense document;
- Profit announcements and forecasts;
- Dividend increase announcements; and
- Revaluation of assets.

13.8 Estimating the Economic Gains and Cost of Mergers

There is an economic gain in a merger situation if the sum of the whole is greater than the sum of the individual parts, i.e., A > A + B. The following relationships are worth noting:

> Gain = PVAB − (PVA + PVB)
> Cost = Cash payment − PVB (victim)
> NPV = Gain − cost
>
> Where;
> PVA is the present value of the acquirer
> PVB is the present value of the acquiree
> NPV is the net present value

Illustration 13.1

The worth of Company A is GHS400 million, whereas Company B is valued at GHS140 million. The two just completed a merger, and cost reductions estimated to be about GHS50 million are anticipated. Company B's whole paid-up capital was paid in cash by Company A in the amount of GHS170 million.

Required:
  a. What is the total value of the two firms after the merger?
  b. Calculate the cost of the merger to the shareholders of company A
  c. What is the portion of the Gain due to company A's shareholders?

Solution

a. Total Value of the two Companies

	GHS
Value of company A	400
Value of company B	140
Present value of costing savings	50
	590

b. Cost of the Merger

	GHS
Present value of company B	140
Cash payment to company B	170
Cost to predatory	**30**

c. Gain to the shareholders of A

	GHS
Total value of A and B	590
Less: NPV of A and B (400 + 140)	540
Gain	**50**

	GHS
NPV Gain	50
Less: cost	30
	20

13.9 All-Share Transaction

Acquiring companies often pay a premium on their stock market value due to synergy, as it is beneficial to shareholders when the price of post-merger shares increases. Buyers must pay a premium regardless of pre-merger valuation, while sellers value the premium as representing their company's prospects. The premium represents post-merger synergy for buyers, and the equation calculates the minimum required synergy, determining if a deal makes sense by enhancing the buyer's value.

A cash acquisition alters the shareholders' portfolio by holding cash instead of shares, while an all-share transaction shares the value creation or destruction of combining two businesses based on the relative values negotiated by both sets of shareholders. Selling shareholders does not bear the risk of implementation. To merge two companies, determine the exchange ratio, compute earnings per share, cash flow per share, dividend per share, book equity per share, and share prices if they have similar activities. For dissimilar activities, perform a full valuation on a standalone basis, with synergies valued separately. Use the same valuation methods for each company to ensure a successful merger.

Illustration 13.2

The following information is provided related to the acquiring firm X Ltd. and the target firm Y Ltd.:

Table 13.2: Data on Acquiring Firm (X Ltd.) and Target Firm (Y Ltd.)

Details	Firm X (GHS)	Firm Y (GHS)
Earnings after tax	2,000	400
Number of shares outstanding	200	100
Earnings per share	20	8
P/E ratio (times)	20	10
MPS	GHS 200	GHS 40

Required:
a. What is the swap ratio based on current market prices?
b. What is the EPS of X Ltd. after acquisition?
c. What is X Ltd.'s anticipated market price per share (MPS) following the acquisition, presuming that Firm X's P/E ratio stays constant?
d. Determine the market value of the merged firm.

Solution

a. Exchange ratio based on market prices = $\frac{GHS\ 40}{GHS\ 200}$ = 0.2: 1

For every one share of Firm Y, 0.2 shares will be issued in Firm X. Based on this ratio, the number of new shares issued by Firm Y will be = 100 × 0.2
= 20

b. EPS after the merger = $\frac{2,000 + 400}{200 + 20}$ = $GHS\ 10.91$

c. Expected MPS after merger = EPS after the merger * New shares issued
= 10.91 * 20
= **GHS 218.2**

d. Market value of merged firm = GHS 218.2 × (200 + 20 shares)
= **GHS 48,004.**

Illustration 13.3

Piepeaye Ltd. is currently evaluating the potential acquisition of Tuyakiye Ltd. With Piepeaye Ltd. valued at GHS40,000 and Tuyakiye Ltd. at GHS20,000, the acquisition is being carefully considered. The consultants at Piepeaye Ltd. have projected that the acquisition could lead to annual administrative cost savings of GHS1,000 indefinitely. Two settlement-term options are being explored as part of the evaluation process.

a. Piepeaye Ltd. to pay cash of GHS28,000 for the entire paid value of Tuyakiye Ltd. OR
b. Offer 50% holdings in the combined firm to shareholders of Tuyakiye Ltd.

The opportunity cost of capital applicable to Piepeaye Ltd. is 10%

Required:
i. What is the Gain from the Merger?
ii. What is the cost of the Merger, assuming Piepeaye Ltd. offered cash?
iii. What is the cost of the Merger, assuming Piepeaye Ltd. offered stock?
iv. What is the Net present value of the acquisition under the cash offer?
v. What is the Net present value of the acquisition under the stock offer?
vi. Explain why Piepeaye Ltd., shareholders will insist on stock offer instead of cash.

Solution

i. **Gain from the Merger**

PV Piepeaye and Tuyakiye	GHS
PV of Piepeaye	40,000
PV of Tuyakiye	20,000
	60,000
PV of Savings (1,000 / 0.10)	10,000
PV Piepeaye and Tuyakiye	**70,000**

Therefore, Gain = PVPT − (PVP x PVT)
= 70,000 − (40,000 + 20,000)
= **10,000**

335

ii. **Cost of the Merger**

Cost = Cash payment – PV of Tuyakiye
= 28,000 - 20,000
= **8,000**

iii. **Cost of Stock Offer**

Stock offer = 50% x 70,000
= 35,000
Cost = 35,000 – 20,000
= **15,000**

iv. **NPV of cash offer**

NPV = Gain – Cost
NPV = 10,000 – 8,000
= **2,000**

v. **NPV of Stock Offer**

NPV = Gain in cost
NPV = 10,000 – 15,000

= **(5,000)**

vi. The preference of Piepeaye Ltd. to finance the acquisition of stock may be informed by the following factors:
1. Availability of cash, Piepeaye Ltd. may not have cash to finance the merger transaction; and
2. Pessimistic view of the outcome of the merger. The predatory (Piepeaye Ltd.) insists on stock offer, it means it is pessimistic about the gains from the merger.

On the other hand, Tuyakiye Ltd., the victim may prefer stock payment for the following reasons:

1. **Tax consideration.** Acquisition by exchanging stock is generally task-free;
2. **Optimum.** If the victim is optimistic about the gains, it will prefer to accept stock payments that can participate in future distributions; and

3. **Control.** The victim company may still want to have some control in the merged firm.

Illustration 13.4

Pukyee Ltd. is to take over Kobiri Ltd., which is badly managed. The shareholders of Pukyee Ltd. would pay 0.4 of their own shares for each share of Kobiri Ltd. The acquisition is not expected to yield economies of scale and operating synergy. The relevant financial data for the two firms is shown below:

	Pukyee	**Kobiri**
	GHS	GHS
Net sales	167,500	59,000
Profit after tax	29,000	6,000
No. of shares	6,000	1,500
Price per share	15	10
PE ratio	3.25	2.5

For the combined company, you are required to calculate:
a) EPS;
b) Weighted Average PE ratio;
c) Market value per share;
d) Total market capitalization; and
e) Calculate the premium received by Kobiri shareholders.

Solution
a. EPS

$$EPS = \frac{Combined\ earnings}{New\ number\ of\ shares}$$

$$EPS = \frac{29,000+6,000}{6,000+(0.4*1,500)}$$

= **GHS 5.30**

b. **WA PE ratio** = $\frac{(29{,}000 * 3.25) * (6{,}000 * 2.5)}{29{,}000 * 6{,}000}$

$$= \underline{8.13}$$

c. **Market Value Per Share** = EPS x PE ratio

$$= 5.30 \times 8.13$$

$$= \underline{43.09}$$

d. **Total Market Capitalization (TMC):**

TMC = No. of shares x market price

= 6,600 x 40.09

= $\underline{264{,}594}$

e. **Premium Received**

Value before merger (1,500 x 10)	15,000
Value after merger (0.4 x 1,500 x 40.09)	24,054
Premium received	**9,054**

Illustration 13.5

Wotaa Yese Ltd. is being acquired by Wongukuaahe Ltd. On a share exchange basis. Their selected data are as follows:

	Wongukuaahe	Wotaa Yese
	GHS	GHS
Profit after tax	28,000	10,500
EPS	2,800	1,250
No. of shares	10	6.2
PE ratio	6.5	4

Required
   a. Determine the pre-acquisition market value per share of each company.
   b. Determine the maximum exchange ratio Wongukuaahe Ltd. should offer without diluting it EPS.
   c. Determine the maximum exchange ratio Wongukuaahe Ltd. should offer without diluting its market value per share.

Solution

a. Pre-Acquisition Market Value per Share:

Price = EPS x PE ratio
   Wongukuaahe Ltd.: 2,800 x 6.5
      = GHS 18,200

   Wotaa Yese Ltd.: 1,250 x 4
      = GHS 5,000

b. Determine the maximum exchange ratio without dilution of Wongukuaahe Ltd. EPS

Combined Earnings = 28,000 x 10,500
      = 38,500

Let x = New No. of shares in the merged firm

$$EPS = \frac{Combined\ earnings}{New\ number\ of\ shares}$$

$$2,800 = \frac{38,500}{x}$$

x = 13.75

New EPS	13.75
Less: own shares	(10)
Maximum shares to offer	**3.75**

Maximum exchange ratio = $\frac{Offer\ shares}{Victim's\ shares}$

Maximum exchange ratio = $\frac{3.75}{6.2}$

= 0.605

c. Maximum Exchange Ratio without diluting Wongukuaahe Ltd. Market value
Pre-acquisition market capitalization:

Wongukuaahe (18,200 x 10)	182,000
Wotaa Yese (5,000 x 8.4)	42,000
	224,000

Price = $\frac{Combined\ price}{New\ number\ of\ shares}$

$18,200 = \frac{224,000}{x}$

x = 12.31

New EPS	12.31
Less: own shares	(10)
Maximum shares to offer =	**2.31**

Maximum exchange ratio = $\frac{Offer\ shares}{Victim's\ shares}$

Maximum exchange ratio = $\frac{2.31}{6.2}$

= 0.373

13.10 Chapter Review Questions

1. Nzue Pukyee Ltd. (Nzue Pukyee), a hotel and leisure company, is currently considering taking over a smaller private limited liability company, Kobiri Ltd. (Kobiri). The board of Nzue Pukyee is in the process of making a bid for Kobiri but first needs to place a value on the company. Nzue Pukyee has gathered the following data:

Nzue Pukyee	
Weighted average cost of capital	24%
P/E ratio	24
Shareholders' required rate of return	30%
Kobiri	
Current dividend payment (GHS)	0.54
Past five years' dividend payments (GHS)	0.30, 0.34, 0.36, 0.42, 0.46
Current EPS	0.74
Number of ordinary shares issued	10 million

The shareholders of Kobiri demand a rate of return that is 20% greater than that of Nzue Pukyee, reflecting the higher risk profile of Kobiri. Nzue Pukyee forecasts cash flows of GHS 5 million at the end of the initial year, with a projected annual growth rate of 5%. Additionally, Nzue Pukyee anticipates generating GHS 10 million in two years by divesting surplus hotels owned by Kobiri.

Required:
Estimate values for Kobiri using the following valuation methods:
   a. Price/earnings ratio valuation.
   b. Gordon growth model.
   c. Discounted cash flow valuation.

2. Global corporations are constantly seeking methods to enhance their efficiency and productivity in order to thrive in the competitive global market. In response to this, Gynayee Ltd. and EEI HUMM Ltd. have decided to merge and establish EBIE TRA EBIE Ltd. The agreement states that Powell's shareholders will receive three shares in Gynayee for each share they currently hold in EEI HUMM. Additional information is provided below:

	Gynayee Ltd.	EEI HUMM Ltd.
Number of shares	20m	5m
Annual earnings	GHS5m	GHS2.9m
P/E ratio	8	5

The combined company's yearly profits following the merger are anticipated to increase by eight percent compared to the total profits of the individual companies prior to the merger, thanks to economies of scale and other advantages. EBIE PLC is projected to have a P/E ratio of 4.5 in the market.

Required:
Determine the extent to which the shareholders of EEI HUMM will benefit from the proposed merger.

3. Afua Adjoe PLC is currently evaluating the potential acquisition of Ewoserbo Ltd. As part of the proposed deal, Afua Adjoe PLC plans to offer 10% of its shares to the shareholders of Ewoserbo Ltd. for each share they currently hold. Below are the financial details for both companies:

	Afua Adjoe Ltd. GHS	Ewoserbo Ltd. GHS
Profit after tax	300	60
No. of shares	50	16
EPS	12	7.5
Price per share	156	67.5
PE ratio	26	18

The Finance Manager at Afua Adjoe PLC has made an estimation that the combined firm will experience a reduction of GHS 20 in operating costs as a result of the economy of scale. Additionally, it has been projected that the Foreman at Ewoserbo Ltd., who was earning a salary of GHS 24, will unfortunately lose their job and receive GHS 14 as compensation to equalize the job loss. It is important to note that a corporation tax rate of 30% will be applied.

Required:
   a. Calculate EPS of the surviving firm after the merger.
   b. If the PE ratio falls to 24 after the merger, what is the premium received by Ewoserbo Ltd. shareholders, using the surviving firm's new price?
   c. Is the merger beneficial to the shareholders of Afua Adjoe PLC?

4. Mewoyefeer PLC (Mewoyefeer) and Fawonye Diyesiin PLC (Fawonye Diyesiin) are two competing companies listed on the Ghana Stock Exchange. Fawonye Diyesiin has faced uncertainty in its earning power due to poor managerial decisions, leading shareholders to consider selling the business. Despite this, Fawonye Diyesiin's management has implemented defensive strategies to prevent any hostile takeovers.

During the recent Annual General Meeting (AGM), Fawonye Diyesiin's shareholders decided to proceed with selling the company. Shareholders of Mewoyefeer have shown interest in acquiring Fawonye Diyesiin and have proposed to the board to prepare a formal proposal for the upcoming extraordinary meeting. The board of Mewoyefeer has compiled the following information to assist in the development of the proposal:

	Mewoyefeer	**Fawonye Diyesiin**
Earnings per share	GHS 0.25	GHS 0.25
Retention ratio	0.30	0.20
Price per share	GHS 5	GHS 2.50
Number of shares	12,500	12,500

Required:
a. Assuming the acquisition will be financed with shares, how many shares of Mewoyefeer should be exchanged for all the shares of Fawonye Diyesiin based on market value?
b. Assuming the share price of the combined business after the acquisition is the same as the share price of Mewoyefeer, calculate the market value, earnings per share, and price/earnings ratio of the combined business.
c. Calculate the cost of the acquisition if Mewoyefeer pays GHS65,000 in cash for Fawonye Diyesiin.
d. Explain four (4) defensive tactics the management of Fawonye Diyesiin can employ to prevent Mewoyefeer from acquiring the company.

13.11 Chapter References and Bibliographies

[1] Bessler, W., Drobetz, W., & Zimmermann, J. (2011). Financing corporate mergers and acquisitions. *Capital structure and corporate financing decisions: theory, evidence, and practice*, 15, 419.

[2] Smith, K. W., & Triantis, A. J. (1995). The value of options in strategic acquisitions. *Real options in capital investment*, 135-149.

[3] Gödecke, T. (2024). Ownership Structure and Corporate Decisions: Capital Structure, M&A Activity, and Acquisition Financing.

[4] Hong, E., Park, M. C., & King, T. H. D. (2023). The effect of option listing on financing decisions. *Journal of Business Finance & Accounting*, 50(3-4), 858-891.

[5] Speechley, T. (2015). *Acquisition finance*. Bloomsbury Publishing.

[6] Dittmar, A. K., & Dittmar, R. F. (2008). The timing of financing decisions: An examination of the correlation in financing waves. *Journal of Financial Economics*, 90(1), 59-8.

GLOSSARY

Account payables' Turnover Rate (CTR): This ratio analyzes the link that exists between credit purchases and the average amount owed to account payables. The result of the calculation is used to determine whether or not the company is meeting its obligations to its account payables on schedule.

Acquisition cost: The cost of the inventory itself and is determined by multiplying quantity purchased by supplier's price per unit.

Acquisition: Also known as a takeover is the buying of one company (the 'target') by another. An acquisition may be friendly or hostile.

Acquisition: An acquisition refers to a corporate transaction where one company buys a portion or the entirety of another company's shares or assets.

Aggressive Working Capital (AWC) Financing: An AWC occurs when a company's current assets and the components that make up its working capital are insufficient to meet the firm's trading needs. The company faces a serious working capital issue. Although an entity's short-term investments are financed by its short-term debts, the company's aggressive working capital strategy restricts its ability to finance current asset investment by only its short-term debts.

All-share transaction: During an acquisition, a stock-for-stock merger takes place when the shares of one company are exchanged for the shares of another company.

Beta Co-efficient: Amount of systematic present in a particular risky asset relative that of an average risky asset.

Beta: A measure of the sensitivity or the level of volatility of an individual security's or portfolio's return (basically dividends and capital gains) in relation to changes in the overall inventory market return.

Bid: In corporate actions, a takeover bid occurs when a company presents a proposal to acquire another company.

Bond: A long-term contract under which a borrower accepts to make periodic payments of interest and principal to the holder (bond holder) on specified dates.

Borrower's Risk: The risk associated with firms as a result of the firm not using debt to finance its assets. It refers to the riskiness of the firm's assets as it fails to use debt as a component of the capital structure to finance its total assets.

Business Risk: The term "business risk" refers to the question of whether or not a company will be able to make sufficient sales and generate sufficient revenues to cover its operational expenses and turn a profit. This is the question that determines whether or not a business will be viable.

Capital Assets Pricing Model (CAPM): A model that is based on the preposition that any security's required rate of return is equal to the risk-free rate of return in addition to a risk premium. CAPM enables for total risk to be categorized into relevant risk and diversifiable risk.

Capital Budgeting: The process of planning, choosing and implementing and monitoring an expenditure on non-current assets whose cash flows are expected to extend beyond one accounting year. It involves the decision, whether to invest in specific capital assets or not given the available data.

Capital Market: An organized market that deals in long-term finance; mainly through the inventory exchange. Such market usually involves financial claims with relatively high degree of price risk. Individual investors, companies, and governments can raise long-term funds to finance investments

Capital Structure: Capital structure refers to the mix (combination of debt, preferred inventory and common inventory composition in the capital base of the firm required to finance total assets.

Capitalization: The total amount of money that has been invested in an organization is referred to as its "capitalization." The invested capital of a company is included in the calculation of its capitalization, along with the company's debt, which is typically of the long-term variety. Capitalization is a term that refers to investments that are made with the intention of them being long-term, as opposed to loans that have terms that are long-term.

Cash Conversion Cycle: The time duration in which a firm is able to convert its resources into cash. Cash conversion cycle measures the length of time between the company's outlay on raw materials, wages and other expenditure and the inflow of cash from sale of goods.

Cash Management: A systematic process of ensuring that there is optimum cash level available to take care of day-to-day operations of the firm. It relates to an efficient processes ensuring adequate cash resources are available to cater for routine expenses as well as maturing liabilities, and surplus cash invested in short-term marketable securities.

Cash Offers: An acquirer presents a cash deal to purchase all the stock of the target company using only cash.

Certainty Equivalent Method (CEM): CEM addresses the risk aspects associated in capital budgeting, in which potentially dangerous future cash flows are stated in terms of specific cash flows that investors are ready to accept now. Using Certainty Equivalent is essential when doing risk assessments.

Conservative Working Capital (CWC) Financing: The conservative working capital financing strategy is whereby a firm has excess current asset components, more than what its level of current liabilities can finance. Thus, the components of current assets are always financed jointly by short-range and long-standing financing sources.

Control: The parent or any of its Subsidiaries may acquire a controlling interest of over 50% in the voting power of a business, corporation, partnership, association, or business organization through merger, consolidation, or purchasing an equity interest.

Counterparty Risk: The potential or probability that one party to a transaction would fail to keep its contractual commitments is known as the counterparty risk.

Credit Analysis: Credit Analysis is the process of determining the probability that customers will fail to pay the debt owed to the firm. Firms use a number of devices and procedures to determine the probability that customers will not pay. Credit Analysis also involves deciding on who gets the credit.

Credit Assessment: The analysis of the prospective customer's current business situation and credit history, derived from information obtained from the following available sources.

Credit or Default Risk: Credit risk is the probability that a person or business may be unable to make contractual interest or principal payments on the debt it owes. Bond-holding investors are the ones who should be the most concerned about this specific form of risk.

Cumulative Capital Requirement (CCR): The aggregate capital needed to finance the entire business activities (both short-term and log-term) of a firm for a given period of time.

Current Assets: Assets that are current in nature. They are assets that will normally be transformed or converted into cash within an accounting period (within one year). They are constantly been used by the firm in the transformation process. The current assets form the basis of measuring the company's liquidity position. They include cash and cash-equivalents, inventory of raw materials, work-in-progress and finished goods, marketable securities such as treasury bills, and amounts receivable from account receivables etc.

Current Liabilities: The financial commitments that are payable within one accounting year. Current liabilities include: account payables falling due within one year, and may involve; amounts owed to trade account payables, taxation payable, dividend payments due, short-term loans, long-term debts maturing within one year etc.

Current Ratios: The term "working capital ratio" is another name for this concept. It is used to demonstrate whether or not a company's current assets are capable of covering its short-term liabilities in a manner that is sufficient and adequate.

Decision Tree: A decision tree is a graphical depiction of all the possible solutions or outcomes for resolving a specific problem or taking advantage of a prospective opportunity. It is a handy piece of financial equipment that visually simplifies the task of categorising all of the probable outcomes for a specific situation. It may also be viewed as a flowchart, with a primary concept at its base and numerous branches resulting from your actions. The model is referred to as a "decision tree" since its structure frequently resembles tree branches.

Dividend Policy: The set of rules and procedures that are set out by a firm to govern its dividend decision with respect to dividend payout and retention. Dividends are payments made periodically by companies to equity investors.

Economic Gains: Economic gain is when revenue arising from the takeover is higher than the costs involved

Ethics: The principle of right and wrong that can be used by individuals acting as free general agents to make choices to guide their behavior. ethics may be regarded as the study of moral behavior and the establishment of right and wrong in an individual's acts based on the declared and established norms of moral conduct by society in a specific field of endeavor.

Finance Lease: is a lease that transfers substantially all of the risks and rewards of ownership of an asset to the lessee.

Financial Management: Financial management as the decision-making process that is concerned with planning, acquisition and utilization of funds in a way that achieves the firm's desired goals.

Financial Planning: The task of systematically, determining how a business can afford to achieve its long-term (strategic) financial goals and objectives. Usually, a company creates a financial plan immediately after the vision and objectives have been set.

Financial Risk: The addition risk placed on the equity shareholders as result of the firms' decision to use debt to finance its total assets.

Financial System: Financial system refers to all the various financial components (entities) that ensure for the smooth and efficient operation of the financial markets.

Foreign Exchange Risk: When investing in other nations, it is vital to remember that the price of the asset may also be affected by fluctuations in the currency exchange rate. All financial instruments denominated in a currency other than the native currency of your nation are susceptible to foreign exchange risk,

Gross Working Capital (GWC) GWC indicates overall short-term assets that are turned out repeatedly in a recurrent manner by firms.

Holding Cost: Cost incurred in keeping a given level of inventory or inventory; such as storage cost, insurance, deterioration, obsolescence, pilferage and warehouse upkeep.

Horizontal Integration: When a firm in the same industry; and usually, in the same stage of production is being taken-over or perhaps merged with another firm which is in the same industry and in the same stage of production.

Interest Rate Risk: Interest rate risk is the possibility that the value of an investment may fluctuate owing to a change in the absolute level of interest rates, the spread between two rates, the yield curve's form, or any other interest rate connection.

Interim Dividend: A dividend known as an interim dividend is one that may be distributed to shareholders at any time throughout the course of a company's fiscal year. Interim dividends are not required to be paid out. It is the practice of a firm to distribute dividends prior to a yearly audit of the company's financial reports.

This is the most fundamental definition of the term. The amount of the yearly distribution is substantially more than that of the interim dividends, which are often given out on a regular basis, such as once a month or once a week (paid more than once).

Internal Rate of Return: A discounted cash flow technique that equates the Net Present Value (NPV) to zero (0). It is the rate of discount which equates the present value of the expected initial cash outlay with the present value of the expect cash flows.

Inventories Conversion Period (ICP): This ratio determines the relationship between the cost of goods sold and the average inventory at cost by calculating the number of days it takes the company to turn its inventories into cash through sales.

Inventories Turnover Ratio (ITR): This ratio determines the degree to which the average inventory cost and the cost of goods sold are related to one another. This metric is utilized to determine how rapidly (in terms of the number of times) sales are generated from available inventory.

Inventory Dividend: The distribution of extra shares to existing shareholders on a pro-rata basis in lieu of cash dividend. Essentially, this is the transfer of a number of additional equity shares without the shareholders having to subscribe additional cash.

Investment Decision: It involves the selection of asset or investment drive and committing surplus cash into it.

Irregular Dividend Policy: In a firm that adheres to an irregular dividend policy, the choice of whether or not to pay dividends is left totally up to the discretion of the company. In other words, the company may choose to pay dividends at any time they see fit.

Just-in-Time (JIT) Inventory Management Model: The "JIT" inventory management model is viewed not only as a technique that brings about operating efficiency but also as a philosophy that can eliminate all aspects of waste in a company's production setup. This is because JIT is an abbreviation for just-in-time, which stands for Just-in-time inventory management. JIT is not just a method that can improve operational efficiency but also a concept that can be applied to the process.

Leasing: is a contract between a lessor and a lessee for hire of a specific asset by the lessee from a manufacturer or vendor of such assets.

Lessee: has possession and use of the asset on payment of specified rentals over a period.

Lessor: has ownership of the asset and so provides the initial finance for the asset.

Liquidating Dividend: A special dividend payment made to shareholders during the process of liquidation and it usually implies that part of the business or all of the business is been liquidated. This refers to the distribution of proceeds from liquidated business and such proceeds (after payment of all liabilities) are paid to shareholders based on their shareholding capacity.

Liquidating Dividend: This refers to the distribution of proceeds from liquidated business and such proceeds (after payment of all liabilities) are paid to shareholders based on their shareholding capacity. A special dividend payment made to shareholders during the process of liquidation and it usually implies that part of the business or all of the business is been liquidated.

Market Risk Premium: The difference between the expected market return, $E(R_m)$, and the risk-free rate of return R_f. The market risk premium is converted to a risk premium for individual security by multiplying by the security's beta (β_i).

Market Risk: A type of risk that affects every security traded on an inventory market. Hence, market risk cannot be eliminated through diversification.

Merger: A merger involves the consolidation of companies into a single legal entity, forming a unified corporate strategy.

Moderate Working Capital (MWC) Financing: Moderate working capital strategy refers to a technique of financing that seeks perfect weights between the conservative and aggressive working capital financing methods. The emphasis of a modest strategy for financing working capital should be on making a well-balanced investment in working capital components given the risk profile level.

Net Present Value: A technique of evaluating investment proposal bringing into today's term the proposed cash inflows and outflows for the relevant years that they occur. What it means is that, this technique takes into consideration the concept of time value of money by the marginal cost of capital. The Net Present Value is estimated to be the difference between the Present Value (PV's) of relevant future cash inflows and the present value of the initial outlay, discounted at the firms cost of capital

Net Working Capital (NWC): NWC refers to total current assets minus all short-term debts owed by the firm. GWC is indicated by the classification of working capital components that are considered current assets in nature and that are required in the process of generating cash flow from recurrent activities.

No Dividend Policy: If a company decides that it will not pay dividends as part of its standard practice, this is an indication that the company plans to keep all of its profits for its own use and has consciously decided not to distribute any of them to its shareholders.

Operating Gearing: A measure of the relationship that exists, between the level of fixed costs and the variable costs incurred by the firm over a given period of time. Relatively the higher the level of fixed costs incurred, the greater is the proportion of revenue required to recoup those costs.

Operating lease: is a lease where the lessor retains most of the risks and rewards of ownership

Operating Lease: Type of leasing where the lease period is described as short-term, hence, the lease agreement covers a period lesser than the economic life span of the asset and thus, the net cost of the asset to the "leasor" is not fully recovered.

Ordering Cost: The cost associated with placing an order for inventory of goods. It includes costs associated with requisitioning, purchase ordering, transporting, receiving, inspecting, freight, handling and quantity discounts forgone.

Overcapitalization: A situation known as overcapitalization occurs when a company raises more money than is required for the level of business activity and requirements it currently satisfies. The term "business activity" refers to the typical operations that are carried out by the company. If a company's total owned and borrowed capital is greater than its fixed and current assets, then the company is said to be over-capitalized. This means that the company is making use of more capital than is actually required, and the funds are not being used effectively.

Over-the-Counter market: A large collection of brokers and dealers, connected electronically by telephones and computers that provides for the trading in unlisted securities.

Over-trading: A phenomenon that indicates that, a firm has inadequate finance to support its level of activities or trading. In order words, where a firm tries to undertake more trading or business than what its financial resources would allow. When a firm grows rapidly in terms of its trading activities but there is no corresponding increase in its financial base to support such rapid growth then the firm becomes strapped for cash and it is swallowed up in Over-trading.

Permanent Working Capital (PWC): The proportion of working capital that remains constant regardless of sales or business activity over any given period is termed fixed working capital. Consequently, PWC is the part of your company's working capital that must be kept by a firm to maintain its operations regardless of the operational cycle.

Point of Indifference: The point of indifference under capital structure refers to the level of earnings before interest and taxes (EBT) at which earnings per share (EPS) remain the same regardless of the debt-equity mix or the composition of the capital structure. This level can be reached when EBT reaches a certain level.

Portfolio Beta: The portfolio beta measures the portfolio's reaction to macroeconomic variables, namely, interest rates and inflation. A security's beta represents basically the part of a security's risk called systematic or market risk which represents the risk element that cannot be diversified away.

Portfolio: A collection of two or more financial or physical assets held by one investor. Portfolio investment is held to eliminate unique risk.

Predatory: In the world of business, a predatory is a slang or colloquial term used to describe a financially robust company that gobbles up or engulfs another company through a merger or acquisition.

Premise of Value: This refers to the value that is related with the assumptions, such as the going-concern. It is based on the most likely scenario involving a collection of transactional events that may be important to the subject property's worth. The facts and circumstances related to the asset to be valued, as well as the motivation for completing the valuation, should be expressed in the valuation assumption.

Present Value: It measures the value today of a future sum (cash flow) or series of cash flows over a given number of periods (years). Here, the current value of future cash flows or payments discounted at a given rate of interest.

Primary Market: A market concerned with raising financial assets such as inventories for the first time. Initial Public Offer (IPO) prices are quoted on the Primary market.

Probability Technique in Capital Budgeting: In statistics, the probability distribution is used to characterize the likelihood of each conceivable outcome of a random event or experiment. It provides probability for each of the conceivable outcomes. Probability is a measure of uncertainty applicable to several phenomena, whether they are probabilistic or deterministic.

Property Dividend: There are some scenarios in which a company may opt to deliver non-monetary benefits to its shareholders rather than distributing cash dividends to those who own shares of the company.

Quick Ratio (QR)/Acid-Test Ratio: This is a measurement of the ratio between the company's quick assets and current liabilities. This ratio is also known as the acid-test ratio or the liquid ratio. It is measured as, and indicates, the immediate liquid position of the company, and its values are as follows.

Receivables Conversion Period (RCP): When it comes to credit sales, this ratio determines how many days in a year the company's receivable, also known as account receivables, are handed over or rotated. It communicates the connection between the average accounts receivables period and the total net sales on credit for a given year.

Receivables Turnover Ratio (RTR): In terms of credit sales, it is a measurement of the number of times that receivables, also known as account receivables, are handed over or rotated in a given year. It conveys the relationship between the total amount of credit sales made and the annual average amount of accounts receivable for a particular year. This ratio determines how effective the company's overall credit management strategy is.

Regular Dividend Policy: A "regular dividend policy" is a policy that mandates the payment of dividends to shareholders on a continuous and ongoing basis. This type of policy is known as a "regular dividend policy." In accordance with this policy, a predetermined share of the annual earnings of the business (for instance 40% or 50%) must be distributed in the way described.

Relevant Risk: The risk associated with a security, which cannot be diversified away. The relevant risk shows a security's contribution to the riskiness of a portfolio.

Reverse takeover: A Reverse Takeover (RTO), also known as a reverse IPO, is the procedure in which a smaller private company becomes publicly traded by acquiring a larger company that is already listed on the stock exchange.

Risk Premium: The difference between the expected rate of return on a particular risky asset (security) and on the expected return on less risky assets (security). Price changes usually cause in expected rate of return on two given securities. It refers to the expected additional return for making a risky investment instead of investing in a less risky investment.

Risk: "Risk" refers to the chance that actual profits from an event or investment may differ from the anticipated outcome or return. The danger of losing a portion or the entirety of an original investment falls under the notion of risk. It is usual practice to examine prior behavior and its outcomes when assessing risk.

Risk: A chance that an unfavorable event will happen. Risk is viewed as how we characterize the level of uncertainty that exist. Accordingly, risk measures the degree of uncertainty.

Risk-Adjusted Discount Rate (RADR): A risk-adjusted discount rate is the rate achieved when evaluating the present value of a hazardous investment by adding an estimated risk premium to the risk-free rate. The purchase of real estate or the launch of a new business are examples of hazardous investments since they involve greater degrees of risk than other investments.

Risk-adjusted discount rate: A risk-adjusted discount rate is the rate achieved when evaluating the present value of a hazardous investment by adding an estimated risk premium to the risk-free rate. The Risk-Adjusted Discount Rate, often known as RADR, is composed of two components. The total consists of two components: the risk-free rate and the risk premium.

Sale and leaseback: is when a business that owns an asset agrees to sell the asset to a financial institution and lease it back on terms specified in the sale and leaseback agreement.

Scrip Dividend/ Stock Dividend: The great majority of dividends are dispersed to shareholders in the form of cash distributions. This method is the one that is utilized the most regularly and is the one that is recognized the most extensively. A dividend is a payment that is made by the firm and then distributed to each shareholder. This payment is known as a dividend.

Sensitivity Analysis: Sensitivity Analysis is a tool used in financial modeling to analyze how the different values of a set of independent variables affect a specific dependent variable under certain specific conditions.

Sensitivity Analysis: The sensitivity analysis of a project is an all-encompassing evaluation of the likelihood that a project will be successful based on data-driven projections. In addition to this, it distinguishes between high-risk and low-risk tasks, identifies risks, and quantifies the impact of those risks. Sensitivity analysis, thus measures how sensitive the net present values or the internal rate of return in relation to changes in the variables that affect the cash flows. Sensitivity Analysis is a tool used in financial modeling to analyze how the different values of a set of independent variables affect a specific dependent variable under certain specific conditions.

Simulation Analysis: it refers to a computer model that seeks to recreate a real-world event. Simulation analysis is a methodology used in the field of finance to analyze big projects and discover how changes to input factors influence target variables. This type of model is called a simulation.

Stable Dividend Policy: The establishment of a predetermined number of dividend payments that are to be distributed on a regular basis to shareholders is an essential component of a dividend policy that is steady.

Stand-alone Risk: The risk an investor will face if that investor should hold only one asset. Stand-alone risk is seen to be part of the total risk

Standard of Value: This refers to the hypothetical conditions that will be used to calculate the company's valuation. It is concerned with determining the type of value used in a certain transaction. Depending on the circumstances, each of these four company valuation factors will yield a different figure indicating the value of the firm.

Stock Split: A means of increasing the number of shares held existing shareholders (by dividing their existing unit share held into number of parts to increase the quantity of shares) without raising any new funds. The procedure is to reduce the par (nominal) value of each share. It is a means of dividend payment.

Stock-piling: The means of accumulating inventory in reserve to meet unforeseen demand for inventories. This ensures the purchase of inventory at the right time, at the right price and of the right quantities.

Strategic financial management: The study of finance with a perspective of a long-term view in line with the strategic goals of the business. It refers to the process for identification, collection, selection and analysis of the financial data for the assistance to the team of management for the strategic decisions and effectiveness organizational assessment.

Synergy: The idea of synergy suggests that when two companies come together, their combined value and performance will exceed the total of their individual parts.

Systematic risk: A type of market risk that cannot be diversified away. This type of risk is caused by events that affect the entire inventory market. Risks caused by macro-economic factors that affect all firms and businesses irrespective of their size or the industry the find themselves.

Takeover: A takeover bid occurs when an acquiring company makes an offer to a target company, aiming to gain control over it through a corporate action.

Target: A target company is an appealing organization that is being pursued for a merger or acquisition. The progress of a transaction is contingent upon the consent of the target company's management, shareholders, and Board of Directors to the takeover.

Temporary Working Capital (TWC): This working capital category represents working capital requirements that are typically much higher than permanent working capital as a result of factors such as favorable trade cycles, seasonality peaks, and thriving business conditions.

Undercapitalization: It is said that a company is in a state of undercapitalization when the expected earnings of the company are significantly lower than the profits that the company actually made. In other words, an under-capitalized company does not have sufficient cash on hand to carry out its functions and, in most cases, is unable to qualify for loans from financial institutions due to the unacceptably high debt-to-equity ratio that the company carries.

Valuation of Businesses: Valuation of Business refers to the process and set of procedures used to measure or estimate the economic worth (value) of an owner's interest in a business. Valuation is a concept used by financial market participants to estimate the price that they (buyers) are willing to pay or received (sellers) to affect the sale of a business.

Valuation: The valuation of a company involves the assessment of its worth. In the context of mergers and acquisitions, the process of business valuation aims to assign a monetary value to a business by considering various factors and aspects of its operations.

Working Capital Cycle: The simple movement of cash to inventory, to accounts receivable, and back to cash. Various activity and working capital ratios can be calculated to ascertain the working capital cycle.

Working Capital Management: The set of policies and procedures aimed at managing the current assets (generally cash and cash equivalents, inventories and account receivables) and the short-term financing, such that cash flows and returns would be at their generally acceptable levels to ensure business growth and expansion.

Working Capital: The total short-term resources available to the firm (current assets and current liabilities). It is comprised of the totality of current assets and current liabilities, which are constantly recycled in the course of day-to-day operations of the business.

Zero Coupon-rated bonds: Bonds which do not attract any annual rate of interest to the bond holders, but to compensate the investors, zero company rate bonds are issued at a discount (that is below par value) as a form of capital appreciation. Hence, the difference between the face value (par value) and the issue price constitutes the total amount of return to the investors.

Zero Working Capital (ZWC): This is where the size of the current asset components is the same as the current liabilities to indicate parity between the two main elements of working capital.

SUBJECT INDEX

Account Payables Management, 34
Account Payables Period, 53
Account Payables' Turnover Rate, 53
Account Receivables Management, 34
Account Receivables Turnover Ratio, 52
Accountability, 240
Accounts Payable, 49, 53
Accounts Receivable, 49
Acquisition, xii, xiii, 97, 250, 251, 271, 274, 275, 284, 321, 336, 344, 345
Aggressive Working Capital Policy, vii, 40
Alternative Branches, 190
Attitude of Investors, 111
Attitude of Management, 110
Beta, 150, 345
Board of Directors, 72, 234
Budget, 28, 144, 255
Business Cycle, 42
Business Ethics, xi, xii, 237, 239, 242, 244, 246, 247, 248
Business Growth, 44
Business Risk, 147, 346
Capital Allowances, x, 185

Capital Budgeting, ix, x, 142, 147, 160, 166, 169, 179, 180, 185, 201, 346, 355
Capital Investment Decisions, 5
Capital Market, 85, 111, 346
Capital Requirements, 17
Capital Structure, viii, ix, 5, 18, 105, 108, 112, 113, 114, 115, 117, 123, 133, 134, 344, 346
Capitalisation, viii, 96, 97, 102, 346
Cash Conversion Cycle, vii, 41, 44, 46, 50, 347
Cash Flow, xi, xii, xiii, xiv, 144, 153, 157, 159, 162, 163, 164, 165, 167, 168, 172, 173, 174, 181, 197, 198, 201, 203, 204, 207, 229, 258, 259, 307
Cash Inflows, 152, 157, 158, 208
Cash Management, 32, 68, 347
Cash Ratio, 52
Certainty Equivalent, x, 143, 154, 157, 160, 347
Certainty Equivalent Method, x, 143, 154, 347
Chance Nodes, 190
Code of Ethics, 239
Commercial Paper, 114
Competitive Environment, 12
Conglomerate Merger, 276

Conservative Working Capital Policy, vii, 40
Corporate Tax Position, 108
Cost of Capital, 83, 111, 125, 184, 211
Counterparty Risk, 148, 348
Cumulative Capital Requirement, vi, 24, 348
Current Assets, 32, 52, 59, 61, 63, 319, 348
Current Liabilities, 59, 61, 63, 348
Current Ratios, 51, 349
Debentures, 105, 108, 111, 125, 139, 319
Debt Capital, 114, 129
Decision Nodes, 190
Decision Tree Technique, 143, 198
Declining Firm, 88, 91
Default Risk, 147, 348
Degree of Control, 108
Depreciation, 63, 98, 177, 181, 183, 185, 209, 265
Dividend Payout, vii, viii, 6, 72, 79, 83
Dividend Policy, vii, viii, 71, 79, 82, 85, 93, 349, 353
Earnings, xi, xiv, 84, 86, 87, 88, 92, 98, 120, 122, 123, 131, 224, 298, 302, 303, 305, 311, 321, 334, 339, 343
End Nodes, 190
Equivalency Point, 118

Expected Cash Flow, 155, 167, 168, 169, 204
External Environment, 13
Fair Capitalisation, viii, 101
Fair Market Value, 215
Finance, iv, xii, 10, 68, 69, 93, 94, 102, 103, 139, 140, 211, 212, 248, 252, 253, 322, 343, 344, 349
Finance Lease, xii, 253, 349
Financial Budgets, 18
Financial Decision, 20
Financial Flexibility, 110
Financial Goals, 20
Financial Management, iii, vi, 4, 68, 211, 349
Financial Objectives, 26
Financial Plan, 108
Financial Planning, vi, 17, 18, 21, 23, 26, 28, 349
Financial Strategy, 9
Financing, vii, xii, xv, 8, 37, 38, 83, 84, 102, 111, 250, 254, 259, 281, 296, 325, 326, 344, 345, 347, 352
Foreign Exchange Risk, 148, 350
Friendly Takeovers, 276
Gross Working Capital, vii, 35, 350
Growth Firm, 87, 88, 90
High-Geared Firm, 106
Horizontal Merger, 275
Hostile Takeovers, 276
Inflation, x, 74, 169, 170
Interest Rate Risk, 148, 350

Interim Dividend, 80, 350
Inventories Turnover Ratio, 53, 351
Inventory Conversion Period, 52
Inventory Management, 33, 351
Investment, ix, 74, 140, 143, 148, 151, 158, 162, 163, 164, 165, 200, 216, 329, 351
Investment Value, 216
Irregular Dividend Policy, 78, 351
Just-in-Time, 351
Lease, xii, xiii, 71, 93, 250, 254, 255, 258, 259, 261, 263, 264, 267, 270, 271
Liberal Dividend Policy, 98
Liquidating Dividend, 77, 352
Liquidation Value, 217
Liquidity Risk, 148
Location Decisions, 6
Matching Resources, 7
Mergers and Acquisitions, xiii, 6, 102, 282
Most-Likely, 162, 163, 164
Negative Working Capital, 39
Net Income (NI) Approach, ix, 124, 129
Net Operating Income Approach, ix, 129, 130
Net Present Value, 157, 158, 173, 184, 188, 351, 353
Net Working Capital, vii, 35, 59, 61, 63, 353
Normal Firm, 88, 90
Operating Efficiency, 43

Operating Lease, 252, 353
Optimistic, 161, 162, 163, 164
Over-Capitalisation, 26
Pecking Order Theory, ix, 136
Permanent Cash Deficit, 26
Permanent Working Capital, vii, 36, 354
Point of Indifference, ix, 117, 118, 120, 121, 122, 123, 354
Political Risk, 148
Positive Working Capital, 39
Probabilities, 143
Production Cycle, 42
Profitability, 74, 219
Quick Ratio, 51, 356
Regular Dividend Policy, 78, 356
Regular Working Capital, 36
Reserve Working Capital, 36
Retained Earnings, 113
Reverse Takeovers, xiii, 276, 285, 286
Risk, ix, x, 115, 116, 142, 143, 146, 147, 149, 150, 151, 153, 155, 158, 159, 212, 296, 346, 350, 352, 356, 357, 358
Risk Premium, 155, 352, 356
Risk-Adjusted Discount Rate, x, 149, 357
Risk-Free, 151
Savings and Investments, 19
Scope of Working Capital, vii, 32
Scrip Dividend, 76, 357

Seasonal Working Capital, 37
Sensitivity Analysis, x, 143, 160, 161, 165, 166, 358
Simulation Technique, 143, 201
Social Responsibility, 242
Stable Dividend Policy, 78, 358
Standard of Value, xi, 215, 358
Strategic Financial Management, iii, vi, 2, 4, 5, 7, 9, 10, 12, 14
Super-Profit Approach, xi, 226
SWOT Analysis, 144
Technology Ethics, 243
Temporary Working Capital, vii, 36, 37, 359

Trade-Off Theory, ix, 135
Under-Capitalisation, viii, 100, 101
Valuation of Business, xi, 214, 219, 360
Values of Business Ethics, xii, 240
Vertical Merger, 275
Working Capital, vii, 31, 32, 35, 37, 38, 39, 41, 51, 54, 57, 59, 61, 63, 345, 347, 352, 360, 361
Working Capital Cycle, 57, 360
Working Capital Management, vii, 31, 360

www.ingramcontent.com/pod-product-compliance
Ingram Content Group UK Ltd.
Pitfield, Milton Keynes, MK11 3LW, UK
UKHW060216240426
12048UKWH00030BB/1686